Chiefs and Councils in Rhodesia

in Rhodesia

Transition from Patriarchial to Bureaucratic Power

A. K. H. WEINRICH

(Sister Mary Aquina, O.P.)

Senior Lecturer in Sociology
University of Rhodesia

UNIVERSITY OF SOUTH CAROLINA PRESS
Columbia, South Carolina

First Edition

Published 1971 in Great Britain by
HEINEMANN EDUCATIONAL BOOKS LTD.
London, England

and in the United States of America by
UNIVERSITY OF SOUTH CAROLINA PRESS
Columbia, South Carolina

International Standard Book Number: 0-87249-239-7
Library of Congress Catalog Card Number: 76-163907

Suggested Library of Congress classification furnished by
McKissick Memorial Library of the University of South Carolina:
HN793.W

Manufactured in Great Britain

This book is dedicated
to my Father
and my Mother
and my Sister, Elisabeth

Contents

Contents

List of Plates

List of Tables and Figures

Foreword

by

MARSHALL W. MURPHREE
Professor of Race Relations
University of Rhodesia

The publication of this book is an important event for Rhodesian ethnography and social anthropology. Most of the literature published to date on rural, small-scale politics in Rhodesia has suffered from fragmented, discontinuous publication in articles and papers, many of them obscure and of difficult access to readers outside this country. Now, for the first time, we have a detailed case study of an extended succession dispute of the type which has been endemic in Shona society for many years, placed within the context of a more general study of the Rhodesian chiefs and their difficult inter-hierarchical role. An interesting historical section traces the changing status of these chiefs against the background of national politics and an examination is made of the position of the chiefs vis-à-vis their subjects, government and African nationalist politicians. A reading of this material, together with that published recently by Holleman,[1] gives a much clearer picture of the salient features found in rural Rhodesian African politics today.

In her analysis Dr Weinrich draws on the Wilsons' insights concerning scale and social change and, more especially, on the theories of Max Weber. However, Dr Weinrich is not here attempting a systematic and comprehensive application of Weber's theories to Karanga society; she is rather using Weber's schemata as a useful framework within which to present and analyse her own materials. In this respect this book is yet another tribute to the perspicacity of a mind which could produce theoretical constructs of such general validity that, after over 50 years, they are still analytically seminal in a social arena far removed from Weber's Germany.

Ethnographically, this work is of value in that it draws its field data from the Karanga, one of the largest and historically most signifi-

[1] Holleman, J. F. (1969). Holleman's material was published after this book was written, and the two studies are independent of each other. Written against the background of different data, and with somewhat different perspectives, they are however in the best sense complementary.

cant Shona groupings. Most of the recent anthropological studies of the Shona have focused on the Zezuru and Korekore, and it is most useful to have this Karanga material placed alongside them.

The question arises as to how representative the Karanga data is of the Rhodesian Shona as a whole, a point taken up by Dr Weinrich herself. I would agree with her conclusion that much of the material does, with certain qualifications, have a measure of general validity. I would however add two reservations. One has to do with the pervasive influence of Christianity which Dr Weinrich sees in the Tribal Trust Lands. My own studies of the Budjga indicate a much smaller Christian component to the population. While a general typicality cannot be claimed for the Budjga figures either, some caution is, I believe, indicated concerning the extent of Christian influence, particularly in the light of the nominal nature of much Christian affiliation in the rural areas.

The second reservation has to do with the strong emphasis on group action seen in the case study which forms the focus of this book. While individual motivation is given recognition, it is the houses that are the units centrally involved in competition for power in the succession dispute. On the other hand, recent unpublished field data from the north and east of Rhodesia indicates that several contemporary succession debates have been primarily a matter of individual struggle for chieftainship, with only sporadic and unenthusiastic support being given by the contestants' houses. Although Dr Weinrich's case study is a continuing one, its focal events took place some time ago, and the critical variable may be a chronological and not an ethnographic one. If this is the case, one may see here a further erosion of the patronage aspects of chieftainship and a continued trend towards the bureaucratization of the position.

I have commented on the importance of this book in an academic context. Its publication is also an important event within the context of current changes in Rhodesia's social and political structures. As Dr Weinrich points out in her introduction, considerable interest has been focused on the Rhodesian chiefs by the events surrounding Rhodesia's unilateral declaration of independence. For some spokesmen of the Rhodesian Government the chiefs are leaders who command the almost universal respect and support of the rural African population. For some spokesmen of the African Nationalist cause, the chiefs are nothing but government lackeys, entirely compromised by their participation in the current administration. The position of both these groups is understandable, since both have short-term vested political interests in the interpretation given to the current position of the chiefs in this country. In reviewing the tremendous disparity between these two views and the dogmatic assertions made as to their validity, one comes to the rather gloomy conclusion that the degree of distortion involved in the stereotypes of any public issue varies in direct proportion to the political importance of the issue concerned. Ignorance and misconception, we are prone to think, stem from inattention and indifference. It may be more accurate to suggest that, within the political sphere at least, they may arise from the prejudices that the emphasis of politically sectarian perspectives give.

This has certainly been the case with regard to public opinion on the position of the Rhodesian chiefs. But the longer, more enduring vested interest that all concerned with Rhodesian society have in this issue is in a realistic and relatively objective appraisal of their position based on facts, and an understanding of the implications that their position has for a wide range of problems that face Rhodesian society—social, political, economic and demographic. To this kind of appraisal Dr Weinrich has made a significant contribution, and it is hoped that many members of the general public will read this book, which sheds valuable additional light on one of the more central political issues of our time.

Salisbury, May 1970   M.W.M.

Preface

This book arose partly from field research done for my Ph.D. thesis, and partly from later research which I conducted as a lecturer at the University College of Rhodesia. Research techniques differed during the first and second spell of my fieldwork. Between 1962 and 1964 I was free to devote all my time to my investigations. I chose two tribal trust lands and one purchase area, all located in the centre of Rhodesia and inhabited by the Karanga-speaking people. I was accompanied by a young African companion. She had completed her primary education and introduced me to her own society. We generally slept at mission stations, but spent our days in the villages and fields with the Karanga.

I tape-recorded most of my conversations with the people and all the public meetings which I attended. With the help of my assistant I transcribed the tapes into notebooks. This word-by-word record of my informants' responses enables me to quote literally whatever they said. The Karanga were very willing and proud to have their words tape-recorded.

In addition I obtained statistical information on the communities through a population census and an agricultural census. In 1968 I had these censuses brought up-to-date and extended.

During 1966, 1967, and 1968 teaching commitments prevented me from continuing full-time research, but I was able to employ two research assistants from the School of Social Work. These I had personally trained in social anthropology, and I visited them every four to six weeks in the field. Under my close supervision they included three more communities in which I had not personally worked. Civil servants had drawn my attention to these communities because of significant differences in their social processes.

During 1968 I concluded the research by personally visiting a large number of chiefs and other leaders to fill in the gaps in the fieldwork.

The information in chapters two and three is predominantly based on my census data and investigations during the early part of my fieldwork. Most of the field data presented in chapters four and five were collected during 1962–1964 and in 1968; some data were added by my field assistants.

B

During the earlier period of my research I spent much of the time gathering extensive field data on a succession dispute which had already lasted over twenty years. I personally interviewed all the actors in this social drama and was present at many of the events described. Information on the earlier decades was primarily derived from a diary kept by one of my informants; his entries were carefully cross-checked with other informants who had played leading parts in the succession dispute. The development between 1964 and 1968 was recorded by one of my field assistants. These findings are analysed in chapters six to eight.

The field data presented in chapters nine and ten were partly collected by myself, partly by my field assistants. The community development campaign described there began in one of the tribal trust lands in September 1962 and gathered momentum in 1964. I personally recorded the events which led to the rejection of the new government policy in this area. In the other tribal trust land and the purchase area, the community development campaign started only in 1966 or later. The majority of the case histories were therefore collected by my assistants. The last case history recorded in this book was added after all the other research had been completed because I found that none of the communities included in my sample had a long-established and well-functioning council.

The identities of all the individuals, European as well as African, who are mentioned in this book, have been purposely kept anonymous. All individuals and communities are referred to by fictitious names in order to focus attention on the structural implications of the changing political system of the Karanga. At no time has it been my intention to disparage any of the individuals concerned, since this book is intended purely as a social-anthropological study.

Throughout my research I received co-operation from civil servants of the ministries of Internal Affairs and Agriculture, who put at my disposal statistical data of the districts in which I worked, and volunteered other advice. The hospitality of missionaries enabled me to greatly reduce the expenditure on my research. My first spell of fieldwork, between 1962 and 1964, was generously financed by the Dominican Missionary Sisters of Rhodesia. Later research, carried out between 1966 and 1968, was financed by the University College of Rhodesia. I wish to express my sincere gratitude both to my missionary superiors and to the University.

Between 1962 and 1964 Professor J. C. Mitchell, then head of the department of Social-Anthropology at the University College of Rhodesia, who earlier on had initiated me as an undergraduate into

Social Anthropology and later encouraged me to specialize in this discipline, supervised my research and gave me valuable advice. During 1965, Dr A. L. Epstein, then senior lecturer in Social Anthropology at Manchester University, guided me in the preparation of my Ph.D. thesis. During my later research at the University College of Rhodesia I received stimulating comments from my colleagues, especially from my professor, D. H. Reader, and Professor M. W. Murphree. Mr T. McLoughlin of the English department read my manuscript and helped me—as my mother tongue is German—to present a readable account of my research findings. Sr Mary Matthia Stigler O.P. accompanied me on most of my later supervisory trips and shared with me the strain but also joy of those years. Her constant assistance and encouragement greatly lightened the visits, which were often strenuous, and still more the taxing task of writing up the material. To all these I wish to extend my sincerest thanks.

University College of Rhodesia
Salisbury
June 1971

A. K. H. Weinrich
[Sister Mary Aquina O.P.]

Introduction

1. THE PURPOSE OF THE BOOK

Rhodesian chiefs, almost unknown to the Rhodesian public until the 1960s, suddenly received wide newspaper coverage when the Rhodesian Government began negotiating independence with Great Britain. The Rhodesian Government claimed that African chiefs were the true representatives of over five million unenfranchised Africans. When Great Britain did not accept this claim, the Rhodesian Government made strong efforts to publicize its attitude in order to acquaint Europeans with the roles and functions of the African chiefs. After the unilateral declaration of independence in 1965, several parliamentary acts were passed which conferred greater powers on African chiefs. These new powers drew the chiefs more closely into the bureaucratic administration of Rhodesia, but by doing so they altered the chiefs' relationships with their own people.

This book traces the changes which have taken place in the position of Rhodesian chiefs during the twentieth century; it examines the tensions which chiefs experience in contemporary society, and it shows the options open to chiefs in situations in which their traditional patriarchal powers are challenged by a modern bureaucracy. Since the shift in the power basis of Rhodesian chiefs from their people to European superiors, that is, a change in sovereignty, finds its clearest expression at the accession of new chiefs after the death or deposition of their predecessors, this book focuses on a detailed case study of a succession dispute in a Rhodesian chiefdom. The different functions which modern chiefs are expected to perform, and the new roles in which they have to meet their subjects, are most clearly evident in situations alien to traditional life. Consequently this book examines the reactions of chiefs to a new government policy in which they are expected to take an active part.

Max Weber's theory of bureaucracy provides the general framework in which the transition from patriarchal to bureaucratic power of Rhodesian chiefs is analysed. Another useful concept for an understanding of the changing position of chiefs is that of scale, first clearly formulated by Godfrey and Monica Wilson in 1945. An elaboration of

Weber's theory with the help of the Wilsons' concept of scale throws new light on the changing position of chiefs in a multiracial society.

2. ANALYTICAL FRAMEWORK

Max Weber was struck by the fundamental differences in the power structures of patriarchal and bureaucratic societies.[1] He states that whereas a patriarch's power and authority are based on personal dependants, many of whom are related to him by blood, the bureaucrat's power and authority are based on his position in an impersonal administrative system. Moreover, whereas the patriarch provides leadership not only in the political, but also in the economic and religious spheres of his followers' lives, the bureaucrat's influence extends to clearly circumscribed aspects of a particular social system, be it political, economic or religious.

Not only the basis and scope of a patriarch's and bureaucrat's power vary, but also the values associated with their positions. This difference derives from the origins in which the two systems of control are rooted. Weber writes that because patriarchalism is the oldest and most widespread form of domination, it has become legitimate by tradition and has acquired a sacred character.[2] No such character attaches to bureaucracies, most of which are of recent origin. Bureaucracies are ideally organized on the basis of efficiency, and their officials are appointed because they possess professional qualifications, not because they are related by kinship or friendship to leading administrators. As a result bureaucrats are cogs, moving along together, and individually unable to bring the machine to a halt. Bureaucracies, therefore, are the most powerful form of social control yet invented, and are resistant to change. They seem to be the end-product of a long political evolution.

Bureaucracy was almost universally preceded by patriarchalism because it could only evolve after certain preconditions prevailed. Chief among these rank a money economy and an extended communication system; a concentration of power over large territorial units; and an educational system which provides experts to staff the offices created by the bureaucracy.

A developed money economy is essential for the establishment and continuation of a bureaucracy, because without money to reward its officials and to pay for the cost of administration, a bureaucracy is likely to turn into some other form of domination. In order, therefore,

[1] Gerth and Mills, eds. (1961) *From Max Weber.* See especially pp. 196–245.
[2] ibid., p. 296.

to preserve the administrative structure, bureaucrats impose taxes on the people. For the older forms of administration, such as patriarchalism and feudalism, money is not essential. Tribute could be paid to the leader in the form of labour or wealth, and the leader in turn could reward his followers with various privileges. When tribute and privileges were replaced by taxes and salaries, the older structures gave way to bureaucracies.

A money economy reflects a developing or developed economic system. Intense economic progress, moreover, requires a network of communication to distribute the goods it produces. As soon as this network has been established to further economic enterprise, another precondition for bureaucracy is achieved. Centralized control of a large area now becomes possible. Means of communication can, therefore, be seen as 'pacemakers of bureaucratization'.[1]

Centralized control of a country is essential for bureaucratic administration. The police can assure conformity of all citizens to government instruction and an army can repress rebellion and defend people from outside attack. Yet at the same time the 'political master' finds himself in a power position which is 'overtowering'.[2] The machine of administration soon becomes so complex that he needs expert advisers to whom he can turn and to whom he can delegate responsibilities, In a highly developed bureaucracy, Weber states, the political master becomes a mere 'dilettante' dependent on his trained staff. Consequently bureaucratic power, however great, does not necessarily mean great personal power for individual leaders. It is an impersonal power, the rule of law and not the rule of men.

Because of the emphasis on efficiency in a bureaucracy, education assumes key importance. It selects through its examination system men who can fill positions in the administration. This contrasts with the patriarchal system where political office depends on kinship ties with the patriarch. This difference led Weber to observe: 'Today, the certificate of education becomes what the test for ancestors has been in the past.'[3]

To ensure a smooth-running bureaucracy, educational opportunities should not be evenly available, otherwise positions in the administration can no longer be monopolized.[4] Weber assumes that monopolization of office is a characteristic of all systems of domination; they only differ in regard to the circles that control the monopolies. In patriarchal

[1] ibid., p. 213.
[2] ibid., p. 232.
[3] ibid., p. 241.
[4] ibid., p. 201.

systems these circles consist of family members of the patriarchs; in bureaucracies of the owners of educational certificates. Both patriarchal and bureaucratic systems, therefore, are inherently anti-democratic.

Once the economic, political and educational preconditions for bureaucracy have been established, a change from patriarchalism to bureaucracy may take place. Such a change, however, is generally accompanied by many tensions. A most acute tension centres round the position of the former patriarch who tries to become, or is forced to become, a bureaucrat, for bureaucrats are appointed by their superiors, but patriarchs rise to power with the consensus of their followers because of their structural position in a kinship system.

Max Weber's theory may be amplified by Godfrey and Monica Wilson's concept of social scale. As early as 1945 they drew attention to the importance of differences in scale between primitive and civilized societies.[1] They argued that if the scale of a society expands rapidly, the various sections of the society are likely to change unevenly. Such an uneven change would lead to a disequilibrium in the society, and the disequilibrium to a radical opposition among the society's component parts.[2]

3. RHODESIAN BACKGROUND

In terms of Weber's theory, the African population of Rhodesia is undergoing during the twentieth century the transition from a patriarchal to a bureaucratic social structure. This change began when the first European settlers arrived at the end of the nineteenth century and successfully attempted to establish between the Limpopo and Zambezi rivers political and economic systems that were patterned on those of Western European societies. Immigration policies contributed to a steady inflow of Europeans, who consolidated the emerging Rhodesian bureaucracies. By 1969, there were some 228,000 Europeans in Rhodesia.[3]

The African population, numbering over five million in 1969, had to adapt itself in the economic sphere to European expectations. In 1931 the country was divided into African and European areas,[4] in which the

[1] Wilson, G. and M. (1968), p. 24; first published 1945.
[2] ibid., pp. 133–134, 127.
[3] *The Rhodesia Herald*, 23.5.1969.
[4] In 1931 the Land Apportionment Act was passed, which legalized the division of land between different racial groups. Fifty per cent of the country was declared 'European area', 30 per cent 'Native area', and the rest was classed as unassigned or forest land. In 1969 50 per cent of the land was declared European, 50 per cent African area. Cf.: *Second Report of the Select Committee for the Resettlement of Natives*, 1960, p. 15; and: *Proposals for a New Constitution for Rhodesia*, 1969.

two races were encouraged to live according to their own customs and values. Land shortage in African areas, however, and the need for unskilled labour among Europeans, brought about a steady flow of African men into European areas. Africans left their villages in order to earn a living for their families. Yudelman estimates that in 1958 the average gross output per family holding in African rural areas was less than £80 per year, and the average gross money income less than £15. If costs for labour, seed, and other expenditure were taken into account, the return was close to zero.[1]

Labour contributed by Africans to Rhodesia's economy is of great importance, 88 per cent of all Rhodesian employees being Africans.[2] By 1967, Africans in European employment earned a total of £123·7 million; their average income per year was £138, or 10 per cent of the average European income. Since at any one time about 40 per cent of all African men are employed as labour migrants, their wages make an important contribution to the living standards in rural areas and help the rapid spread of a money economy among African people. Through this incorporation of African labour into the Rhodesian economy, the first precondition has been established for the extension of bureaucracy in the tribal areas, generally known as tribal trust lands.[3]

To advance their economic interests, Europeans immediately began to establish a network of communication. By 1899 the railways had reached Salisbury, the capital of the new country, linking it to both Portuguese East Africa and South Africa. Roads soon connected European settlements and gradually extended to African areas, though roads within African areas were generally inferior and often impassable in the rainy season. By 1969 roads had mostly improved and most areas could be reached by car throughout the year. The groundwork for a central administration of the whole country had therefore been laid.

Administratively Rhodesia is divided into seven provinces, each province being subdivided into six to eight districts. Their administrators are called provincial commissioners and district commissioners respectively. These officials are members of the ministry of Internal Affairs, one of the most important ministries of the country and directly

---

[1] Yudelman (1964), pp. 90, 261. Data derived from unpublished manuscript in the Central Statistical Office (1958).

[2] *Economic Survey of Rhodesia* (1965), p. 38.

[3] African areas were known as native areas or native reserves until 1962. Since then they have been renamed tribal trust lands. Tribal trust lands are areas where Africans are considered to live according to their own customs under their traditional chiefs. In reality most of their customs have been modified by cultural contact with Europeans, as this book shows. Cf. chapter 1, p. 10.

responsible for African administration. Most public and private services for Africans are channelled through this bureaucracy. The traditional African system never contained such a large administrative unit. Confronted with the power of the new 'Government' in the form of commissioners the rural people are often overwhelmed, and many react through outward conformity or withdrawal. Their apparent patient submission frequently conveys to the European officials the impression that the people they rule are content with the administration. It is likely, however, that this apparent submission reflects a latent period preceding some major changes.

The final precondition for a successful bureaucratization of society is education. The Rhodesian Government has introduced compulsory education for all European children between the ages of seven and fifteen; in fact almost all European children aged five to eighteen are in school. By contrast, only 44 per cent of all African children in this age-group are in school. African education is voluntary; it depends both on the financial ability of parents to pay for their children's education and on vacancies in overcrowded classes. Limited capital prevents a more rapid expansion of the African educational system.[1]

Great differences exist not only between the percentages of African and European children attending school, but also in the type of education available to them. To enable a person to participate effectively in the economic and political life of Rhodesia, secondary education is desirable and often essential. Only ten per cent of all Europeans enter the labour market with primary education and no more; 90 per cent attempt secondary education, and of these 10 per cent reach university level. Of African pupils, on the other hand, only 2 per cent attend secondary schools, and only 0·04 per cent reach university level. Moreover, of the African children who do attempt primary schools, 78 per cent leave during the first five years and consequently are at most able to read and write in an African language, but not in English. This means that very few Africans are educationally qualified to take an active part in public life.

Weber's observation that in bureaucracies the owners of educational certificates try to monopolize positions in the administration partly accounts for the limited access African children have to schools. This is

[1] Social reasons too may influence government allocation of funds for African education. These, however, are difficult to establish. Barber made the following comment on African education in Rhodesia: 'Education policy cannot be divorced from a country's political and constitutional development. Given certain conditions educational development could dictate political development.' Barber (1967), p. 88.

borne out by the fact that 90 per cent of all African children are in private, mostly mission schools, and only 10 per cent in government schools, whereas European education is almost exclusively provided by the Rhodesian Government. Only 17 per cent of all European children attend private schools. But for the efforts of missionaries, therefore, to provide Africans with education, African people would be even more handicapped in their attempt to adapt themselves to the many social changes confronting them.

The extent of missionary influence, apart from education, can be gauged by the following figures. In the 1960s about one third of the African population were active church members, and at least another third were affiliated to Christian denominations without, however, regularly attending religious services. A very large proportion of the African people, therefore, has been influenced by Christianity.

The Africans' confrontation with Christianity has partly been achieved by Europeans resident in Rhodesia and partly by missionaries from Europe and America. Ninety-two per cent of all Europeans[1] in Rhodesia are at least nominally Christian, though different denominations have contributed in varying degrees to the evangelization of their African neighbours. Roman Catholics, who constitute 13 per cent of the European population, have proportionally the largest African following, counting 10 per cent of the total African population as active church members.[2] Anglicans and the various other Protestant denominations, accounting for 79 per cent of all Europeans, have affiliated some 22 per cent of the total African population as active church members.[3]

CONCLUSION

The Rhodesian setting, within which the transition from patriarchal to bureaucratic power takes place, consists therefore of a racially composite society which has evolved during the last eighty years. A small minority of Europeans controls the economic life of the country and dominates the political scene. This minority, rich and well educated, rules over five million Africans, most of whom are little educated, politically unenfranchised and economically poor.

The transition from patriarchal to bureaucratic power in the tribal trust lands is brought about by a large variety of structural changes.

[1] 1961 *Census*, p. 13.
[2] 1963 *The Catholic Directory of Southern Africa*, Statistical Appendix for the Year 1962.
[3] 1962 *Southern Rhodesia Christian Conference Statistical Record*.

Money has penetrated village life everywhere in Rhodesia; some education has been acquired by Africans; and Europeans have provided the broad administrative framework for the new bureaucracy. Moreover, the scale of the African people's social universe has rapidly expanded. The foundation for bureaucratic government has, therefore, been laid.

CHAPTER 1

Chiefs and Councils in Rhodesia: 1890–1969

INTRODUCTION

The administration of African rural areas in Rhodesia, and especially the status of chiefs, has undergone major changes over the last eighty years. This chapter, based on government documents and historical studies, presents a brief survey of the most important events of Rhodesian history, the different attitudes expressed by government towards African chiefs, and the emergence of African councils.

Rhodesian history can be divided into four major periods: the first period, extending from the arrival of the first European settlers in 1890 up to 1923, represents the 'Period of Company Rule', when Rhodesia was administered by the British South Africa Company. The second period, extending from 1923 to 1953, can be called the 'Period of Internal Self-Government'. The third period, extending from 1953 to 1963, represents the 'Federal Period' when Rhodesia formed part of the Central African Federation of Rhodesia and Nyasaland. The fourth period, commencing with the dissolution of the Federation in 1963, and continuing through the country's subsequent unilateral declaration of independence, has not yet come to an end by the time this book is written. It may be called the 'Post-Federal Period'.

1. 1890–1923: COMPANY RULE

(a) *Historical Background*
The new country of Rhodesia, lying between the Limpopo and Zambezi rivers, began as an economic enterprise. Until it obtained internal self-government in 1923 it was administered through a legislative council composed of representatives of the British South Africa Company and settlers. Final authority over Rhodesian politics rested with the British High Commissioner for South Africa in Cape Town.[1]

This early period set the pattern for the economic and political development of the country. The British South Africa Company's fore-

[1] Leys (1959), pp. 11–12.

most concern was to administer the country on a profit basis so that dividends could be paid to shareholders. Its directors hoped to strike rich gold deposits in Rhodesia, but when mining proved less profitable than was expected they turned their attention to agriculture. To enable the new settlers to make a profit from farming they needed land. Indiscriminate allocation of land to Europeans was prevented by an Order-in-Council of 1898 that requested the Company to provide adequate and suitable land for the indigenous population. The Order led to the creation of native reserves, which in 1962 were renamed tribal trust lands. By 1902 most boundaries of African areas had been defined. This delineation set the pattern for African settlement in Rhodesia until the present day.[1]

European enterprise in mines and on farms required cheap labour. At the turn of the century few Africans were willing to work for Europeans because their own social system had as yet been little affected by cultural contact and still provided for all their needs. Consequently in 1896 the government introduced a tax of ten shillings, which was raised to £1 in 1904,[2] in order to induce Africans to seek employment.

The collection of taxes was the duty of field cornets, later renamed native commissioners, who were given a roving commission over large areas and instructed to get to know their people and ensure that violence ceased and government instructions were obeyed. In 1902 the Native Affairs Department was formally established, and with it the bureaucratic framework through which African areas are still administered.

The native commissioners' authority extended over the whole economic and political life of the African people. The most important powers which the African chiefs had traditionally exercised were transferred to native commissioners. Native commissioners allocated land to African people, issued them with cattle permits, and at the same time procured labour for European settlers. They decided who was allowed to settle in a chiefdom and so controlled the Africans' contact with missionaries and businessmen. In 1910 they received both criminal and civil jurisdiction over Africans through the High Commissioner's Proclamation.[3] The same Proclamation defined the powers and duties of chiefs to be the same as those of police constables in their areas.

(b) *The Position of Chiefs*

The effective replacement of chiefs by native commissioners as local

---

[1] 1969.
[2] The Native Tax Ordinance No. 21; cf. Leys (1959), p. 10 and Gann (1965).
[3] Rhodesia: *Robinson Report* (1961), p. 13.

rulers and the consequent decrease in prestige and power of chiefs had its origin in the suspicion and fear which Europeans had of the leaders of two native uprisings in the 1890s. Rhodesia's African population consists of the Ndebele tribe in the west of the country and the Shona people in the centre and east of Rhodesia. The Ndebele constitute approximately 20 per cent of the indigenous population and the Shona 80 per cent. In 1893 the Ndebele rebelled against Company rule, and in 1896 many Shona chiefs also rose in rebellion. Both uprisings were repressed, but among the Shona individual chiefs kept up resistance until 1902.[1] The extensive powers granted to native commissioners were intended to limit the influence of chiefs among their people and to make Africans directly dependent on European administrators. In 1913 the success of this policy was recorded in the Chief Native Commissioner's Report:

> Chiefs complain that they no longer control their followings as they did in the past and that the young people are gradually breaking away from tribal control. . . . The increased powers granted to Native Commissioners materially assist in breaking up these tribal methods of control, and I am glad to say results have so far proved satisfactory.[2]

In order to facilitate administration, African chiefs were asked to register with the nearest native commissioners. It seems that several chiefs refused to present themselves, and that some local leaders, who were not recognized as chiefs by their neighbours, registered as chiefs.[3] By 1941, 323 men had registered as chiefs[4] and the list of their names formed the basis for the subsequent tribal administration.

The period of Company rule, therefore, is the period during which African chiefs lost much of their power and prestige. They were effectively replaced by European bureaucrats and ordered to serve them as constables. They had become the dependent leaders of a conquered people.

2. 1923–1953: INTERNAL SELF-GOVERNMENT

(a) *Historical Background*

The period of Company rule closed in 1923 when the settlers voted by a small majority in favour of responsible government. Forty-one per cent of the electorate would have preferred inclusion into the Union of South Africa.[5] The strong ties by which many Rhodesians felt bound to South Africa derived from pioneer days, when a significant number of

[1] Ranger (1968), p. 217.
[2] *Chief Native Commissioner's Report* (C.N.C.), 1913.
[3] Information based on personal fieldwork.
[4] Garbett (1966), p. 118.
[5] Leys (1959), p. 13.

Afrikaners took part in the occupation of the new country.[1] Consequently the racial policies of Rhodesia were modelled on those of the
South. In 1933 a member of parliament outlined a 'two-pyramid' policy
of racial separation[2] which provided the ideological framework for
future legislation and retrospectively justified past legislation. The 1923
Constitution had already made provision for racially segregated areas,
and the Land Apportionment Act of 1931 had legalized the actual
division of land between Africans and Europeans. In 1934 the Industrial
Conciliation Act was passed which protected European workers from
African competition and indirectly introduced job reservation and
racial segregation into industry.[3] This restrictive legislation against
Africans was partly influenced by unemployment among Europeans.
During this period Rhodesia was struggling for economic survival. With
rapid economic development during the Second World War and the
post-war years[4] the Europeans' economic position in Rhodesia improved. Many immigrants came into the country after the war and the
political power of the white minority was strengthened. Under these
conditions racial attitudes broadened. Expanding industries required
more labour and politicians began to speak of partnership between the
races.

From the beginning of self-rule in 1923 until 1962, the government
party never changed hands though it often altered its name. It may be
described as 'moderate' in the Southern African context, and always
faced an opposition on its right which asked for racial separation in all
spheres of Rhodesian life.[5]

(b) *The Position of Chiefs*

As long as Europeans in Rhodesia were economically insecure, Africans
were regarded with suspicion and fear, and their chiefs were largely
ignored by the administration. With the outbreak of the Second World
War and a new prosperity among Europeans, however, individual native
commissioners began to take more notice of chiefs in their districts,
as can be seen in various extracts from the Reports of the Chief Native
Commissioners of the period.

[1] Gann (1965), pp. 90–95.

[2] Leys (1959), p. 163.

[3] By the Act Africans were prevented from bargaining and from learning industrial
skills (Rayner, 1962, p. 197). They were specifically excluded from its definition of an
'employee' and 'in practice excluded from the greater part of the available skilled
employment' (Leys, 1960, p. 30).

[4] Tindall (1968), p. 214.

[5] Leys (1959), p. 203.

The Chief Native Commissioner's Report for 1940 stated that African chiefs showed a complete lack of initiative and that one chief had to be removed from office.[1] In 1941 it was reported that several chiefs had provided men for the war effort and that this had increased the chiefs' prestige among their own people. Yet some chiefs had defied the law and that year one had been deposed for misconduct,[2] and a third in 1942.[3] The 1943 Report recorded that by and large chiefs had preserved peace among their people, but that they lacked leadership qualities.[4] The 1946 Report contains the bitter comment: 'Our aim is to eliminate many of the old diehards and replace them in time by fewer and better chiefs.'[5] The 1949 Report commented more approvingly: 'Though some are ultra-conservative and quite unable to adjust themselves to the tempo of modern progress, the majority of chiefs and headmen have carried out their difficult duties well within the limits imposed by the loss of authority and prestige arising from disruption of tribal controls.'[6] The last years of the period of internal self-government were influenced by propaganda for a Central African Federation. Contact with Africans in the northern territories of the proposed Federation awakened nationalist aspirations in Rhodesian Africans.[7] In 1950 the Chief Native Commissioner's Report stated for the first time that 'some self-seeking Native agitators' had visited African areas and that it would be advisable to increase the power of chiefs.[8] From then onward, as nationalism spread in African areas, government policy was to fortify the position of chiefs. The year 1951 saw a complete restructure of African chieftainships. Of the 323 chiefs who had registered their chieftainships in 1914, '89 were abolished, 11 were pensioned off, and 37 lost rank altogether'.[9] The remaining chiefs received a salary increase and were organized into provincial assemblies through which they could express their views to government officials. According to the Chief Native Commissioner's Report the reorganization was appreciated by Africans.[10]

In 1952 the Chief Native Commissioner recorded that chiefs were receiving greater respect from their subjects than in the past decade, but

[1] C.N.C., 1940, p. 10.
[2] C.N.C., 1941, p. 11.
[3] C.N.C., 1943, p. 64.
[4] C.N.C., 1945, p. 217.
[5] C.N.C., 1946, p. 27.
[6] C.N.C., 1949, p. 27.
[7] For further examples, cf. Rotberg (1966).
[8] C.N.C., 1950, pp. 20, 6.
[9] Garbett (1966), p. 118.
[10] C.N.C., 1951, pp. 34–35.

C

he admitted that many chiefs were old and inefficient, and some even obstructed government policies. He expressed concern that 'political agitators' were winning the support of chiefs.[1] The government grew alarmed and about thirteen chiefs were deposed during these years: seven had criminal charges brought against them, and six were removed for unsuitability and drunkenness.[2]

This brief survey shows that during the last years of internal self-government, which coincided with the rise of African nationalism, the government raised the chiefs' status. Provincial assemblies gave them for the first time the experience of corporate identity and drew them into closer co-operation with administrators. Their increased salaries encouraged loyalty to the government.

(c) *Councils*

The period of internal self-government awakened in educated Africans a political awareness, and as early as the late 1920s African political associations were formed in Rhodesian towns.[3] To counteract independent African political organizations in 1931, the government established native boards 'to meet the legitimate desire for the united expression of native opinion'.[4] These boards consisted of chiefs and subchiefs who represented the traditionally orientated Africans, and of an equal number of elected Africans, who were thought to represent the educated section of the African population. The boards were allowed to make recommendations to government, but had no authority to see that their recommendations were carried out. Consequently they turned into debating societies and found little support among the African people.

In 1937 native boards were replaced by councils which were chaired by native commissioners. In 1944 these councils were given limited power of taxation and of passing by-laws. They were entitled to look after roads and bridges, water conservation and primary education.[5] Forty-three African councils had been established by 1952[6] but in spite of encouragement by native commissioners Africans failed to show enthusiasm for councils. One reason was that old uneducated chiefs and young educated men served together on these councils. The Chief Native Commissioner's Report stated that 'the younger and better educated Africans are coming

[1] C.N.C., 1952, p. 33.
[2] *The Rhodesia Herald*, 22.10.1964.
[3] Ranger (1966), pp. 171–193.
[4] C.N.C., 1930, p. 2.
[5] Passmore (1966), p. 36.
[6] C.N.C., 1952, p. 31.

to resent the rule of old and illiterate Chiefs, who cannot command their respect.'[1] Chiefs feared that councils would undermine their traditional position and nationalistically inclined men refused to serve on councils which were chaired by government officials. The work undertaken by the councils was of such limited nature that it failed to capture the imagination of those who strove for progress.

3. 1953–1963: THE FEDERAL PERIOD

(a) *Historical Background*
The Federal period begins with the establishment of the Federation of Rhodesia and Nyasaland and ends with its dissolution. For Rhodesia it was a period of economic expansion and rapid European population increase. The government changed its policy of separate development to partnership between the races, a partnership, however, in which Europeans were the senior partners. Several Africans were admitted to parliament. Colour restrictions were lifted in public buildings, and many barriers preventing the races from mixing in social life were removed. A multiracial university was established in the capital.

Yet, whereas a number of educated and wealthy Africans were partially accepted into European society, the majority saw no alteration in their economic, social and political condition. In fact, the rural population was antagonized by the Land Husbandry Act, passed in 1951 to preserve the soil through conservation methods and destocking. By disqualifying Africans who worked in urban areas from cultivating land in their home villages, the Act aimed at creating a stable rural and a stable urban population and hoped that through increased productivity of both sections labour migration might be prevented. However, the peasant population, as well as the labour migrants, rebelled against the Act and caused great unrest in rural areas. They were unwilling to engage in destocking schemes and to construct soil conservation works. Above all they objected to the law that those who did not cultivate land at the time of the Act's implementation would in the future be prevented from farming. The disturbed peasantry rallied behind African nationalist leaders.

(b) *The Position of Chiefs*[2]
The Federal period proved a turning point in the position of Rhodesian

---

[1] C.N.C., 1952, p. 33.
[2] For an independent account of chiefs during this period see Holleman (1968), pp. 342–345.

chiefs. Whereas in the past they had been rejected as leaders of rebellions or as inefficient old men, during the Federal period chiefs were wooed by both government and African nationalists.

According to the Chief Native Commissioner's Report of 1954, Africans had hardly noticed that the Federation had been established, there was no 'nationalist organization of any consequence'[1] in the country, and race relations were excellent. A year later, however, the Report admitted that nationalists were winning many chiefs to their side and that provincial assemblies were used by the administration to guarantee the loyalty of chiefs.[2] Nevertheless the old image of contented Africans still maintained itself in the Chief Native Commissioner's Reports. In 1956 it stated: 'The time has not yet arrived when our policy of "benevolent paternalism" can be shelved; the majority of Africans, particularly in the rural areas, still demand and expect it.'[3]

A change occurred in 1957 when Africans founded the first effective nationalist party in Rhodesia, the African National Congress.[4] The Native Affairs department became alarmed and more consideration was given to chiefs. Their salaries were again increased,[5] and the Chief Native Commissioner's Report commented favourably on the chief's loyalty. In 1958 government arranged excursions by plane for chiefs to lake Kariba to see the new dam, and to the large cities to show them the industrial development of the country. Chiefs also attended the opening of parliament and visited the University College of Rhodesia and Nyasaland.[6] The chiefs' public appearance on those occasions caught the passing attention of Europeans in Rhodesia.

The government, with its power to reward and punish,[7] proved more successful in winning the support of chiefs than African nationalists. In 1959 the chiefs sided for the first time openly with the government against the nationalists, when they petitioned the government through their provincial assemblies to ban nationalist meetings in their areas.[8] The reason was that peasant discontent had increased the support for the African National Congress, and men began to look to the new leaders for guidance rather than to their chiefs. Nationalists reacted to

[1] C.N.C., 1954, p. 18.
[2] C.N.C., 1955, p. 5.
[3] C.N.C., 1956, p. 2.
[4] C.N.C., 1957, p. 9.
[5] C.N.C., 1957, p. 5.
[6] C.N.C., 1958, p. 6.
[7] For example, by deposing a chief from office.
[8] C.N.C., 1959, p. 17.

this prohibition, which became law, by accusing government of 'stealing' the chiefs from the people.[1]

The Chief Native Commissioner became aware of the conflicting demands made on chiefs and reported:

> The position of Chiefs is a difficult and ambiguous one; the very duality of their role as representatives or custodians of traditional authority, and, at the same time, as agents in some functions of Government, makes them peculiarly susceptible to criticism of the most varied quarters.[2]

This is the first reference in government documents to the intercalary position of chiefs. The positive evaluation of the chiefs' dilemma, moreover, shows that government had begun to rely on the support of chiefs for a successful administration of rural areas.

In 1960 the African National Congress was banned, but immediately reorganized itself as the National Democratic Party. It continued to spread in the rural areas and its followers ridiculed and defied chiefs as well as government officials.[3] The National Democratic Party was banned in 1961, but emerged again the same year as the Zimbabwe African People's Union. Tensions between chiefs and nationalists increased. The Chief Native Commissioner commented that many chiefs were singled out for specific attack by nationalists, and gave as reasons that chiefs:

> Are experts in articulating genuine feelings, not in arousing artificial ones; and their conception of their role as Chiefs is that of ironing out differences, ... not of stirring up passions. ... This is the point of their collision with the modern politicians. ... To this, of course, must be added the fact that Chiefs tend to move with their people, not with the times. They are the conservative element.[4]

Never before had chiefs been praised so unambiguously as in this report. Even the reference to their conservatism has a positive ring against the background of African nationalism. The same year the chiefs were consulted by the government about a new constitution for the country. They assured the government that it had their 'mandate to go ahead'.[5]

To consolidate the chiefs' position still further, a National Council of

---

[1] Cf. *infra*, p. 178.
[2] C.N.C., 1959, p. 17.
[3] C.N.C., 1960, p. 2.
[4] C.N.C., 1961, p. 16.
[5] C.N.C., 1961, p. 2.

Chiefs was formed in 1962, consisting of twenty-six delegates from the seven provincial assemblies.[1]

In 1963 a section of the Zimbabwe African People's Union split off to form the Zimbabwe African National Union; faction fights occurred between the two parties throughout the country, and both parties were banned. All legal African nationalist activities came to an end. An uneasy peace was restored in the rural areas and the chiefs remained as the only official African leaders.

An interesting phenomenon characterizes the Federal period: the government improved the chiefs' position as African nationalism spread in Rhodesia. Relatively little attention was paid to chiefs by the administration in the early 1950s, and nationalists won the support of a significant number of chiefs. Awakening to the danger to European domination presented by a united African opposition, the government drew the chiefs into its orbit by bestowing on them privileges and rewards. This trend, which alienated the chiefs from the nationalist leaders, reached its culmination in 1962 and 1963 when the National Council of Chiefs was formed and all nationalist parties were banned. The chiefs were becoming politicians, because through their council they could represent African aspirations at a national level.

(c) *Councils*

Not only chiefs but also African councils, another channel through which Africans were invited to express their wishes, received special attention during the Federal period. The failure of councils under the 1937 Act had led to a reconsideration of the legislation, and in 1957 a new African Councils Act was passed, which differed from its predecessor in that it presented councils as a privilege granted to progressive communities. Councils were no longer imposed on a community by the native commissioner. Provisions were also made that the chairmanship be handed over to elected Africans at the earliest opportunity. Yet even with these provisions, the number of African councils increased by only twelve, from forty-three in 1952 to fifty-five in 1962.[2]

Because the composition of councils was not altered by the 1957 Act the Africans' opposition remained unchanged. Chiefs still resented the presence of elected members on the council, and progressive young men refused to co-operate with uneducated old chiefs and with district commissioners. In 1959 the Chief Native Commissioner's Report stated that the government did not intend to transfer authority from

[1] C.N.C., 1962, p. 4.
[2] C.N.C., 1952, p. 31; C.N.C., 1962, p. 90.

'a mystical and hereditary Chief to a new elective body'.[1] It presented the problem not as:

> That of substituting new roles and functions in place of ancient duties, but of consolidating the Chief in his traditional sphere while at the same time channelling the needs of a money economy and an uneducated, partly individualised society, through new elective institutions.[2]

The 1962 Report admitted that the native council system had further deteriorated, and that it had to be completely rebuilt under a new government policy of community development.[3] Chiefs and people had unanimously rejected councils. Since the co-operation between chiefs and government was a recent event, government did not yet press chiefs hard to accept a modern institution to which they had manifested open aversion.

4. 1963–1969: THE POST-FEDERAL PERIOD

(a) *Historical Background*

The dissolution of the Central African Federation in 1963 was preceded in 1962 by the election defeat of the former government party of Rhodesia. For the first time in Rhodesian history, a right-wing party which looked to South Africa for inspiration came to power. At first the new government had a narrow majority in parliament, but at a second election in 1965 it captured fifty out of sixty-five seats; all but one of the opposition members were Africans, and the one European who did not belong to the government party was elected to represent a predominantly African electoral district as an independent.

The new government immediately began to negotiate for independence from Great Britain, but because of its reluctance to allow Africans a larger participation in the political life of the country, negotiations proved fruitless. When Great Britain made it clear that it would not grant independence before the majority of Africans were legally represented in parliament, the Prime Minister declared Rhodesia independent in 1965 without Great Britain's consent. As a result economic sanctions were imposed on Rhodesia by the world community. No nation officially recognized Rhodesia's independence. Meeting greater opposition than originally expected, Rhodesia encapsulated itself,

[1] *Note:* The Chief Native Commissioner expresses here his awareness of chiefs as patriarchs, who are the religious leaders of their followers; yet at the same time he expects them to fill the position of bureaucrats.

[2] C.N.C., 1959, p. 158.

[3] C.N.C., 1962, p. 9.

strove to diversify its industry, with the help of South Africa, in order to become less dependent economically on the rest of the world, and followed an internal policy of racial segregation, culminating, at the time of writing, in the 1969 proposals for a new constitution, which the Prime Minister himself declared to be a 'racialist Constitution'.[1] The European population accepted the proposed constitution at a referendum by a large majority.[2]

Economic sanctions affected all sections of the population. Among Africans it created large-scale unemployment when the Rhodesian tobacco industry closed down and dismissed 30,000 Africans. Secondary industry expanded only slightly, and by 1967 there were 21,000 fewer Africans in employment than in 1965.[3]

Internal security was threatened by a small-scale invasion of guerrilla fighters. Armed Africans, termed 'freedom fighters' by fellow Africans and 'terrorists' by most Europeans, crossed the Zambezi river and engaged units of the Rhodesian army along the northern border of the country. They exerted little influence, however, on the rest of Rhodesia. Security was maintained by a continued state of emergency, declared in 1965, which empowered the government to arrest, detain or restrict any person deemed to endanger the peace. Yet even from prisons and detention camps African nationalists kept in touch with their people, as was proved by the trial in 1969 of the leader of the Zimbabwe African National Union.[4] In the absence of legal nationalist parties, African members of parliament became more outspoken in their criticism of government.

(b) *The Position of Chiefs*[5]

If during the Federal period African chiefs rose to power, during the post-Federal period they were propelled into prominence. One act after another was passed by parliament to increase their power. New legislation was strongly criticized by African members of parliament, who argued that chiefs could not be simultaneously civil servants and politicians.[6] In 1968 an African member of parliament stated: 'We are

[1] *The Rhodesia Herald*, 29.5.1969.

[2] *The Rhodesia Herald*, 23.6.1969; 72·5 per cent of the electorate voted in favour of the new constitution.

[3] *Economic Survey of Rhodesia*, 1967, pp. 55–56.

[4] *The Rhodesia Herald*, 4.2.1969–13.2.1969.

[5] For an independent account of chiefs during this period see Holleman (1968), pp. 345–370.

[6] *The Rhodesia Herald*, 23.7.1966; 30.7.1966; 4.8.1966; *Hansard* 22.2.1967, col. 1937–2143.

alarmed by the political powers awarded to African chiefs and, through them, to the Internal Affairs Department.'[1]

In order to increase both the experience of chiefs and to augment their esteem among their people, in 1964 and 1966 the Rhodesian Government sent two parties of chiefs on a world tour, which ended with a visit to South African Bantustans. A member of the first tour recorded the major impression of the chiefs as follows: 'With their knowledge of what had happened to African Chiefs in countries to the north of us and having learnt of the disappearance of chiefs in Pakistan, our Chiefs were heartened by the strong position of their opposite numbers in the Transkei.'[2]

In 1963, the Secretary for Internal Affairs[3] paid tribute to the loyalty of chiefs who had 'courageously asserted their leadership and co-operated with Government. Many of them have had to face up to politically inspired threats and to actual violence.'[4] This tribute implies that there was, nevertheless, active support among the African people for the nationalist cause, because by that time all nationalist parties had been banned and their leaders could not organize their followers.

The provincial assemblies discussed the proposed legislation affecting the powers of chiefs, and the National Council of Chiefs analysed this legislation in detail. Yet even among chiefs nationalist aspirations still existed, in spite of their co-operation with government. In 1963 the first president of this council was forced by his fellow chiefs to resign because of his strong support of African nationalism.[5]

In 1964 all chiefs were assembled at the capital to discuss the independence of Rhodesia from Great Britain. The Report of the Secretary for Internal Affairs recorded that their 'unanimous support for Government at this meeting will probably be a milestone in the history of this country'.[6] The chiefs recognized their strong bargaining position and asked for representation in a new Rhodesian parliament. They condemned African nationalism and claimed to represent all Africans not on the voters' roll.[7]

[1] *The Rhodesia Herald*, 26.7.1968.
[2] Inkomoyahlaba (1965), p. 68.
[3] In 1962 the administration of African areas was reorganized: native commissioners were renamed district commissioners, the Chief Native Commissioner became the Secretary for Internal Affairs, and the Native Affairs Department became the Ministry of Internal Affairs. African rural areas, in the past known as reserves. were called tribal trust lands.
[4] Secretary for Internal Affairs (S.I.A.), 1963, p. 4.
[5] S.I.A., 1963, p. 5, and information derived from personal fieldwork.
[6] S.I.A., 1964, p. 7.
[7] Rhodesia: *Domboshawa Indaba*, 1964, pp. 16–33.

In 1965 the British Prime Minister came to Rhodesia to ascertain the views of the people on independence. Reluctantly he agreed to meet some chiefs. After his interview he commented. 'I have seen the chiefs. They cannot, by the widest stretch of imagination, be said to be capable of representing the African population as a whole.'[1] The chiefs in their turn informed the government that they had no confidence in Great Britain and expressed 'satisfaction ... over the firm action taken by Government'.[2]

In 1966 the African Affairs Act was amended, and the section of the old act which described chiefs as constables in their tribal areas was deleted.[3] In 1967 the Tribal Trust Land Act was passed, which returned to chiefs the power to allocate land to their subjects, and held them responsible for soil conservation. In 1969 the African Law and Tribal Courts Act was passed, returning to chiefs most civil and limited criminal jurisdiction. Under both acts the Minister of Internal Affairs retained final control in tribal trust lands and could invalidate or intervene in any decisions reached by a chief. Yet even so these acts present a great increase in the powers of Rhodesian chiefs. Since the two most essential functions of chiefs in the past had consisted in land allocation and trying court cases, and since these functions had largely been removed from them when the first commissioners were appointed,[4] their return reconstituted the chiefs in their traditional roles.

The constitution of 1969 includes chiefs in both the Rhodesian parliament and senate. It suggests a senate consisting of twenty-three members, ten of whom are African chiefs, and a parliament of sixty-six members, eight of whom are chiefs or their representatives.[5] With the acceptance by the electorate of this constitution chiefs obtained their request of 1964, when they asked the Prime Minister that they be represented in parliament as a condition for their support of independence. With their lift into the country's legislative assembly Rhodesian chiefs have completely changed their image, from leaders of rebellions at the end of the nineteenth century to parliamentarians in a racially composite society.[6]

[1] S.I.A., 1965, p. 2.

[2] S.I.A., 1965, p. 4.

[3] *African Affairs Amendment Act*, No. 44, 1966.

[4] Chiefs were allowed to try minor civil cases; but every litigant had the right to have any civil case tried by a commissioner.

[5] *Proposals for a New Constitution*, 1969, para. 7 and 9.

[6] The rising self-esteem of chiefs, resulting from these changes in their scope and influence, can be seen from the following demands.

In 1969 several groups of chiefs asked the Secretary for Internal Affairs for an

(c) *Councils*

The period after 1963 showed a rapid spread of councils. This increase
was brought about by the vigour with which the government publicized
and implemented the new policy of community development. In 1962
the Prime Minister had announced in parliament that district commissioners would become the spearhead of the new policy of community
development,[1] and in consultation with experts in the field of community development in America and England the Rhodesian Government worked out in detail what community development was to mean
in Rhodesia. In 1965 the Prime Minister issued the following statement
on the new policy:

> Community development is . . . an active, planned and organized effort to
> place responsibility for decision-making in local affairs on the freely chosen
> representatives of responsible people at community and local government
> levels, and to assist people to acquire the attitudes and knowledge, skills
> and resources required to solve, through communal self-help and organisa-
> tion, as wide a range of local problems as possible in their own order of
> priority.[2]

Councils were to be the organs through which the new development
was to be channelled; yet, as this statement shows, community development went beyond council activities as they were envisaged under the
1957 African Councils Act.

Community development immediately ran into many difficulties.
In 1963 the Report of the Secretary for Internal Affairs recorded much
opposition to the new policy from missionaries, African nationalists,
teachers and peasants. The first three groups feared that community
development was apartheid in disguise, and the peasants objected
because they saw in it another means by which government extracted
taxes from them.[3] The link between community development and
councils hardened African attitudes.

Yet the government was determined to succeed, and embarked on an

---

increase in salaries. They argued that since they had to perform more work than in
the past, such as allocating land and travelling far, both within and outside Rhodesia,
above all since they had to maintain law and order in the country and so assist
government, they had a claim to higher wages. They also took it amiss that when the
salaries of members of parliament were increased in 1969 (*The Rhodesia Herald*,
5.7.1969), their own were not increased. They claimed that their income, which was
lower than that of their more educated subjects, caused them social embarrassment.
(Information from an African clerk employed by the Ministry of Internal Affairs.)

[1] S.I.A., 1963, p. 8.
[2] Prime Minister, 1965, para. 7.
[3] S.I.A., 1963, pp. 6, 83–85.

extended training programme. Four district commissioners were sent to
America to study community development and two training advisers
from the States were invited to advise on local implementation. Four
hundred and forty African civil servants working for the department of
Conservation and Extension attended courses in community development and 252 accepted transfers to the department of Internal Affairs
as untrained 'community advisers'.[1] These men, however, had little
experience in community guidance and soon encountered serious
obstacles. In 1964, therefore, a training centre was opened near Salisbury
at which 61 community advisers underwent a longer training. By 1966
their number had increased to 230.

The training centre also ran courses for secretaries of African councils.
The government aimed to replace all unqualified staff as soon as possible. To the surprise of the officials of Ministry of Internal Affairs,
however, council members refused to accept trained strangers to replace
their untrained local secretaries. Again the government insisted, and
from 1964 onwards the number of trained secretaries increased.

Secretaries formed a minor hindrance to the popular acceptance of
councils. Again and again Reports of the Secretary for Internal Affairs
quote numbers of secretaries who had been dismissed for theft. For
example, in 1963 the Report of the Secretary for Internal Affairs stated:
'The standard of integrity is low and six secretaries were suspended for
dishonesty during the year, of whom three ended up in the courts on
criminal charges';[2] and in 1967 it recorded that there was 'an unfortun-
ate "wastage" amongst the trained men, for they prove too young and
inexperienced to carry the responsibilities, whilst others crack under the
strain of finance, and turn to dishonesty'.[3] The number of trained
secretaries rose from twenty-two in 1964 to sixty-seven in 1967.

In spite of training programmes, few councils were established in the
early 1960s. According to the 1964 Report the first council since 1959
had been established in that year, yet six councils were completely
inactive. Like earlier Reports, it noted that conflicts existed between
traditional leaders and elected councillors, and that these difficulties
were so widely known that other chiefs had forbidden the establishment of councils in their areas.[4] By 1965 a lessening of opposition to
community development was recorded and four more councils were
established.[5] During 1966 and 1967 sixteen new councils opened. The

[1] S.I.A., 1963, p. 84.
[2] S.I.A., 1963, p. 86.
[3] S.I.A., 1967, p. 21.
[4] S.I.A., 1964, p. 28.
[5] S.I.A., 1965, p. 12.

1967 Report stated that twenty-three further communities had asked for councils in the next few years.[1] This means that by 1970 there are likely to be some hundred African councils, providing about a quarter of all African rural areas with local government.

By the late 1960s the majority of councils had their own African chairmen. The move to replace district commissioners by elected Africans had begun earlier. By 1963 nine councils had their own chairmen; by 1965 forty-two and by 1967 sixty-six. This transfer of responsibility to Africans accelerated the acceptance of community development. Also the great increase of community agents contributed to this change.

TABLE 1
African Councils, 1963–1967*

Year	No. of councils	No. of African chairmen	No. of trained secretaries	No. of community agents
1963	55	9	—	252†
1964	56	25	22	61
1965	60	42	46	163
1966	68	49	50	230
1967	76	66	67	226

* S.I.A., 1963–1967.   † Untrained.

By 1965 the basic framework for community development had been established. More and more councils took over local services, such as cattle dipping, road and bridge building and maintenance, water supplies, primary education and clinics. The 1967 Report gives a list of all the services provided by councils. Table 2 lists major services:

TABLE 2
Community Services Rendered by Councils, 1967*

Services	No. of councils involved
Animal husbandry and dipping	46
Beer-halls, bottle stores, etc.	43
Roads and bridges	41
Water supplies	36
Primary education	30
Clinics and first-aid posts	23

* S.I.A., 1967, p. 24.

[1] S.I.A., 1967, p. 8. By October 1969 ninety-eight councils had been formed. *The Rhodesia Herald*, 2.10.1969.

Many of these services rendered by councils are directly related to the spread of bureaucratization in African areas: roads and bridges not only help people in their economic pursuits, but they also provide the means for a more thorough administration; water supplies, animal husbandry and dipping increase production, and together with business enterprises such as beer-halls and bottle stores bring money into circulation; schools produce the future bureaucrats.

By 1967 government had exempted the people living in twenty-three council areas from personal tax and allowed them to collect its equivalent for local development. The Report of the Secretary for Internal Affairs concluded that this concession provided a great incentive for responsible administration. The revenues collected increased rapidly: in 1962 all African councils together collected a revenue of £124,726; in 1966 they collected £275,101; in 1967 £438,684.

Another major factor, though not recorded in the Reports of the Secretary for Internal Affairs, is a change in attitude of chiefs towards councils. In several tribal trust lands district commissioners made council activities dependent on the wishes of chiefs and their traditional advisers. This assured chiefs that the new system would not necessarily undermine their position, but could be used to increase their status. Hence several chiefs became spokesmen for community development.[1]

After initial opposition, therefore, the post-Federal period has witnessed a steady spread of councils in Rhodesia. Opposition was overcome when chiefs began to support community development. The relationship between chiefs and councils is analysed in the last chapters of this book.

CONCLUSION

This chapter has traced the changing position of chiefs and the growth of councils against the broad background of Rhodesian history. The development of European politics determined the structure of administration in African areas and the changes in the indigenous political system. As long as fear of African uprisings dominated European consciousness at the turn of the century, African chiefs were suppressed; when the country struggled for its economic survival in the early 1930s Africans were separated from Europeans and a policy of separate development propagated; with increased prosperity for an ever-growing European population and the need for labour, Africans were accepted as junior partners in a multiracial society.

[1] Cf. *infra*, pp. 166–227.

By this time, however, African nationalist consciousness had awakened, a development not expected by European administrators. To repress nationalism, African chiefs were organized into provincial assemblies and a National Council of Chiefs, and their salaries were increased. The introduction of salaries, replacing the tribute chiefs received in the past from their subjects, marked an important stage in their transition from patriarchs to bureaucrats. The banning of all African nationalist parties convinced the chiefs that their future lay in co-operation with the European government. International isolation after the unilateral declaration of independence united Rhodesian European politicians and African chiefs. Legislation was passed to increase the chiefs' powers, and both within Rhodesia and without, chiefs became identified with the Rhodesian government.

The aim in creating African councils was identical to that which inspired government to increase the chiefs' powers. Councils were intended to provide an outlet for the views of educated Africans and thus divert them from national politics. This is proved by an early Chief Native Commissioner's Report, which states that the first African councils in Rhodesia, called community boards, were created to counteract the emergence of nationalistically inclined African voluntary associations. The policy of asking chiefs and elected members, that is representatives of the uneducated older tribal population and young educated men, to serve on the same councils, precluded success. Repeated attempts through new legislation to strengthen the council system failed, until under the policy of community development in the 1960s a new framework had been established and the district commissioners' influence over chiefs had increased to such an extent that chiefs consented to co-operate.

The system of administration in African rural areas that evolved from these changes is as follows. The Secretary for Internal Affairs, himself responsible to the Minister of Internal Affairs, is assisted by seven provincial commissioners. Each provincial commissioner supervises the work of six to eight district commissioners in his province. District commissioners are in direct contact with the chiefs in their districts, and through the chiefs deal with subchiefs, village headmen and people. This structure represents the bureaucratic hierarchy through which administrators communicate with the people.

To ensure an exchange of views between government and the chiefs', provincial assemblies and the National Council of Chiefs have been established. Here European officials can convey government policies to Africans, and chiefs may voice the requests of their people. According to repeated references in the Reports of the Secretary for Internal Affairs, new policies affecting Africans are first discussed at these assemblies before parliament votes on final legislation. Under the 1969 constitution, eight African chiefs or their representatives will be elected by eight electoral colleges,[1] whose relationship to provincial assemblies has not yet been defined. It is clear, however, that through participating in these gatherings chiefs influence politics. They are both administrators and politicians.[2]

Through serving on community development councils, chiefs also influence the economic life of their areas. Community development councils are part of a third hierarchy connecting African villages with parliament, because local government itself consists of councillors operating at village subchiefdom, chiefdom, district, provincial and national level.[3] In addition to being administrators and politicians, therefore, chiefs are economic planning officers for their areas.

The final picture of Rhodesian chiefs which emerges from this survey shows them as occupying key positions in different systems of domination. Because they link together in their own persons the institutions of patriarchalism and bureaucracy they are caught in a role conflict. Weber's theory that the most acute tensions during a period of changing political structures centres round the position of the former patriarch who wants, or is forced, to become a bureaucrat, explains the dilemma in which Rhodesian chiefs find themselves.

---

[1] *Proposals for a new Constitution for Rhodesia*, 1969, para. 9b ii.
[2] S.I.A., 1966, p. 1.
[3] Prime Minister, 1965, para. 17–22. cf. *infra*, p. 170.

CHAPTER 2

Material and Ideological Preconditions for Bureaucratization

INTRODUCTION

The study of chiefs and councils presented in this book is based on field-work undertaken among the Karanga section of the Shona-speaking people. The Karanga have been chosen because they constitute the largest culturally homogeneous group of Africans in Rhodesia. With well over a million people, they account for approximately 27 per cent of the indigenous population. They are, moreover, the oldest and traditionally most important group of Africans in this country. Archaeologists have established that the proto-Karanga probably arrived south of the Zambezi river about the year A.D. 1000,[1] and historians confirm that the Karanga had certainly settled there by the early fourteenth century,[2] built the famous stone structures or *zimbabwe*, and founded the Mutapa empire, which dominated the country between the Zambezi and Limpopo rivers for about 500 years.

1. GENERAL BACKGROUND

Karangaland covers approximately 14,400 square miles and lies within a radius of about 80 miles around Fort Victoria. It presents a typical cross-section of Rhodesia. Its altitude varies between 5,000 and 3,000 feet above sea level. The high veld in the north is predominantly inhabited by Europeans; in the middle veld Europeans and Africans live in adjacent blocks of land; and the low veld is almost exclusively occupied by Africans.

Most of Karangaland consists of light sandy soil, occasionally interspersed with dark loam. Uncertain rainfall, varying between 20 and 30 inches per annum, but reaching 40 inches in the higher and dropping to 15 inches in the lower-lying areas, makes crop production hazardous. The land is eminently suited for ranching, but population pressure as

---

[1] Robinson (1966), p. 7 *et alia*; Summers (1961), pp. 1–13.
[2] Abraham (1966), pp. 28–46; Stokes (1966), p. xv; Tindall (1968), p. 28.

D

well as preference among the Karanga for a mixed farming system militate against a pastoral economy.

Fig. 1. Map of the indigenous people of Rhodesia

The communities[1] on which this study is based live in six chiefdoms and one subchiefdom in three tribal trust lands, the nearest within a radius of about twenty miles from the provincial capital, Fort Victoria, some within a radius of fifty miles, and the most distant within a radius of eighty miles. In 1967 a census was taken of thirty-nine villages, consisting of eight neighbourhood groups[2] in six chiefdoms and one subchiefdom. The aim was to test whether the communities studied were representative of the whole of Karangaland. These groups, called Hove (Fish), Shiri (Bird), Ngara (Crocodile), Shoko (Monkey)—subdivided into the Shoko Murewa and Shoko Museamwa communities—Nzou (Elephant), Mhofu (Eland) and Shumba (Lion),[3] were thoroughly sur-

[1] The term 'community' is used here in a very loose sense. It applies to a group of people 'sharing a limited territorial area as the base for carrying out the greatest share of their daily activities' (Sjoberg, 1964, p. 114). These communities are not self-sufficient economic units, nor are they politically independent; they are the constituent parts of a chiefdom. Most communities centre around a village school (cf. *infra*, pp. 48–49). The term 'community' in this context means a smaller social unit than in Rhodesian Government literature on 'community development' (cf. *infra*. pp. 166–227).

[2] The neighbourhood groups were the cores of local communities.

[3] See Appendix A, p. 237.

veyed and every person belonging to these villages was enumerated. The statistical data presented in this chapter are based on this census.[1]

In addition to these tribal trust land communities, two purchase areas, called Guruuswa and Mutadza, have been surveyed. Purchase areas are blocks of land, set aside under the Land Apportionment Act of 1931, in which proficient African farmers can obtain freehold titles to land; they are administered by farmers' committees and are independent of the control of African chiefs. The Guruuswa purchase area consists of 146 farms and the Mutadza purchase area of sixty. Both lie between the tribal trust land communities of this study and are linked to them by close social ties.

All nine communities border on European farm-land, and their inhabitants occasionally interact with Europeans in economic and political contexts.[2]

All communities are connected to tarred main roads by reasonably good dirt roads, and regular bus services link them to all the main centres of Rhodesia, to Fort Victoria, Bulawayo, Gwelo, Salisbury and Umtali. None of the communities, therefore, is isolated from the wider life of Rhodesia, and all are penetrated by economic enterprise and bureaucratic administration. All communities are provided with local stores. They are frequently visited, too, by civil servants of the various government ministries.

2. DEMOGRAPHY

The political development of Rhodesia has in part been influenced by a rapid African population growth. Whereas at the turn of the century Africans were estimated to number half a million, by 1969 they numbered over five million. Political and social developments in tribal trust lands are to a large extent determined by population pressures.

The census result of the selected Karanga communities shows that population densities differ greatly between one community and another. The 1967 census is based on 5,631 men, women and children, of whom 3,300 live in tribal trust lands and 2,331 in purchase areas. The Shiri community, which had lost land to European farmers at the beginning of the twentieth century, and had to absorb a large number of people when an adjoining block of land was declared a purchase area, has the high population density of 148 persons per square mile. The other communities

[1] Several of these groups had already been surveyed in 1962, and occasional reference will be made to the earlier census.

[2] Cf. *infra*, pp. 76–165.

have population densities of just over 70 persons per square mile, and the two purchase areas have 20 persons per square mile.[1] The overall population density of Rhodesia is 30 persons per square mile. The different population densities result mainly from different government policies regarding tribal trust lands and purchase areas, and to a lesser degree from the natural increase of these communities.

The government treats tribal trust lands as the true home of all African people, and urban Africans who fail to find employment are urged to return to their villages. This means that tribal trust lands have to absorb both the natural increase of their own permanent population and also those people who, having once left their rural areas, cannot find employment among Europeans.

This general trend is occasionally altered when a chiefdom suffers from acute population pressure and the government decides on a resettlement scheme. The Shiri community, for example, lost 531 persons, or 37 per cent of the total population, between 1962 and 1967,[2] when the government offered the people land north of Karangaland. More people would have left if the new area had not been infected by tsetse fly; for the Karanga are reluctant to part with their cattle.

Purchase areas are in a different category. The government considers them part of Rhodesia's cash economy, and in order to preserve economically viable holdings, landowners are forbidden to divide their land among their children. Sons approaching adulthood must leave their parents and either migrate to towns or return to the tribal trust lands which their fathers left. This regulation keeps purchase-area populations more or less constant, but again throws the burden of supporting the surplus population on tribal trust lands.

Karanga people in their tribal trust lands exhibit high fertility rates. The replacement rate for the seven sample communities in the chiefdoms is 2·1, indicating a doubling of the population every twenty years and an attendant increase in population pressure. In the two purchase areas, on the other hand, the replacement rate is only 1·6, so that the population would double every thirty years if emigration did not play a role. Emigration does however drain off increase, and purchase area populations tend to remain constant.[3]

[1] A population density of 148 is very high for local climatic and ecological conditions. All statistics derived from the sample census have been confirmed by information from the department of Conservation and Extension.

[2] Information derived from a census taken in 1962 in which half of the 1967 surveyed communities were included. The Shiri community was one of these.

[3] Confirmed by the 1962 census, which included the Guruuswa purchase area.

Because of their high fertility rates, African areas have youthful, non-mature, populations. The age-structure of the nine sample communities shows that children below the age of fifteen constitute 48

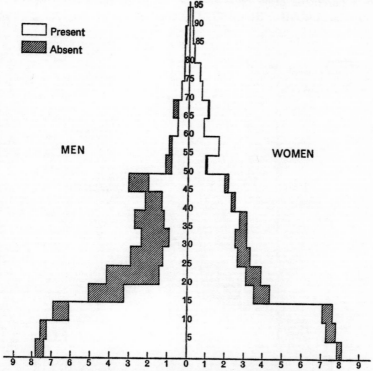

Fig. 2. Population pyramid of tribal trust land populations

per cent of the population. Seventy-four per cent of the people are below the age of thirty, 87 per cent below the age of forty-five, and only 13 per cent are over forty-five years of age. Since the young are less socialized than their elders and more open to change and innovation, especially in the political sphere, the age composition is likely to promote a change towards a political system which is based on other principles than patriarchalism.

3. ECONOMICS

(a) *Dependants*

Prosperity in African rural areas depends in part on the number of dependants a man has to support, and in part on the economic resources available to him. In the tribal trust land communities household heads have to support on the average five dependants, and in purchase areas farmers support nine. The dependants are wives, children, and occasionally a parent or other close relative. Some of these contribute to the family income either by working on the land or by their earnings from

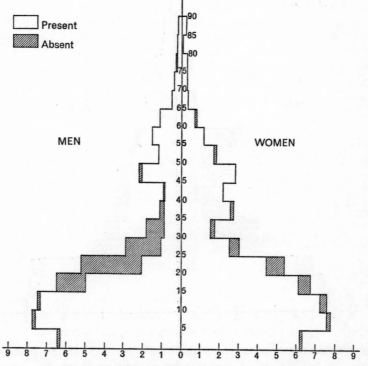

Fig. 3. Population pyramid of purchase area populations

non-agricultural sources. Nevertheless, even if these contributions are taken into account, there still remain a hundred children below the age of fifteen or old people above the age of sixty to be supported by every hundred economically active adults in tribal trust lands, and ninety-five dependants by every hundred active purchase area inhabitants. This is one of the highest dependence ratios in the world.[1] Because African

[1] Blanc gives the number of dependent persons per 100 active persons as 72 for the entire world, but as 100 for tropical and South Africa, 89 for South-East Asia, 77 for South America, 64 for North America, and 61 for Central Europe (Blanc, 1960, table 2).

dependants are mostly children of school age rather than old people, the expenditure for their education imposes a heavy burden on the working population.

(b) *Agricultural Income*
The economic resources of Africans in Rhodesia fall into two broad categories: agricultural and non-agricultural. About half the African male population is engaged in agriculture. In tribal trust lands 31 per cent of all men over the age of fifteen cultivate their land holdings, and 15 per cent assist their fathers in the task. In purchase areas 40 per cent are landowners, and a further 23 per cent help their fathers on the land. This farming population, apart from the youths assisting their parents, is rather old: in the chiefdoms 54 per cent of all peasant cultivators are over the age of forty-five, and so are 81 per cent of all landowners in purchase areas. The average age of the land-working and the land-owning population in these areas is therefore much higher than that of the total community. This means that the core of the stable rural population, especially on the farms, is elderly.

The agricultural resources of the communities are set out in Table 3.

TABLE 3
Agricultural Resources in the Nine Sample
Communities, 1967

	Tribal trust lands	*Purchase areas*
Total acreage	2,669	5,136
Arable acreage per head of population	0·8	2·2
Arable acreage per land-holder	4	25
Head of cattle	2,711	3,854
Beasts per head of population	1	2
Beasts per owner	5	19

The cattle population in the tribal trust lands has increased since 1962, when there were only three beasts per owner. Consequently the grazing areas, which already in the early 1960s carried an animal population in excess of their capacity, are heavily overstocked and eroded. Cattle herds in purchase areas are adjusted to the grazing potential of the farms.

Since land and cattle are more plentiful in purchase areas than in tribal trust lands, their farmers are able to reap much larger harvests than peasants in tribal trust lands. This is borne out by an agricultural survey of 101 tribal trust land peasant cultivators and 108 purchase area farmers in the nine sample communities. No family without a land-holding is included. The value of all their agricultural produce has been converted into current market prices and averaged out per peasant household or farm. The expenditure on seed and fertilizer, but not on labour, transport and the depreciation costs of capital equipment, has been subtracted.

TABLE 4
Average Agricultural Income per
Household or Farm, 1967*

Income	Tribal trust land	Purchase areas
	£	£
Crops harvested	41	145
Cattle sold	6	42
Milk, eggs, vegetables sold	3	9
Total income	50	196
Expenditure	3	3
Profit	47	193

* Cf. *supra*, p. 5: Yudelman gives the gross output per family holding in African rural areas as £80 in 1958.

Table 4 shows that the income of a farm-owner in a purchase area is about four times as large as the income of a peasant cultivator in a tribal trust land. These annual incomes of £47 and £193 respectively are both small when the large number of dependants is taken into account. Peasant families especially often find it impossible to live on their agricultural income.

(c) *Non-agricultural Income*
Non-agricultural employment is therefore essential to subsidize income from agriculture. Table 5 shows that 45 per cent of the men in tribal trust lands and 23 per cent of the men in purchase areas are engaged in non-agricultural activities.

Material and Ideological Preconditions for Bureaucratization 37

TABLE 5
Occupation of Men, 1967

Occupation	Tribal trust lands No.	Per cent	Purchase Areas No.	Per cent
Farming	279	31·0	232	40·4
Assisting parents	132	14·7	129	22·5
Studying	86	9·5	79	13·7
Infirm or old	2	0·2	1	0·2
Unskilled work	225	24·9	82	14·3
Skilled work	45	5·0	8	1·3
Crafts	59	6·5	1	0·2
Business	18	2·0	6	1·1
White-collar work	56	6·2	36	6·3
Total	902	100·0	574	100·0

Non-agricultural work is predominantly sought by younger men who have no land of their own. Apart from students, who are all below the age of thirty, 30 per cent of the unskilled workers and businessmen and 40 per cent of the white-collar workers in tribal trust lands are below the age of thirty; so are 67 per cent of the businessmen, 74 per cent of the white-collar workers, 86 per cent of the unskilled workers, and 87 per cent of the unskilled workers in purchase areas. Forty-five per cent of the craftsmen, 41 per cent of the skilled workers and 50 per cent of the white-collar workers in tribal trust lands are between thirty and forty-four years of age. This means that a fairly clear age division exists, especially in purchase areas, between the types of occupations a man is likely to follow. Whereas old men take to agriculture, the young provide the skills and services that their communities require.

This age division of occupations is in part a function of the labour migration system. The majority of labour migrants are young. The population pyramids[1] show that in tribal trust lands most men aged fifteen to fifty, and in purchase areas the majority of the men aged twenty to thirty-five, are absent as labour migrants. Labour migration draws 43 per cent of all men from tribal trust lands, and 33 per cent of all men from purchase areas. The different migration rates from these two types of settlement are due to the different social structures in these communities, to the differences in their economic potential, and to different Government policies controlling residence rights.

The departure of labour migrants rarely affects agricultural production

[1] Cf. *supra*, pp. 33–34.

because many of them have no land, and those who do have can easily call on landless neighbours to help their wives in the fields while they are away. Of 2,381 labour trips, which represent the combined labour histories of all men in the sample, 20 per cent lasted less than one year, 44 per cent between one and three years, and only 36 per cent more than four years. Only the agricultural help of men who stay away longer than four years is seriously missed by their families. Yet these men frequently hold the most remunerative jobs in European employment, and the money remittances which they send home more than compensate for the labour they could have provided.

Contributions which labour migrants and locally employed non-agricultural workers make to their families' income is substantial. The survey of 101 peasant and 108 farm households shows that people in tribal trust lands rely heavily on non-agricultural incomes, but that in purchase areas this source is insignificant.

TABLE 6

Average Non-Agricultural Income per Household, 1967

Source	Tribal trust lands	Purchase areas
	£	s. d.
White collar work	22	—
Skilled and unskilled work	6	5 0
Crafts	2	6 0
Total	30	11 0

The highest contribution by white-collar workers in tribal trust land communities is in part due to the large number of teachers employed in rural primary schools. Teachers occupy key positions in Karangaland. Not only do they bring more money into local circulation than any other group, but they are also looked up to socially as leaders, especially in the political sphere, and their ideas and values influence many peasant farmers. Their relative economic affluence consolidates their leading position. Money from skilled and unskilled work derives predominantly from remittances sent home by labour migrants. Most money from crafts is locally earned and therefore does not inject new money into the rural economy, but merely redistributes what others have earned from outsiders.

A comparison of Tables 4 and 6 shows that men in tribal trust lands and purchase areas rely for their income on different sources. These sources have significant effects on the spread of bureaucratization in their communities: purchase area farmers derive their annual income of just over £193 almost exclusively from agriculture. Their dependants employed in other occupations make hardly any positive contribution to the family budget. In the tribal trust lands, on the other hand, where agricultural income is low, fathers, sons and brothers contribute substantially through outside employment to the family budget. Their wages and salaries amount to two thirds' of the income derived from agriculture and raise the total annual income from £47 to £77.

These different economic patterns are linked to structural differences. Purchase-area farmers, richer and older than tribal trust land peasants, have frequent contact with European officials, on whom they depend to market their agricultural surpluses. They are familiar with the workings of the African Farmers Union and co-operative societies, and through them with bureaucratic procedures.[1]

Apart from administrative contact with district commissioners, men in tribal trust lands associate less frequently with bureaucrats. Instead they meet a large variety of Europeans—missionaries, farmers, industrialists and businessmen and from these they receive a more varied picture of European life than their purchase area neighbours.[2] In their home villages social life is still regulated through chiefs, whose domination many of the younger men resent. Tribal trust land peasants are poorer than purchase-area farmers. Living hardly above subsistence level in a patriarchal social system, these men with a wider experience of life are predisposed to object to a political structure which bars them from access to leadership. Their discontent, in turn, predisposes them to social change. For them too, entry into the money economy has been a 'pacemaker' for bureaucracy, though in quite a different sense than for purchase area farmers. Young white-collar workers and manual labourers experience patriarchalism as an anachronism in the twentieth century.[3]

4. RELIGION AND EDUCATION

According to Weber, the final pre-condition for bureaucratization is education. In Rhodesia African education is closely linked with religion

---

[1] Cf. *infra*, pp. 51–54.

[2] Purchase area farmers had the same varied experience before they settled on their farms. Conditions of purchase, however, prevent them from seeking outside employment, so that their knowledge of European life is becoming a thing of the past.

[3] Cf. *infra*, p. 198.

because Christian missionaries first established the African school system and still control it to a very large extent. With the exception of one council school in Mutadza purchase area, all educational facilities in the nine Karanga communities are provided by Christian missionaries. The most active missionary group among the Karanga is the Roman Catholic church, which employs some 360 full-time missionaries, has affiliated some 100,000 Karanga as practising members and runs some 240 schools in Karangaland. The next largest group of missionaries is the Dutch Reformed church, whose local branch working among the Karanga is called the African Reformed church. It engages some 112 full-time missionaries, has a membership of some 36,000 Karanga, and runs some 400 schools. A third active mission church in the area is the Methodist church. Other Christian denominations are less active in Karangaland. Table 7 sets out the religious affiliation of African adults in the nine communities. This Table includes both practising and non-practising church members.

TABLE 7

Religious Affiliation in Seven Tribal Trust Land
and Two Purchase Area Communities, 1967

Religion	Tribal trust lands		Purchase areas	
	No.	*Percentage*	*No.*	*Percentage*
Roman Catholics	825	44·9	326	24·9
Anglicans	13	0·7	64	4·9
African Reformed	394	21·4	174	13·3
Methodists	30	1·6	300	22·9
Other Protestants	200	10·9	262	20·0
African Independent Churches	101	5·5	58	4·5
Traditional Religion	276	15·0	124	9·5
	1,839	100·0	1,308	100·0

Table 7 shows that the majority of Africans in these communities belong to one or other of the major mission churches. Some 5 per cent follow African independent churches. African independent church members, as shown elsewhere,[1] share many of the social characteristics of Africans still practising their traditional religion; they are less educated than members of mission churches and economically poorer. Only 15 per cent of all people in tribal trust lands and 10 per cent in purchase areas still

[1] Aquina, Sister Mary, O.P., 1966, pp. 1–40; 1967, pp. 203–219; 1969, pp. 113–137.

practise their traditional religion. Many children of religious traditionalists have joined one of the mission churches, and the percentage of
Christians in each generation increases. This trend began some generations ago. For example, whereas 86 per cent of the present adult population are Christians, only 50 per cent of their parents have joined a Christian denomination.

The first Roman Catholic and Reformed missions were opened in
Karangaland at the end of the nineteenth century and beginning of the
twentieth. They soon developed a large variety of social services, such as
hospitals with nurses' training centres, and primary, secondary and
craft schools. From these centres missionaries spread their influence
throughout the surrounding tribal trust lands. Each of their stations
became a focal point for a wide net of out-schools, that is village schools
founded from a central mission station. These village schools provide up
to five or eight years schooling for the rural people. All central mission
stations are situated in tribal trust lands or at their borders, but never
within purchase areas, because there population densities are too low
to warrant a large concentration of services. Hence either purchase areas
are served by some out-schools attached to mission stations outside
their areas, or they run their own council schools.

The educational facilities of each denomination are co-ordinated. The
Roman Catholic church in Karangaland, for example, has three
teacher-training colleges on central mission stations, and seven secondary schools and an art school on other stations. Three missions have
large hospitals, with nurses' training schools, and all missions have at
least a clinic and an upper primary school. One Roman Catholic mission
is the economic centre, where missionaries from other stations buy their
goods at wholesale prices, and still another is a cultural centre, where
new missionaries from Europe study African language and culture.

If a child from one mission opts for an educational course not available
at his nearest mission, he is transferred to the particular mission at
which the skills he desires are taught. Most missions, therefore, accom-
modate large numbers of boarders, and higher education in Karangaland is for most students only available at boarding schools. This greatly
increases education costs for parents, who have to contribute to the
maintenance of schools since missionaries receive very low subsidies
from government, apart from their teachers' salaries.

Education is therefore linked to the economic position of parents,
but above all to religion. Consequently the future bureaucrats trained
in these schools are imbued with some of their missionaries' values. This
influence becomes socially decisive when religious leaders and African

nationalists share the same attitude towards a government policy, such as community development.[1]

The education of adults in the nine sample communities is set out in Table 8.

TABLE 8
Education in Seven Tribal Trust Land and
Two Purchase Area Communities, 1967

| Education in years | Tribal trust lands | | | | Purchase areas | | | |
| | Men | | Women | | Men | | Women | |
	No.	Per cent	No.	Per cent	No.	Per cent	No.	Per cent
Nil	139	15·4	330	35·3	40	7·0	180	24·5
1–5	418	46·4	479	51·2	216	37·7	374	51·0
6–8	270	29·9	102	10·8	231	40·3	161	21·9
9–11	62	6·9	21	2·2	71	12·3	19	2·6
12 and over	13	1·4	5	0·5	16	2·7	—	—
Total	902	100·0	937	100·0	574	100·0	734	100·0

Table 8 shows that the purchase area population is more highly educated than the tribal trust land population and therefore implicitly better prepared for bureaucratic administration. Of great import for the spread of bureaucracy in African rural areas is the age-structure of the highly educated and of illiterates. If the latter are mostly old, illiteracy declines. If the young are highly educated, then the African population becomes ready to accept clerical and administrative posts in modern bureaucracies. Table 9 shows that the educational preconditions for bureaucratization are being established.

TABLE 9
Percentage Distribution of Illiterate and Educated Africans, 1967

| Age | School attendance in years | | |
	Nil	9–11 years	12 years and over
15–29	8	65	100
30–44	24	24	—
45 and over	68	11	—
Total	100	100	100

[1] Cf. *supra*, p. 23, and *infra*, pp. 168–169.

The uneven distribution of education among the African age-groups has both economic and political consequences. In the economic sphere young educated people are able to earn higher wages than their less educated elders; this results in the dependence of older adults on the young. In the political sphere the wisdom of the old is less respected than in the past because their lack of formal education undermines their standing in communities that regard education as one of the highest social values. Even in rural areas controlled by chiefs, the educated young are taking over some key positions on modern administrative bodies, because the old men are unqualified to serve as secretaries and treasurers. Hence social change in rural areas is accelerated. Only legislative protection of traditional leaders and a concentration of authoritative positions in the hands of elders still arrest a structural revolution.

CONCLUSION

By implication chapter two has shown that the nine sample communities of Karanga tribal trust lands and purchase areas are representative of the whole of Karangaland because the statistics derived from the sample survey coincide with the general statistics prepared by government for Rhodesia. A minor difference occurs in the religious, and consequently educational spheres. Karangaland has had more intensive contact with Christian missionaries than some other areas of Rhodesia, so that a larger number of people have become Christians; the educational achievements of these people are therefore slightly higher than the average in the rest of the country.[1] This means that the Karanga are slightly better qualified to take up positions in new bureaucratic structures. Because mission work extends throughout Karangaland, this difference does not affect the representativeness of the sample communities.

Throughout Karangaland the system of communication is adequately developed; the money economy has been generally accepted, and diverse economic sources have been tapped. Government has provided the basic administrative framework, and missionaries have prepared Africans to accept European values. The material and ideological preconditions for bureaucratization have therefore been created.

---

[1] *Final Report of the April/May 1962 Census of Africans in Rhodesia*, p. 24.

CHAPTER 3

Organization and Community Structures in Rural Karanga Areas

1. EXTERNAL RELATIONSHIPS BETWEEN CHIEFDOMS

The three tribal trust lands in which the sample communities of this study are situated consist of chiefdoms related to each other by kinship ties or by mere geographical contiguity. Present inter-chiefdom relationships are the result of the conquest, fission and fusion that characterized Karanga politics before European occupation.

During the nineteenth century, population increase and pressure on natural resources caused chiefdoms to split up. Sections of established chieftainships which through their structural positions found themselves barred from political office tended to break off and settle in new territory. These splits resulted in constant migrations of people across the country between the Limpopo and Zambezi rivers. Most of the chiefdoms sampled in this study were established by this process in the nineteenth century. Local legends record in stereotyped form how family disputes in the country of origin precipitated secession and the creation of new chiefdoms.[1] They generally point to an uneven economic or political growth among the branches of the ancestral groups. These upset the customary equilibrium and balance of power. Fission restored the equilibrium in both the remaining and departing sections.

With the advent of European settlers such population movements became impossible, and internal conflicts had to be solved within narrowly confined territorial units. Inability to secede limited leadership positions and intensified competition for chieftainships.

Most areas were originally peacefully occupied because land was plentiful. Later arrivals, who were less numerous than those who had come before them, tried to settle at some distance from a larger chiefdom or established affinal ties with a powerful chief; that is, kinship ties through marriage. The three tribal trust lands in which the sample communities are situated provide examples of these alternatives.

The Shiri chiefdom, containing the Shiri community, is a young chiefdom. The ancestors of this chiefdom arrived in their present territory

[1] Cf. Vansina (1965), p. 96, for similar processes among other African tribes.

during the second part of the nineteenth century and asked a powerful chief, Ngara, for land. Chief Ngara accepted them. Some years later the leader of the Shiri people married two daughters of chief Ngara and so became his son-in-law. At the turn of the century, when commissioners asked chiefs to register their office, the leader of the Shiri people presented himself to the commissioner as chief and was accepted. Chief Ngara protested against his son-in-law's action but was unable to invalidate the registration. The relationship between the two chiefs has become traditional, and the successors of chiefs Shiri and Ngara still call each other 'father-in-law' and 'son-in-law'. Any dispute which the junior chief fails to settle is referred to the 'father-in-law'. The two chiefdoms form today one tribal trust land. Chapter Nine demonstrates how this traditional link influences modern politics in the area.[1]

Such positional succession[2] is common in Karangaland. In another tribal trust land chief Nzou recognizes agnatic ties, that is, ties with persons related to him through blood in the male line, with two chiefdoms in a neighbouring tribal trust land. Legend records that the three groups arrived together from the east. Chief Nzou was son and elder brother to two men who settled in adjoining tracts of land. The present chiefs still address each other by the titles of 'father', 'son', 'elder' and 'younger brother'.

The tribal trust land in which chief Nzou rules consists of three unrelated groups. Chiefs Shoko and Mhofu arrived independently of each other long before chief Nzou, and settled next to each other without entering into special relationships. When African areas were separated from European land, these three chiefs found themselves in the same unit. They have never co-operated, and jealously guard their independence from one another. This independence was temporarily abolished when in 1951 the government reduced chiefdoms Shoko and Mhofu to subchiefdoms under chief Nzou, who has a larger number of taxpayers than the other two. This loss of status intensified the animosity between the chiefdoms. Chief Mhofu and his people refused to recognize the demotion. Because of their early settlement in the area and the strong support given by the people, their chieftainship was restored to them. The Shoko chiefdom, however, had to struggle for many years with the help of lawyers and members of parliament to regain its chieftainship, a struggle which is analysed in chapters six, seven and eight.[3]

The third tribal trust land under review consists of one large chiefdom.

[1] Cf. *infra*, pp. 173–180.
[2] Cf. Cunnison (1956), for the role of positional succession in Central Africa.
[3] Cf. *infra*, pp. 106–165.

E

Chief Shumba, who arrived early in the nineteenth century, was invited by a local group to help them fight other newcomers who threatened to take their territory. Chief Shumba accepted the offer, defeated the incoming group in battle, and forced it to settle further south. Instead of becoming a subchief under his host, however, chief Shumba subjected the former to his own domination as soon as his people outgrew the earlier settlers in number. The Shumba chiefdom, therefore, was established through conquest.

2. INTERNAL GROWTH OF CHIEFDOMS

Whether a group is able to become an independent chiefdom or remains subject to another chief, depends on numbers. The establishment of a chiefdom is connected with population increase. The growth of the Shiri chiefdom typically exemplifies the emergence of a chiefdom.

When the Shiri people had arrived in Karangaland, they settled on a hill south of chief Ngara's territory. Threatened by Ndebele raids, they stockaded their village and took refuge in caves. In the centre of their village they erected a land-shrine as a symbol of their unity and political autonomy. A land-shrine consists of a circle of sticks surrounding a small sacred enclosure, which forms the religious centre at which people pray to God for rain and protection against dangers threatening the whole group.[1]

The settlement on the hill was soon unable to support its increasing population. Fields had to be cultivated at ever-increasing distances from the settlement, and the lives of cultivators were thus endangered during Ndebele raids. These economic and security anxieties were frequently reflected in competition for leadership. Two brothers, A1 and A2, moved out with their families and established their own villages on two other hills. Each reproduced the layout of their parent village by fortifying his village against raiders and erecting a land-shrine in its centre. Later they claimed the status of subchiefs, but the descendant of chief Shiri successfully opposed their claim.

By the turn of the century the leader of the Shiri people had married the daughters of chief Ngara; Ndebele raids had ceased, and the commissioner recognized Shiri as chief. A new era began. The early administrators found it difficult to collect taxes from people who disappeared in caves or barricaded themselves in stockaded villages. They therefore ordered them to leave their fortified villages and to live in the plains. Since the government was prepared to use force to disperse mountain

[1] Aquina, Sister Mary, O.P. (1968), pp. 152–153.

villages – in some parts of Rhodesia villages were blasted with dynamite[1] – people began to scatter. This dispersal caused new village splits.

Sons of each of the three village leaders, Aa, A1a and A2a, split off to form their own villages. Between 1910 and 1940 each of these villages split further and gave rise to twenty-three new villages. In 1943 the government precipitated further village splits when it ordered people to build their villages in lines above the rivers, separating grazing and arable land. Most villages had to build anew, and again sons took the opportunity to start their own villages. Thirty-seven new villages were founded. In 1956 the Land Husbandry Act was implemented in the Shiri chiefdom. This implementation necessitated yet another resiting of villages, and fifty more new villages came into being. At the same time land south of the chiefdom was declared a purchase area and the people living there were ordered to leave. Many migrated into Shiri chiefdom and established sixteen new villages. This immigration greatly increased population density in the chiefdom.

TABLE 10

Village Proliferation in Shiri Chiefdom

c. 1880		c. 1900	1910–1940	1943	1956	Immigrants 1956	Total
	A1	1	1	3	6	4	15
	A2	1	7	2	5	—	15
1A	A	—	1	11	8	5	26
	Aa	1	4	7	9	4	25
	A1a	1	7.	13	18	3	42
	A2a	1	3	1	4	—	9
Total village increase		5	23	37	50	16	132
Cumulative increase		6	29	66	116	132	—

This survey of village fission in Shiri chiefdom shows that over a period of eighty years the first village had given rise to 115 new villages, and absorbed a further sixteen immigrant villages. The present villages are much smaller than the early villages and their headmen resemble commoners more closely than chiefs. The village chief of the past is replaced by a chief ruling a large number of villages scattered over many square miles. This change in the position of Rhodesian chiefs has

[1] Thomson (1898), pp. 147–157.

generally been overlooked in the literature on Rhodesian chiefs. In other parts of Rhodesia large chiefdoms existed in the past,[1] but for most of Karangaland the development of Shiri chiefdom is typical.

All the villages in this area recognize chief Shiri as leader. The successors of A1, A2, Aa, A1a and A2a have become recognized as senior headmen by all the new village headmen who split off from them. They frequently press for government recognition, but have not been officially appointed as subchiefs. The people however look to them for leadership, and several of them try court cases and perform other functions that exceed the authority of village headmen.

The multiplication of villages has resulted in a territorial clustering of sections of the chieftainship descended from distinct ancestors. The Karanga call these sections 'houses'. The first village of each group is situated near a hill with a land-shrine, and surrounded by a circle of villages founded by the sons or friends of the first village headman. A second concentric circle of villages consists of villages that split off from the 'sons' ' villages. The successors of the first six village headmen are regarded as 'fathers' by all the headmen who sprang from them, whether or not they are his agnates. The sample communities analysed in chapter two are based on sections of such village clusters.

Fusion also characterizes inter-village relationships. In the early 1960s, for example, the government moved many people out of the Shoko Museamwa community, which had become heavily overpopulated. Since movement was voluntary, it so happened that six village headmen refused to accompany the majority of their people. They stayed on their original land, forming one large village, but none of them gave up his headmanship badge. The twin processes of fission and fusion, therefore, which operate at chiefdom level, apply equally at village level. Because of constant population increase fission is more frequent than fusion.

3. THE SOCIAL STRUCTURE OF LOCAL COMMUNITIES

The effective communities in Karangaland, then, are clusters of villages centring around the village of their leader, whose residence is marked by a land-shrine. This land-shrine is the symbol of the political identity of the group. The leader's village is always the largest in a neighbourhood.

When the first Christian missionaries arrived and opened their schools they tended to look for sites near large villages. The first school, which later became the central mission station in Shiri chiefdom, was

[1] Rennie (1966); Wheeler (1967).

built in 1908 next to the chief's village. By 1940 out-schools had been erected near the homes of all six local leaders, so that every local community centred from then onwards not only on its land-shrine, but also on its school. Missionaries did not at first realize that the educational system would follow traditional groupings and reinforce them.

As the people became more orientated towards the new cash economy education assumed greater importance in their lives. Soon the local school outstripped the land-shrine as the focal point of communal activities, since it became a meeting place for children and adults of the community. Neighbouring groups began to compete with one another to expand their schools, and people referred to their home area by the name of their school rather than by the name of their traditional leader.

Various factors have contributed to the close identification of the people with their schools. Firstly, the people themselves have usually helped to build their schools by making bricks and contributing labour and funds. Secondly, each school has its own committee, on which parents of schoolchildren discuss school administration with the teachers. In this way schools have not only become training grounds for future bureaucrats, but they have also been training adults in bureaucratic procedures.[1] School committees are now democratically elected, and traditional leaders are only represented on them if their own children are in the school and other parents vote for them. This means that they are not *ex officio* members, and that they are obliged to work together with other parents on a democratic basis.

The schools themselves have grown into village communities because the teachers' families have come to live in special houses on the school ground, and the head teacher performs the same functions among his teachers that a village headman performs among his villagers. Complaints against teachers are brought to the head teacher, who tries minor offences. He negotiates as an equal with headmen of surrounding villages in disputes concerning his teachers and villagers. Cases exceeding his authority are brought before the school committee and the parents advise on suitable action. Although schools are a modern institution, they are not regarded as an alien body in the community. They have been fully absorbed into local life and become one of its vital organs.

Apart from providing the focal point of local communities, schools are also an important link through which communities are integrated into larger social groupings. Head teachers are regularly visited by school managers residing at the central mission station; these are

[1] See also Murphree (1970).

responsible to school inspectors for the schools' efficiency, and school inspectors in charge of larger districts are in turn responsible to the government's African education department. In addition, all teachers are members of the Rhodesian African Teachers' Association, a national association that looks after the interests of teachers. Up to 1962, moreover, most teachers living in the nine Karanga communities were members of African nationalist parties. Teachers pass on much of the information they receive through these channels to their local communities, so that through their schools people become acquainted with and interested in country-wide and even international issues.

Schools also unite different local communities by spreading religious interest. All out-schools founded by a central mission entertain close ties with their mission. Religious and educational ties are strengthened through many voluntary church organizations, which have their administrative centre at the mission church. Since 12 per cent of all Roman Catholics belong to one or more religious association, but only 2 per cent of all Protestant Christians, these ties are especially close in Catholic areas.

The unifying functions of a Catholic mission in the social life of an area can be illustrated by a description of regular Sunday activities in Shiri chiefdom. During the early 1960s, every Sunday morning several thousand men, women and children attended religious services at the central mission station, although parallel services were held at distant out-schools. These Sunday-morning gatherings were the largest weekly social events in the chiefdom. They provided opportunities for people to meet their friends, to learn both local and other news, to visit their sick at the mission hospital, and to collect their letters, because the mission remains the only postal address in the area.

The time between the morning services was taken up by voluntary associations. Every month the branch leaders of these associations come to the mission from their out-schools to co-ordinate their work with that of other local communities throughout the chiefdom. On their return they reported back to the members of their local communities the work done at other out-schools. This regular communication served as a link between the Christians of the chiefdom and promoted unified action.

A school community comprises a number of villages, which are the smallest social and political units in Karangaland. The average modern Karanga village numbers some 84 men, women and children. Of these some 37 per cent tend to be agnates of the village headmen, that is, persons related to them by blood in the male line, 32 per cent are other cognates, that is, other blood relatives, 22 per cent affines, that is, kinsmen related through marriage, and 9 per cent strangers or *vatorwa*, that is, unrelated subjects of village headmen. The percentage of strangers has increased during repeated village movements caused by the implementation of various government policies.[1] Strangers are generally at a disadvantage in community enterprises. If they have any land, it is mostly of a quality inferior to that of the headman's agnates; they claim to suffer injustices at the chief's courts, and are often excluded from political decision-making. They therefore live on the periphery of the local community and are more frequently absent as labour migrants than other villagers. They are politically impotent in a patriarchal society.

The social structure of local communities shows that two different bonds link them to larger groupings. Through their village headmen they are united to the chief whose subjects they are. Their relationship to these traditional[2] leaders is part of the patriarchal structure of Rhodesian tribal trust lands. Through their schools and missions people are linked to country, and even world-wide organizations, which are structured along bureaucratic lines. Those villagers who lack kinship connections with local rulers tend to occupy leading positions in these modern organizations. But all participate simultaneously in both systems, and the transition from patriarchalism to bureaucracy is well advanced in tribal trust lands.

4. THE ORGANIZATION AND STRUCTURE OF PURCHASE AREAS

The most important difference between chiefdoms and purchase areas is that the tribal structure does not influence the political processes in the purchase areas. Some chiefs claim political authority over adjoining purchase areas if these had once formed part of their territory; neither farmers, however, nor government, recognizes these claims of tribal leaders.

Purchase areas are administered by democratically elected committees and councils. The farmers come from many different chiefdoms and most are unrelated to one another. This holds true even in purchase areas where a substantial number of farmers come from the same tribal trust land. In Guruuswa purchase area, for example, 25 per cent of all

---

[1] Cf. *supra*, p. 47.
[2] The adjective 'traditional' is here used to refer to the various component parts and aspects of the patriarchal system, even if these are affected by cultural contact.

farm-owners come from Shiri and Ngara chiefdoms, and in Mutadza purchase area 77 per cent come from one tribal trust land. None of them, however, looks to his original home for political leadership; in fact all are proud of their independence from chiefs and eager to elect their leaders and vote them into office.

Connections between purchase areas differ from those between chiefdoms. No traditional links exist between farming communities because all are creations of the modern cash economy and form part of a large farmers' bureaucracy. Every purchase area forms a 'division', though sometimes it is divided into different committees if it consists of many farms. Divisions are organized into six branches. The divisions are represented on these branches by their delegates. The six branch chairmen form a council at the head office of the African Farmers' Union in Salisbury. The union represents the interests of all purchase-area farmers. It issues a monthly newspaper, which keeps them informed of economic developments in Rhodesia and advises them on farming activities. The organization of purchase areas shows that these farming communities are united on the principle of administrative efficiency; kinship relations play no role. Guruuswa purchase area was first occupied in 1956 by farmers who organized themselves through an African Farmers' Union committee to deal with the administration of their area. Such a committee is not a statutory body and cannot draw on government subsidies. By 1967, 146 farms were occupied, the area was subdivided, and a second African Farmers' Union committee was formed.

All committee members of Guruuswa purchase area were chosen because of their agricultural leadership. In 1967 none of the sixteen office-holders had an income of less than £200 from his farm; four made a profit of over £300 but less than £400 and six of over £400.

Mutadza purchase area is ten years older than Guruuswa purchase area. Since the mid 1950s it has been administered by a council, and its African Farmers' Union committee has become less important. The council is a statutory body and enables the people to draw on government subsidies for their community projects. The farmers formed a council because the area is many miles from the nearest mission and no denominational school had been established in their area. The council therefore had the express aim of establishing a school. The school was built and soon provided full primary education for the farmers' children. As soon as this aim had been achieved, people lost interest in their council and by 1968 it was closed.[1]

[1] Cf. *infra*, pp. 201–203.

Council members in Mutadza purchase area were not chosen for their agricultural abilities but for their political leadership. Farmers described the most important characteristic of council members as the ability to speak in public, and fearlessly to represent the wishes of the farming community before European government officials. In 1967 only three of their eight council members had an income of over £200; two were evicted in 1968 for poor farming practices and arrears in paying their annual rentals. These two men made a total profit from farming in 1967 of £23 and £27 respectively.

The African Farmers' Union committees and the council perform a large variety of functions. They regulate the life of their communities in broad outlines. They organize agricultural meetings and shows, discuss government regulations, plan the development of their areas, and settle community disputes. Their juridical activities are not recognized by the government and their decisions cannot be enforced. Yet because groups of some sixty to seventy farms are small, local pressure assures that litigants abide by the decisions of their committee or council. Farmers are concerned to be as independent as possible from outside control, and resent it if their neighbours take court cases to European magistrates. Their elected leaders perform many of the functions which in tribal trust lands are performed by chiefs. The patriarchal structure of chiefdoms, however, is completely replaced by modern institutions. Through the African Farmers' Union and other agricultural organizations purchase-area farmers are incorporated into country-wide bureaucracies. The transition from patriarchalism to bureaucracy was made easy for them by their geographical move from chiefdoms to purchase areas. They started off among strangers in a new area, unhampered by an inherited patriarchal system.

Because purchase areas have a low population density, farming families do not live as close to each other as do villagers in tribal trust lands. Homes are generally built on little hills in the centre of the 200-acre farms, and visits to neighbours involve long walks. The majority of people spend most of their time on their own farms. Effective co-operation is limited to small groups of three to four farms clustering together. Farmers emphasize that they have plenty to do on their farms and little time for social gatherings. It is mainly for committee sessions and agricultural meetings that farmers come together. Every farm, therefore, is to a large extent an independent social unit.

Kinsmen rarely own farms in the same purchase area. Those kinship ties which are still operated by farmers link them back to the tribal trust lands from which they migrated and to which some of their children have returned. To create links among farmers, voluntary associations have been established which unite people on a common-interest basis. The most widespread formal associations are agricultural. Eighty per cent of all farm-owners belong to co-operative societies or to intensive conservation area committees. Religious associations, on the other hand, are not active because organized church life is underdeveloped. Visiting priests and ministers hold occasional religious services but are prevented by distance from visiting the purchase areas more frequently.

CONCLUSION

Great differences exist between the political and social organization of tribal trust lands and purchase areas. Both types of communities are controlled through European government officials of the various ministries; but whereas in tribal trust lands these administrators work through chiefs, in purchase areas they contact the farmers directly. The farmers' democratically elected councils and committees form part of country-wide bureaucratic systems. Unlike chiefs, who form part of the bureaucratic hierarchy of the Ministry of Internal Affairs, purchase-area councils and committees form a more integral part of these systems because they have arisen from them and are determined by no other structural principle. They had no predecessors in traditional Karanga society. Chiefs, on the other hand, introduce into the administration of the Ministry of Internal Affairs a foreign patriarchal element, which operates on structural principles alien to bureaucracy.

CHAPTER 4

Modern Chiefs and their Self-image

INTRODUCTION

In 1961 the government deposed one of the leading Rhodesian chiefs. A commission of inquiry was appointed to investigate the events leading to the chief's deposition. To provide a background against which the chief's actions could be judged the Commission summarized the position of chiefs in the administrative system of Rhodesia's African rural areas. It first stated that the administration is ideally conceived as a single pyramidal system; it continues:

> In reality it represents two distinct, vastly dissimilar but inter-locking spheres, that of European Administration of Native Affairs and that of local tribal Government, with the Chief as the principal link between the two spheres. It is the Chief's unenviable lot to be both the bottom of the European upper half of the pyramid, and the top of the lower tribal part of the structure. This dual position is fraught with difficulties, because it involves a reconciliation between two inherently conflicting roles (and loyalties): that of faithful servant of an essentially foreign and superimposed Administration, and that of head and representative of an autonomous African tribal community whose support is equally vital to him. When the aims of the Administration and of the tribal community coincide, re-conciliation is no problem, but when these aims diverge (as they often do) the Chief is in the unhappy position of seeking to satisfy one master without incurring the displeasure of the other. Usually a Chief tries to steer a middle course, thereby running the risk of weakening his position on both sides. ... The Chief's role as conveyor of 'Government instructions', un-avoidably tends to outweigh his role as representative of his people. The result is that he stands in danger of losing their confidence and support (the term 'Government stooge' has gained wide currency in African rural circles). Few Chiefs can escape this dilemma, and probably the great majority of Shona Chiefs, by tradition ill-equipped to overcome both their own and their people's conservatism, are unable either effectively to serve the role of progress, or to retain the confidence of their people. With the result that reluctantly (if not resentfully) they have to withdraw into the twilight of their traditional office, leaving it to others to carry the torch of progress.[1]

[1] *Mangwende Report* (1961), para. 166, 167.

This analysis illustrates the dual role of Rhodesian chiefs, who are regarded both as patriarchal leaders of rural communities and as bureaucrats in modern government administration. Such roles conflict, and the conflict is not confined to chiefs in Rhodesia. Fallers writes that in many parts of Africa chiefs live in a disordered and conflict-ridden world because African and European social systems not merely collide head on but interpenetrate each other. The result is that 'new social systems embodying diverse and conflicting elements have come into being'.[1] Fallers concludes that as a result individual chiefs are considered as social deviants by one or other group, depending on the values they emphasize.

Chapter one has presented a historical analysis of the evolution of modern chieftainship. This chapter studies further the conflicts that arise from the unprecedented increase in the chiefs' powers; it examines the social characteristics of chiefs, and finally presents a series of self-images which chiefs entertain of themselves. The last section is based on long interviews with twelve chiefs, representing a sample of approximately 20 per cent of all Karanga chiefs.

1. INCREASE IN THE CHIEFS' POWERS

Chapter three traced the growth of Shiri chiefdom over the last eighty years and showed how a single village split and resplit until the size of the modern chiefdom was 132 villages. In 1969 the tribal trust land consisting of the Shiri and Ngara chiefdoms numbered 45,000 inhabitants. Assuming that the growth rate of this population had been identical with that of the country as a whole,[2] it is likely that at the turn of the century the two chiefdoms numbered at the most some 5,000 people. In fact the number must have been lower, because a substantial number of outsiders had been moved into the area in the 1930s and 1950s. Considering this immigration, and also the fact that the Ngara chiefdom has always been much larger than the Shiri chiefdom, it is likely that the Shiri chiefdom in about 1900 numbered just over 1,000 people, of whom some 300 may have been adult men.[3] Since by that time there existed already four villages, each village is likely to have had approximately 75 men, and a total population of some 250 children and adults. Today chief Shiri rules over 11,000 men, women and children.

[1] Fallers (1955), pp. 294–295.

[2] At the turn of the century Rhodesia had an estimated African population of half a million, and in 1969 of over five million. Cf. *supra*, pp. 31–32.

[3] Estimate based on fertility rates and infant mortality rates.

These numbers show that the position of traditional village chiefs differed substantially from modern chiefs ruling large chiefdoms. In the past a chiefdom was identical with a village and its surrounding land. The power of village chiefs resembled that of modern heads of extended families. They enjoyed great prestige in their own villages, but their followers seldom numbered more than a few hundred men and their dependants. If these early village chiefs ruled as despotically as present chiefs relate, they were despots only of a very minor order. As pointed out in chapter three,[1] this observation applies to the Karanga communities included in this study; it may well be that chiefdoms in other parts of the country were much larger.

With the cessation of tribal warfare, the general pacification of Rhodesia, the disintegration of large villages and the creation of many smaller settlements, the powers of former village chiefs were to a large extent assumed by European commissioners.[2] Yet even during this period of legal impotence the successors of the old village chiefs considered themselves rulers of all the people living in their expanding chiefdoms. This meant that even during these decades, in which commissioners effectively controlled African areas, chiefs extended their influence because of the natural population increase, for the Karanga estimate a chief's prestige by the number of his followers.

Meanwhile chiefs were consulted from time to time by Rhodesian governments. Provincial assemblies and the National Council of Chiefs were established, and new powers were given to chiefs by legislation in the 1960s. These factors increased the chiefs' authority and influence, and effectively included them in the administrative bureaucracy of the Rhodesian government.

The chiefs' powers have therefore been increased by two processes: (a) the number of their followers have been multiplied owing to population expansion. In the past this increase was drained off by constant fission of chiefdoms and ensuing migration. Such subdivisions and movements had become impossible by the turn of the century; and (b) many of those powers exercised by traditional village chiefs over their extended families have been extended to the modern chief. Chiefs have accordingly become more powerful in the second half of the twentieth century than they have ever been in the past, except that they are strictly dependent on European government officials. For whereas in the past chiefs were related only to their people, their integration into the national administration of Rhodesia eliminates their former autonomy.

[1] Cf. *infra*, p. 48.
[2] Cf. *infra*, p. 10.

The real change in the position of chiefs can therefore be described as a change from small-scale patriarchs to large-scale bureaucrats; bureaucrats however, who are hemmed in by surviving values of a passing patriarchal era.

This change in the chiefs' position alters their relationship with their people. Many of these changes, resented by chiefs and people alike, are forced on them by the structural opposition between the old and the new political systems. Max Weber has stated that 'bureaucratic and patriarchal structures are antagonistic in many ways'.[1] The vested interests of chiefs, entrenched through the structural rigidities of the traditional system, prevent them from acquiring the qualifications needed by bureaucratic administrators. To modify or adjust them to a changed social situation is only possible through conflict and opposition.[2] This is shown by the social characteristics of modern Karanga chiefs.

2. THE SOCIAL CHARACTERISTICS OF MODERN KARANGA CHIEFS

The traditional village chief was the eldest male relative of his dependants. His group was undifferentiated by economic skills; all men were peasant cultivators, cattle herders and hunters; what they procured was shared among all; an egalitarian ethic prevailed, which was not disturbed by the greater prestige accorded to the village chief, because even he had the same training, material comforts, and shared the same beliefs as his people.

During the first half of the twentieth century this ethic and economic egalitarianism was gradually replaced by a situation of economic differentiation. Chapter two showed that rural areas have become highly differentiated.[3] Some men have distinguished themselves educationally, occupationally, and economically, so that there are now great differences in wealth and living standards. Many Karanga moreover have accepted the Christian religion, and traditional religious worship, in which chiefs played a leading part, no longer serves as a bond among the people. The chief is no longer *primus inter pares*; in fact, in terms of modern values he ranks near the bottom of the prestige hierarchy.

This assessment is based on the social characteristics of five chiefs and one subchief who were included in the census based on the sample communities in Karagaland. Personal contact with seven more chiefs has

---

[1] Gerth and Mills (1965), p. 245.
[2] This observation is made by Blau (1964), p. 301.
[3] Cf. *supra*, pp. 35–39.

shown that those included in the census were typical of a large number.

Four of the five chiefs claim to have been born in about 1880, and one in 1915. All five chiefs have abdicated the actual administration of their chiefdoms to their sons, either because of old age or because of serious ill health. The four old chiefs still adhere to and participate in traditional religion. The younger chief, however, is a member of a Christian church. None of the four old chiefs has ever been to school, but the younger chief has studied for twelve years and was headmaster of a primary school before his appointment as chief.[1]

Four of the sons acting for their fathers were born in the 1920s, and one in 1939. All of them are therefore of mature age and physically capable of actively administering their areas. All have had some schooling and are literate in the vernacular; the youngest has received secondary education. Unlike their fathers, all are Christians belonging to various denominations: one is a Roman Catholic, one a member of the African Reformed Church, one a Methodist, one a Seventh Day Adventist, and one belongs to an African Independent church.

The subchief was born in 1920, received five years schooling, and belongs to the Roman Catholic church. He is not deputed by his son. He shares all social characteristics with the acting chiefs, that is, with the sons who administer the chiefdoms for their fathers.

These social characteristics show that apart from one chief all traditional leaders belong to that section of the community which is most orientated towards the past. The old chiefs still adhering to their traditional religion represent a strong link with the tribal past, but already their sons cease to constitute such a link. Though not all acting chiefs are practising Christians and some participate occasionally in the traditional religion, the majority take their Christian religion seriously. This means that acting chiefs no longer fulfil their role as guardians of the religious cult of their chiefdoms. As long as their old fathers are still alive and perform these functions, this does not affect their relationship with those followers who are traditionally orientated. At present their church affiliation is to their advantage because it guarantees the chiefs' families support from their Christian followers.

More serious than religious traditionalism is the chiefs' lack of education. Nobody takes it amiss that old retired chiefs are illiterate, but that their acting sons are in most instances unable to read English government documents greatly reduces their prestige in the eyes of their

---

[1] Holleman states that ninety per cent of the 320-odd Rhodesian chiefs were illiterate. Holleman (1968), p. 49.

educated subjects. These subjects reason that in the modern Rhodesian economy chiefs would be unskilled labourers earning very low wages, and if they did not receive large government salaries every one of them would be a 'Mr Nobody', a term generally given to African domestic servants. There are some exceptions to this rule, for example the younger acting chief who has attended secondary school. All except this man have been labour migrants, and their migration histories show that they performed unskilled and lowly paid labour for many years before they began to act for their fathers. This tends to support their subjects' contention that chiefs' families rank low in the modern prestige hierarchy.

Yet if chiefs lack modern prestige criteria they are well endowed with those that conferred esteem and prominence in the past. In the past a great man had many wives. These could cultivate larger fields for him than most men could manage who had fewer dependants. This enabled them to feed and entertain many guests and supporters. As polygynists they had many children, who provided the core of their followers. Wealth was counted in cattle, and this traditional value is still accepted in all rural areas.

Three of the five chiefs are polygynists: one has two wives and two have four wives. Of the two monogamists one is a Christian and the other lives in an almost totally Catholic area. The subchief, a Roman Catholic, is a monogamist. Only one of the acting chiefs, a non-practising Christian, is a polygynist, with three wives.

All Karanga chiefs in the sample possess the legal maximum of land allowed under the Land Husbandry Act, which is eight acres in Karangaland. Some plough more. All have larger herds of cattle than their subjects. The average old chief owns twenty-two head, the average acting chief eleven, and the one subchief twelve. The average commoner owns only five head of cattle. All chiefs therefore have considerable investment in traditional wealth and rank high in all criteria conferring traditional prestige.

Fallers writes: 'A people's stratification system is rooted in its culture, and particularly in its culturally elaborated image of the "admirable man", the man who everyone would like to be.'[1] The problem confronting modern Karanga is that they are unsure of the image of the 'admirable man'. The social characteristics of chiefs show that they still strive for prestige through fostering traditional values. Their 'admirable man' is the wealthy patriarch. Few have striven to acquire prestige symbols, such as higher education, that are not rooted in traditional Karanga culture.

[1] Fallers (1963), p. 162.

Consequently their vested interests cause them to lag behind in the general evolution of their people. This characteristic can be seen in all traditional rulers, among the French aristocracy for example at the time of the 1789 revolution, as well as among the Russian aristocracy in the early twentieth century.

The 'admirable man' of the educated Karanga measures prestige on a different scale. The educated see in chieftainship a divisive force which binds the people's loyalty to narrowly circumscribed localities and so prevents the emergence of national consciousness. Their own incipient commitment to a world culture, manifested in their acquisition of modern prestige symbols, inclines them to shrink back from the particularistic values embodied in chiefs. The educated followers have accepted the modern political system and broken with patriarchalism. The chiefs still stand poised between both. Educational qualifications, which Max Weber listed as a precondition for bureaucratization, have been acquired by the people but rarely by the chiefs.

The Karanga chiefs' lack of modern prestige criteria is not characteristic of all African chiefs. Lloyd observes that in West Africa 'it would be erroneous to imagine these traditional offices as being filled by elderly, illiterate men, impervious and perhaps hostile to Western ideas. The educated among them form a highly significant bridge between the indigenous societies and the modern state.'[1] But in Karangaland only one of the chiefs in the sample census, and a second interviewed in another tribal trust land, are capable of forming a 'bridge' between their peasant followers and the modern state. In most chiefdoms this bridge is provided by commoners who have become alienated from their traditional rulers.

3. LEGITIMIZATION OF CHIEFTAINSHIP

The conservatism of the Karanga chiefs can be largely attributed to their succession rules, which reserve the office for the eldest members of the families of chiefs. Chapter six analyses Karanga succession rules in detail.[2] Here it need only be stressed that brothers, or at least classificatory brothers, succeed each other as chiefs, and that their accession has to be confirmed by traditional chief-makers, called nominators, and legitimated by spirit mediums. Nominators and spirit mediums only name a candidate for office when they have ascertained that he has the general approval of his people, delaying their decision until public

[1] Lloyd (1967), p. 146.
[2] *infra*, pp. 107–110.

F

opinion has crystallized. Even so, few chiefs ever enjoy the full support of
all their subjects because those segments of the chieftainship whose
candidates have competed unsuccessfully always remain ready at any
time to challenge him if he departs from popular expectations. Case
histories that appear subsequently show that the approval of his
followers is vital for a chief to retain his office.[1]

In addition to this traditional method of legitimizing rulers, modern
Karanga chiefs need government approval. This means that they
require a double legitimization, one by the patriarchal system and the
other by European government officials. The government has however
different criteria from traditional chiefmakers by which to judge a
candidate's suitability for office, desiring bureaucratically efficient
chiefs who are willing to co-operate with government. Field data show
that candidates who actively supported African nationalism were
refused government recognition.[2] On the other hand, younger men with
higher education were occasionally preferred to older competitors who
had stronger traditional claims.[3]

Although an amendment of the African Affairs Act states that 'In
appointing a chief in terms of subsection (1) the Officer Administering
the Government shall give consideration to the customary principles of
succession of the tribe over which the chief is to preside',[4] the government is free to use its discretion in the appointment of chiefs. The
African Affairs Act gives full control over appointments and depositions to administrators. It states:

> The chief in charge of a tribe shall be appointed by the Governor and shall
> hold office during pleasure and contingent upon good behaviour and general

[1] *infra*, pp. 88–91. Blau comments as follows on the importance of popular
support: 'Stable leadership rests on power over others and their legitimate approval
of that power. . . . To legitimate a position of power and leadership, however, requires
that a leader be concerned with earning social approval of his followers, which means
that he does not maintain complete independence of them . . . because concern with
being liked prevents him from basing his decisions consistently on criteria of effectiveness alone.' (Blau, 1964, p. 203). Government officials too are occasionally aware of
the importance of local support. When a deputy secretary for Internal Affairs retired
in 1969, he made the following statement. 'Chiefs are not dictators. They do not
even have the powers of Cabinet Ministers (as the Prime Minister seems to imagine).
They derive their tribal standing from their people, whose voice they are, and not
from the Government. They wander too far from tribal opinion at their peril. And
they know it.' *The Rhodesia Herald*, 9.7.1969.
[2] e.g. *infra*, p. 97.
[3] e.g. *infra*, p. 100.
[4] *African Affairs Act*, para. 4 as amended.

fitness. He may be paid such salary and allowances as may from time to time be prescribed by regulations.[1]

And:

The Governor may remove any chief for just cause from his position, and may also order his removal with his family and property from any Tribal Trust Land or other land to other Tribal Trust Land or other land.[2]

Much of the modern Karanga chief's dilemma derives from this dual source for his authority. Modern chiefs have to be legitimated by both the patriarchal and the modern bureaucratic system. The disapproval of either group makes a chief marginal to an important source of legitimacy, so that his position is one of great uncertainty. If a chief takes his obligations towards government seriously and implements unwelcome government policies, he alienates those who are neutral in the traditional power-struggle, so that those segments of the chieftainship that had lost in their struggle for the chiefly office can count on wide support against him. The less a chief succeeds in satisfying his people, the more they tend to withdraw their approval of him, and with this withdrawal of approval his legitimacy is undermined in their eyes. He becomes 'a government chief' and 'a stooge of government'. Only those chiefs who are intelligent enough to understand and balance conflicting demands are likely to succeed. Successful chiefs, therefore, are those who either have a strong traditional backing and a well-balanced personality or those who have no strong commitments to either side but who feel free to shift their allegiance as situations demand.

Beliefs about the legitimation of power are very important because they determine the relative stability of chieftainship.[3] Though many Karanga question the legitimacy of particular chiefs, few if any question the legitimacy of the institution of chieftainship, regarding it as vital to their social life. Even in those tribal trusts lands with strong anti-government and pro-nationalist feelings people view chieftainship as indispensable. On this point the views of government and of the people coincide.

Depending on the recognition of both their subjects and government, the question arises as to how Karanga chiefs interpret their intercalary position and how they see themselves.

---

[1] *African Affairs Act*, para. 17, as amended, para. 7.

[2] ibid.; depositions by Governors, and since 1965 by the Officer administering the Government, have been frequent. Cf. *Hansard*, vol. 45, col. 1150; col. 1348; vol. 57 col. 71; vol. 60, col. 515 *et. alia*.

[3] Cf. Mouzelis, discussion on the legitimacy of systems of domination (1967), p. 16.

4. THE CHIEFS' SELF-IMAGE

The chiefs interviewed fall roughly into two categories: those who support the government and those who pay only lip-service to its orders. This division is not absolute. In reality all chiefs have at one time or another to shift sides when their own or their people's interests demand it. A model of pro- and anti-government chiefs, however, is useful since it has been observed that role conflict is best solved by giving greater emphasis to one or other of two conflicting roles.[1] The categorization here followed refers to the major roles which individual chiefs adopt when not pressurized either by their people or by government representatives.

The chiefs' self-images vary to some extent with their attitudes towards government. The following topics were informally discussed with the chiefs. (a) In what esteem are you held by the young and old men in your own chiefdom, and how do they treat you when you come to town? (b) What are the economic problems in your own chiefdom and how do you intend solving them? (c) What is the relation between you and government officials, and what do you think of government policies towards Africans? (d) What is your attitude towards the British government and towards African nationalism?

(a) *In what esteem do young and old men hold you in your own chiefdom and how do they treat you when you come to town?*

The following opinions were expressed by pro-government chiefs: 'I am highly respected by young and old alike. I have campaigned that our chieftainship be upgraded after government had reduced it to a sub-chieftainship in 1951. I have been successful, and now all people, including our educated sons, respect me. Only the few who have studied overseas ignore me, but because there are only one or two in my chiefdom they do not count.' Another said: 'I have no great difficulties with my people. I am not frightened of them and they are not frightened of me. They respect me. My father, for whom I act, is greatly loved by everybody.' Others felt slightly ambivalent. One commented: 'Young educated people respect me when they come to see me in my house or office, yet they no longer observe our traditional customs. They want to introduce European practices into my chiefdom and I am unable to prevent it. This worries me very much.' Another felt hostile to the government policy of family planning because he linked it with an emancipation of the young from the control of their elders. He com-

[1] Getzel and Guba discuss in addition the personality structure of the role incumbent as a factor in this choice, 1954, pp. 164–175.

mented: 'I like government, but sometimes it does evil things. At present it is introducing family planning in my chiefdom, and European nurses give pills to our young unmarried sons and daughters. Standards of sexual morality have fallen and parental authority is ignored. I doubt whether under such circumstances even I as chief can maintain my position.'

On their visits to town pro-government chiefs feel fairly confident of being accepted by their people. One chief observed: 'When I come to town, the people of my own chiefdom come and buy beer for me. I think that on the whole people in towns think well of chiefs. On my visits there I pin a small brooch with my name on my coat which indicates that I am a chief. I have never been insulted.' Another said: 'When I come to town to try court cases[1] I mix freely with young and old alike. They buy beer for me and tell me that I try their cases better than the District Commissioner.' Or: 'Townsmen still regard us chiefs as their leaders. Only men from Malawi and Zambia do not respect us. But even these obey if they decide to settle in Rhodesia and want a piece of land.'

These comments reveal that pro-government chiefs feel relatively secure in their relationship with their own people and that they believe themselves to be accepted by them.

This is not the case among chiefs who are critical of the government. One anti-government chief stated: 'In the past young people had no respect for chiefs, but now it is better because the Tribal Trust Land Act and the African Law and Tribal Courts Act have given us greater powers. We can now impose our will on our people whether they like it or not. We can force them into submission. If our young men do not obey us, they are the losers. They won't get land for their families.' Another said: 'If my young men cause me difficulties I have the power to throw them out of my chiefdom. Yet quite a number of educated men do not totally reject chiefs. Some would even compete for office if they had a chance because they see that it provides a steady income and more money than clerks and teachers can earn.'[2] One commented: 'I cannot see how Africans could ever do without chiefs.'

The behaviour of these chiefs at social gatherings shows them to be

---

[1] Fort Victoria is the only Rhodesian town where chiefs from the surrounding areas come monthly in pairs to try court cases of townsmen. S.I.A., 1967, p. 9. It is an experiment, following South African practice. Cf. Kuper (1965), p. 170.

[2] 'Government Notice 479 of 1965 states that chiefs whose followers number 500 or more may be paid a salary of £420 a year and those with less than 500 may be paid £240 a year.' *The Rhodesia Herald*, 4.7.1969.

slightly aloof. One anti-government chief was visited by another and went with him to a beer drink near his village. As soon as he arrived he was loudly acclaimed by his people; the women ullulated and the men clapped their hands. The two chiefs were led into a simple furnished hut where they were served with a special pot of beer. The following conversation began. The visiting chief suggested that they should go outside and sit with the people: 'After all, we are all Africans. It will give a bad impression if we remain inside. People will say that chiefs segregate themselves from their people just as Europeans do from Africans.' At this the local chief took a half-crown, gave it to his son and ordered him to buy beer for the people. He added: 'It is more suitable for us to drink in here. A great man must not be seen too much.'

In the towns anti-government chiefs experience a different relation to their people from that of pro-government chiefs.[1] One said: 'Until recently it was not safe for us to go to town. When I had to do so I dressed in shorts so that nobody would suspect that I was a chief. I always stayed with my relatives, who told their neighbours that I was a brother or uncle.' Another said: 'We used to be afraid to go to town because young people disliked the political views publicly expressed by chiefs. But today we are no longer afraid. We can freely go to local beer halls and many buy us a free beer when we wear our chieftainship badge.' A third related an incident he had experienced with young men in town: 'Some young men realized that I was a chief and began to abuse me. I told them that they should not treat us chiefs with disrespect because we only acted as we did because we needed our salaries from the government. I admitted that they were right to fight for their country but begged them to let us, their fathers, enjoy some good days before we die. I assured them that in our hearts we sympathize with them but could not show it openly.' He thought that his argument had satisfied the young townsmen because they left him in peace.

The responses of pro- and anti-government chiefs refer to different periods. Pro-government chiefs spoke only of the near past, in which they received respect from their people. Anti-government chiefs too admit that people accept them today, and the acclamation with which one chief was greeted at the beer drink shows that this acceptance is genuine. Yet anti-government chiefs have not forgotten the past when nationalists were not yet restricted and people were free to express their opinions. A person who abuses a chief today can be charged with a criminal offence. This gives chiefs protection and ensures outward conformity among the broad mass of Africans. Even so, anti-government

[1] Cf. also Mafeje (1963), pp. 88–99.

chiefs frequently convey the impression that they stand more aloof from their people than pro-government chiefs, and that they even dominate them. This behaviour may reflect an insecurity, stemming from their awareness that they are dependent on a government which they reject.[1] Like Albert Luthuli, the South African chief and African National Congress leader, some Rhodesian chiefs would like to combine in their own person traditional and modern leadership,[2] but not all have the necessary strength. As Luthuli wrote: 'The weaker ones go down. Nevertheless, loyalty to the institution of the chieftainship persists.'[3] This is borne out by the remark: 'I cannot see how Africans can ever do without chieftainship.' Rooted in their tradition, yet committed to nationalistic ideals, anti-government chiefs' aspirations go in two different directions. They verge on both the patriarchal and the bureaucratic political systems. Pro-government chiefs do not appear to suffer from similar feelings of alienation and divided loyalties.

(b) *What are the economic problems in your chiefdom and how do you intend solving them?*

This question was asked to assess how seriously chiefs faced the economic problems of their people and what action they had decided on to overcome them. All chiefs were unanimous that land shortage was the most serious problem facing them, but pro- and anti-government chiefs reacted differently towards the challenge of poverty.

A pro-government chief said: 'The situation is hopeless. Almost every man has several sons; his own field is small; where shall his children plough? Government offered to irrigate some of our land but both I and my people are against it. The water rent will be so high that no one will be able to pay it. The land to be irrigated is at present occupied by some old people. These cannot do the hard work. I have no land to move them to. But what can I do? I have advised my people to submit. If we continue to object government may move my people away and bring in outsiders; then we have lost our land completely.' Another chief for whose area no irrigation plans have yet been made rejected the suggestion out of hand. He explained: 'My area is over-populated and I do not know what to do. Perhaps we can start some home industries, such as carving birds from the horns of cattle. Admittedly this will not give a sufficient income to a large number of

[1] Parsons argues that insecurity often reveals itself in the desire to dominate. Parsons (1961), p. 261.
[2] Luthuli (1966), p. 110.
[3] ibid., p. 68.

people. I know that irrigation would increase crop production sub-stantially for many but I shall never consent to it. The reason is that all irrigated land is withdrawn from the direct control of chiefs. We chiefs have just received back the right to allocate land; this is one of the main sources of our present power. We shall never give this right away. We prefer to die of starvation rather than let our people and land be directly controlled by government. We must do everything possible to preserve our present power.' A third chief in this category tried to overcome the land problem by freely allocating land for ploughing in his grazing areas. He allotted land to his subjects and to African squatters on European farms, knowing that each allocation would bring him money. The result was that the cattle of his people were starving and straying on European farms; the European farmers started litigation against the cattle-owners and many tensions arose between European and African neighbours.

None of the pro-government chiefs revealed any intention of actively promoting the economic welfare of his people. Their answers reflected either a fatalistic outlook or a complete disregard for their people. They were concerned only about their own power or their financial profit and seemed not to experience any conflict between personal and social demands. They insisted on traditional farming methods. This guaran-teed them the support of local peasants, who are reluctant to experiment with modern techniques. This may be a reason contributing to their belief that their people trust them. Luthuli's comment: 'Traditional rule by chiefs retards my people'[1] applies to these chiefdoms ruled by pro-government chiefs.

Anti-government chiefs, unless they opt for complete withdrawal, take more positive actions. If they boycott government development schemes their areas stagnate and anti-government feelings increase among an under-nourished population. This alternative was chosen by one old chief who is strongly influenced by his nationalistic sons and relatives. Whenever he is ordered to do something, he does the legal minimum which just prevents his deposition. When government officials suggested a large irrigation project in his chiefdom, he said 'no', and attended none of the meetings which explained the scheme to his people. His subjects attended the meetings but refused to take any decision or to do any work on the scheme because their chief had not authorized them to co-operate. The District Commissioner became very angry and claimed that the old chief was used by nationalists to oppose govern-ment programmes.

[1] Luthuli (1966), p. 68.

Younger anti-government chiefs are often progressive. Two of them have in recent years co-operated with the government's agricultural staff, have paddocked their grazing areas and erected soil conservation works. Both refused to allocate land for cultivation in the grazing areas because they and their people realized that it would mean death to their cattle. One of these chiefs solved part of his problem by encouraging some of his village headmen to emigrate with their people to a resettlement scheme north of Karangaland. This enabled him to redistribute the fields of those who had left among the sons of other subjects. This was a self-effacing action in Karanga eyes because people judge a chief's prestige by the number of his subjects. He willingly lost some of his followers in order to benefit the rest. The other anti-government chief decided on his own accord to start a small irrigation project so that his people could grow vegetables. He was greatly handicapped by lack of money. Like many other chiefs, however, he is opposed to establishing a council under community development and thus qualifying for a government grant.[1]

Anti-government chiefs, therefore, show in general a greater responsibility towards their people's economic progress than pro-government chiefs. In actively supporting agricultural development and urging their followers to co-operate, they may alienate their more conservative subjects; so it seems that their relationship to their people is more distant than that of pro-government chiefs. Both progressive chiefs, however, noted a decrease in resentment as the economic situation of their people improved.

(c) *What is the relationship between you and government officials and what do you think of the government's policy towards Africans?*

This and the following question most clearly crystallize the views of pro- and anti-government chiefs. A pro-government chief stated: 'In recent years government has given us chiefs many powers because it realizes that we stand closer to our people than district commissioners. It knows that we will inform the district commissioner of all important happenings in our areas and it has therefore become convinced that we should take a much larger part in the administration than we did in the past.' Another commented: 'Some years ago district commissioners

---

[1] Chapter 7 shows that community development is the watershed which divides pro-government from anti-government chiefs. Of all the chiefs interviewed only one anti-government chief had established a council; all pro-government chiefs had done so.

regarded chiefs as their messengers. They even corrected us harshly in front of our own people. This no longer happens. If we make a mistake now, district commissioners see us privately and give us advice how to do better. I feel now quite safe with government officials. They pay us some respect.' A third said: 'I think we chiefs should soon take over all the work at present done by district commissioners for Africans. It seems government itself is thinking along these lines. At least this is how I interpret the recent legislation passed by parliament.'

These responses show that pro-government chiefs derive strong support from government and see themselves protected by its officials. This feeling of security may explain their reluctance to develop the agricultural potential of their area. They feel confident that if starvation threatens, government will come to their assistance.

Anti-government chiefs look differently at these issues. One said: 'Look at what happens when an old chief meets a young district commissioner. According to our custom the young man ought to honour the old, but when our district commissioner meets me, age no longer counts. I am just an African and the district commissioner a European. As an elderly chief I have to respect a young white man.' Another commented dryly: 'You think we support government. We would not do it were it not for the money. You read in the report of the Secretary of Internal Affairs[1] that we supported the government's proposal for a school for the sons of chiefs. Government wants to groom our sons for the job they want them to do. But what can we do? Most of us are polygynists and have many children. To have a school for our sons is the cheapest way for us to give them an education. Government uses us for its own purposes. We must in return try to get out of it all we can.'

These answers show a basic opposition of interests between chiefs and government, thinly covered by fringe benefits. Anti-government chiefs view government policies with extreme suspicion. It seems that even their progressive attitude towards agricultural production is influenced by their desire to get the greatest profit for themselves and their people out of the Rhodesian Government. Such attitudes are those of the younger and better educated chiefs who have become aware of national interests.

---

[1] S.I.A., 1963, p. 5; 1966, p. 3. Since the 1950s government showed concern about the old age of chiefs, due to collateral succession, and suggested simultaneously a change in succession rules and the establishment of a school for the sons of chiefs so that African rural areas could be administered by younger, more energetic and better-educated leaders.

(d) *What is your attitude towards the British Government and African nationalism?*

This question was asked to supplement the previous answer and to test how far chiefs understood wider political issues. A pro-government chief said: 'The British Government is bad. It does not agree that chiefs are the real leaders of the African people. Instead it acknowledges young nationalists who will most likely throw us out once they come to power. Nationalists will give all leading positions to their followers and not to us. We chiefs are the real leaders of our people and our government has at last realized this.' To prove his point he referred to an experience he had had while on a government-sponsored world tour. In England Rhodesian chiefs talked to leaders of independent African states. They asked them who of them belonged to a chiefly family. All declared that none of them did; they were politicians, not traditional leaders. This worried Rhodesian chiefs, and my informant concluded: 'The fact that men outside the traditional chiefly families should rule a country seemed outrageous to us.' On the other hand, he greatly approved of what he saw in South Africa: 'We were impressed by the powerful position of South African chiefs. They run their own affairs without any interference from Pretoria. We Rhodesian chiefs desire a similar system.' Another chief said 'We chiefs are politicians. The British ought to admit it because when their Prime Minister and other officials come to Rhodesia they always speak with us. When we go overseas we too meet British politicians. In spite of this the British Government does not accept us as leaders of our people; it only listens to our children, the nationalists. How can children rule their elders?'

These responses show that pro-government chiefs have adopted the attitude of the Rhodesian Government towards Great Britain and that they give the same explanation as government officials do of British policies towards Rhodesian Africans. They realize that they will lose their position should a nationalist government come to power.

As a consequence pro-government chiefs greatly deplore the destructive activities of African nationalists. One admitted that his own brother was a nationalist leader but that since the brother had been imprisoned he had found it his duty as a chief to turn away from him and his family. He deplored the economic hardship his brother's wife and children suffered but did not think it wise to assist them.

Few pro-government chiefs are able to transcend the interests of their own chiefdoms. One chief commented on the suggestion of the Whaley Report[1] that Ndebele and Shona chiefs be given equal representation in

[1] *Report of the Constitutional Commission*, 1968.

parliament as follows: 'The fact that the Ndebele constitute only 20 per cent of all Africans and the Shona 80 per cent does not matter because it does not affect my standing in my own chiefdom. All that counts is that my followers respect me. The country as a whole is too large for me to think about.' Another chief said: 'I cannot visualize what Rhodesia would be like if it were ruled by Africans. As long as my people are happy and live in peace, as long as they can move freely throughout the country and have their beer and sing their songs, I do not see why government should be changed. I do not like the battles now fought in the Zambezi valley. If the fighting spreads to our area, I am sure that my people will help government and hand over the terrorists. We all know that nationalists come only to destroy all that has been built up.'

Pro-government chiefs, because they are so firmly rooted in the traditions of their chiefdoms that they are unable to consider national issues, regard nationalism as a destructive force opposed to the patriarchal organization of their communities.

The attitudes of anti-government chiefs towards the British Government and nationalism were much more positive.[1] Several have large pictures of the Queen and Prince Philip in their houses and they show them with pride to European visitors.[2] One anti-government chief too had joined an overseas tour of chiefs. His account differed substantially from that of the pro-government chief. He reported: 'When we came to England we were not given a reception by the British Government.

[1] The following extract from a recently published statement by Chief Tangwena, who in 1969 was ordered to leave the land on which his ancestors had lived for over a hundred years, reveals a similar negative attitude towards the Rhodesian, but positive attitude towards the British Government: 'The government itself has broken the law in UDI. If I disobey their order, I am just following the example of government. It is impossible for us to look on this illegal government as a father. They have disobeyed the law of the mother Government. We have no conscience in disobeying government's laws as they are no different to us making our own laws. Until the Father, the British Government, tells us what is right, we feel we must stay where we are.

'If it were possible to talk with the British Government we would tell them. The news from this country is that the government is living very well with the Chiefs. But is this the way of Love? We are always being provoked every time.' Clutton-Brock (1969), p. 24.

[2] No chief interviewed had a picture of the Rhodesian Prime Minister in his house. Loyalty of Africans towards the Queen and attachment to her pictures was also shown by an African member of parliament when the Legislative Assembly discussed that Rhodesia should become a republic, *The Rhodesia Herald*, 2.7.1969. A few weeks earlier a leading Rhodesian chief publicly declared that Africans feel closely attached to the Queen, *The Rhodesia Herald*, 2.6.1969.

Instead we were taken to Buckingham Palace where we met the Queen for five minutes. While waiting for the Queen an English gentleman pulled at my sleeve and asked some rude questions about Rhodesia. I pointed to the European leader of our party and told him: "Ask our boss; we chiefs cannot tell you anything." The man then turned away in disgust.' The chief relished this memory because he had proved to an Englishman the inferior position of Rhodesian chiefs.

Another anti-government chief related the chiefs' meeting with the British Prime Minister in Rhodesia prior to the unilateral declaration of independence. He said: 'At the meeting some chiefs asked the British Prime Minister to allow us the use of a tape recorder so that we could later play back to our government all we had said. But he replied that he had his own secretary present and did not need a tape recorder. Pointing to his head he said: "This is my tape recorder." I think the British Prime Minister thought we were big fools. It is good that he thought that.'

This group of chiefs takes delight in demonstrating the absurdity of their own position to the British, even though the process brings ridicule on their own heads. Those quoted have more education than other chiefs interviewed and desire an African government. They expect to play a role in it, either as chiefs or as ordinary politicians. They had close links with the Zimbabwe African National Union before it was banned and could therefore hope for promotion in the party hierarchy.

Their reaction towards nationalism is positive. The two chiefs mentioned above,[1] who enjoyed a quiet beer drink apart from their people, switched on the radio and listened to news from Zambia about how guerrilla fighters in the Zambezi valley were winning the fight against Rhodesian troops. One of them commented: 'Oh yes, these men are freedom fighters and not terrorists as the government tells us. They are fighting for our country which has been seized by Europeans. Europeans are very cunning. At first missionaries came very politely, offering us gifts. We did not know what they aimed at. Later white settlers arrived and took the country from us. At present government still follows the same tactics. It sends us on grand world tours. I have been wondering ever since I have been on that tour what they want from us in return. They handled us so kindly that I knew they wanted something tremendous.' Another chief was forced to resign as president of the Chiefs' Council because he had openly supported the Zimbabwe African National Union and signed a paper demanding majority rule. A fellow chief who was present when he signed the petition foresaw difficulties from government and quietly slipped away to avoid open

[1] Cf. *supra*, p. 66.

confrontation. He is still a member of the Chiefs' Council though he too favours majority rule.

Unlike pro-government chiefs, these men are keenly aware of national interests. They object to an equal number of Ndebele and Shona chiefs in the Rhodesian Legislative Assembly and reject any division of parliament along racial and tribal lines. They desire one common parliament elected by all people on a general adult franchise. Hence their aspirations coincide with those of nationalists.

Anti-government chiefs constantly have to conceal their real attitude towards government officials and so they feel insecure. This may account for their apparent aloofness from their people. Several have established strong bonds of friendship with like-minded chiefs and nationalists outside their own locality.

CONCLUSION

Little mention has been made in this study of the self-image of those chiefs who vacillate between pro- and anti-government sentiments, though repeated mention has been made of pro-government chiefs who are disturbed by certain government policies. Some chiefs constantly fall into this third category, but most are pushed into it from time to time as the pressures from one direction or another vary. Chiefs have been classified as pro- or anti-government according to the choice of their major role. Getzel and Guba's contention that personality traits may determine the major role in situations of role conflict seem to be true, because anti-government chiefs appear more self-assertive, if not aggressive; pro-government chiefs are more submissive, sometimes to the point of fatalism. According to this division pro-government chiefs stress their role as government agents. They communicate to their people what the government expects of them, and in return expect the goodwill of the administration when they inform the government of their people's wishes.

The other group is torn between self-interest and the desire to lead their people to a better future. They would like to see themselves as nationalist heroes, but dare not champion the nationalist cause openly for fear of losing their position on which their economic security depends. Whether they appear outwardly inactive or progressive, in one way or another they secretly support those who oppose the Rhodesian Government.

Of the twelve chiefs interviewed, only two are actively interested in African nationalism, but seven of their sons show such interest. To the old men the social structure of the past is still meaningful and they are unable to adjust themselves to modern trends in their chiefdoms. If they are aware of these changes, they try to ignore them. Their sons, however, who are actively engaged in the administration of their chiefdoms, cannot close their minds to the contradictions inherent in their position. They are not as confident in the patriarchal role as their fathers were, nor are they qualified to break with the past and choose a bureaucratic career.

CHAPTER 5

Karanga Chiefs' Reaction to Government

INTRODUCTION

Karanga chiefs have various options if they are to come to terms with the demands made on them by the government and by their people. A few succeed in harmonizing the often conflicting demands. The majority, however, fail to reconcile them, and deviate from the norms accepted either by their European superiors or by their own followers. Pro- and anti-government chiefs opt for different alternatives, yet most run the risk of alienating one section on whom their power partially depends. Chiefs who unsuccessfully try to satisfy both European bureaucrats and Karanga traditionalists often break down under the strain and suffer personality disintegration. This disintegration may take the form of excessive drinking, sexual promiscuity, or, occasionally, suicide.

To refine the model of pro- and anti-government chiefs presented in chapter four,[1] one can further divide each of these two broad categories into three sub-categories. Pro-government chiefs consist firstly of those who see no contradiction in the demands made on them by the government and their people. They succeed in integrating the demands of both groups. Case history one of chief Mhofu exemplifies this option. Secondly, there are pro-government chiefs who successfully balance the demands made by government and their people without committing themselves to the exclusive support of either side. Case history two of sub-chief Hove exhibits this alternative. Thirdly, a pro-government chief may actively conform to government expectations and completely ignore the wishes of his people. This choice is made by those chiefs whose accession to chieftainship depends on European rather than on Karanga support. Unlike chiefs in the first two categories, a chief who compulsively conforms to government expectations does so because he feels insecure and in need of government protection against his own people. Case history three of chief Shoko illustrates such a case.

Anti-government chiefs too can be divided into three sub-categories. Firstly, chiefs who passively conform to government orders and pass over

[1] *supra*, pp. 64–75.

the objections of their people may do so for fear of deposition. Like actively conforming chiefs, these passively conforming chiefs also feel insecure. This insecurity may derive from lack of certainty about their position. It is often (but not only[1]) found in chiefs acting during an inter-regnum before a new chief is appointed. Case history four of chief Shiri represents such an example.[2] Instead of conforming passively to orders, anti-government chiefs may withdraw from the conflict, boycott govern-ment schemes, and comply with government instructions only so far as to avoid deposition. Case history five of chief Ngara illustrates such anti-government behaviour. In a third category are chiefs who overtly oppose government orders whenever opportunity offers. To opt for this alter-native, however, requires great moral courage because such confront-ation with the power of government can only result in the decline of the chief's power. Case history six of chief Nzou analyses how a strong chief breaks down under such strain.

Fig. 4

Model of Chiefs' Reaction to Government*

	Pro-government chiefs	Anti-government chiefs
1st alternative	Harmonious integration of interests	Passive conformity
2nd alternative	Skilful balancing of demands	Withdrawal
3rd alternative	Compulsory conformity	Great opposition

* For this categorization I am indebted to Parsons (1951), p. 257.

[1] Even the most important chiefs, such as members of the Council of Chiefs, may fall into this category. For example the newspaper *Moto*, in its August 1969 issue, printed the letter of a 'Son of a Chief' to the editor which contained the following statement: 'My father also said that they [the chiefs] were threatened by government authorities that if they should tell their people that they rejected the new Constitution they would be dismissed from their positions of honour.'

[2] Blau writes in his discussion on power that 'people can be made to do things for fear of losing their jobs, of being ostracized, of having to pay fines, or of losing social standing', Blau (1964), p. 116.

G

1. PRO-GOVERNMENT CHIEFS

(a) *Case History 1: Harmonious Integration of Interests*

Chief Mhofu, who has achieved a relatively harmonious integration of his people's and government's interests, rules a chiefdom which differs in a number of characteristics from other Karanga chiefdoms. His people settled in their present territory before any of their neighbours arrived. They therefore consider themselves owners of the land. Their area is agriculturally fertile, has a reliable rainfall and abounds in wild fruit trees; famine is rare. Few men leave the area for outside employment and at the time of the census only just over 20 per cent were absent as labour migrants, against 56 per cent in an adjoining chiefdom. As a result of this relatively low rate of labour migration modern ideas have not made any impact on the chiefdom. Few schools have been opened in the area and none provides full primary education. Consequently most labour migrants perform unskilled work. Since men with little education make very short trips to labour centres and frequently circulate between town and country, they depend as much on their chief for land as those who do not seek outside employment. Their lack of education and ignorance of modern ideas, together with their economic dependence on their chief, predisposes them to obey his instructions.

A traditional orientation, fostered by favourable ecological conditions and a minimum contact with European culture, is further strengthened by the unique position of the chief. Chief Mhofu is the last surviving son of the greatest chief who ever ruled the Mhofu chiefdom. It was only his father, the fourth chief of his people, who established the houses of the chieftainship. His ancestors had few sons, and for four generations father was succeeded by son. The present chief's father, however, was a polygynist with twenty sons, nine of whom held the office of chief in turn. No succession dispute has ever split the chieftainship. Only when the present chief dies will the question arise whether the office of chief should circulate among all the houses founded by the nine brothers, or whether the present acting chief should succeed his father. At the time of this fieldwork the old man was in good health and the question of succession had not been raised.

Chief Mhofu's authority is further strengthened by the belief that he is possessed by two ancestor spirits. It is very rare that a chief is a spirit medium, since Karanga tend to separate political and ritual functions among their leaders.

Because of the structural position of chief Mhofu, his people have strong emotional ties with the past and are proud of their old customs.

They have the reputation of being a peace-loving people and have never shown interest in nationalist activities. This was true even when people in neighbouring chiefdoms stoned dip-tanks and burned hide-sheds in opposition to the implementation of the Land Husbandry Act. Their chief takes pride in being the head of a law-abiding people.

Only once did tensions arise between the chief and the government. In 1951 the government demoted the chieftainship to a sub-chieftainship under a neighbouring chief, a relative newcomer in the area and un-related to chief Mhofu. Several other chiefs in the district had been demoted, but whereas the other chiefs hired lawyers to fight against their demotion, chief Mhofu did nothing. He refused to take off his chiefly emblems, and when the district commissioner had them taken from him he continued to attend all functions for chiefs. His fellow chiefs accepted him as their equal in spite of his demotion. Called to the district com-missioner's office, chief Mhofu was offered the symbols of a sub-chief, but he refused to accept them. Finally, after consultation with the Chief Native Commissioner, the chiefly insignia were returned to him and the people settled down to their normal routine.

The acting chief, like his father, stands firmly behind the Rhodesian government because he believes that the government genuinely cares for the interests of the African people. When he was told about the deposi-tion of an important chief[1] he became very serious and after some reflection remarked: 'Surely this man must have been a nationalist other-wise government would never have deposed him.'

Occasional conflicts over government policies which are opposed by the people are settled through the overwhelming prestige of chief Mhofu. For example, when the people objected to the introduction of community development the chief put pressure on his followers and set up a council.[2] He could do this because he had been convinced by the district commissioner that community development was in the interest of his people, and therefore he experienced no internal conflict. He could act with confidence and draw his people with him. The people respect their old chief as well as his son, who co-operates closely with his father. The son discusses with the father all the events of the chief-dom, and shares his income. So the people trust the acting chief although he lacks his father's spiritual authority. The important trait of this chief is that whenever the government and his people disagree he can side with the government. He always wins his people over to his conviction without much grumbling on their part.

[1] Cf. *supra*, p. 55.
[2] Cf. *infra*, pp. 206–210.

The undoubted traditional legitimacy of chief Mhofu, his close connection with the founder of the chieftainship, and his function as spirit medium, are the factors that inspire respect and obedience in his subjects. Few other Karanga chiefs stand so close to the founder of a long-established chieftainship, and no other has ever combined in his own person the highest political and religious authority over his people. Chief Mhofu's superior status, secured by multiple structural supports, makes him relatively independent of others and puts him in a strong bargaining position with both his people and government. A traditionally weaker chief could not have ignored his demotion as successfully as chief Mhofu did in 1951, nor could he impose unwelcome government policies with little opposition. Meetings of elders in this chief's village are characterized by long discussions about their old customs. This orientation towards the past prevents acute conflicts between the chief and his people.

CONCLUSION

Case history one shows how conflict has been avoided by a chief who succeeds in harmonizing the expectations of government with those of his people. Present government emphasis on traditional values suits the value-orientation of the people in Mhofu chiefdom, who because of their low education and low labour-migration rate have not yet been radically confronted with modern cultures. The main cause for chief Mhofu's success, however, lies in his legitimacy, which is doubted neither by his subjects nor by government. His traditional right to office is unchallenged.

A similarly successful adjustment is found in chiefs who balance the interests of government and their people without committing themselves to the exclusive support of either. Case history two is that of a subchief who tried simultaneously to keep government and people reasonably content by giving in at one time to the wishes of his own group, and at another to the wishes of government.

(b) *Case History 2: Skilful Balancing of Demands*

The case history of this subchief has been included and treated as equivalent to the case histories of chiefs because this subchief is a very strong man and acts in most circumstances as if he were an autonomous ruler. His kinship ties with the chief may account for his relative independence. By positional succession he is the chief's sister's son, and the relationship between a mother's brother and sister's son in Karanga society is always characterized by a great degree of freedom.

Like the area of chief Mhofu, sub-chiefdom Hove is agriculturally more fertile than the surrounding country. It is sufficiently well watered for rice to be grown successfully. In a predominantly maize-and millet-growing area rice is considered a special delicacy, and if sold brings in much money. Hence many men are peasant cultivators and their secure income disposes them to co-operate with government agents, especially with the agricultural staff.

The sub-chiefdom is also well provided with educational facilities, has several upper primary schools and easy access to the secondary school of the chiefdom. Its people are therefore relatively well educated. Those with higher education leave the sub-chiefdom for long periods and earn good salaries in white-collar jobs. The labour-migration rate of 40 per cent is typical for rural Karangaland. Few of the migrants who have gained high status in urban areas return to their villages. The internal power structure is thus not threatened.

Sub-chief Hove himself is relatively young. Since childhood he has been an active member of the Roman Catholic church. Educationally he is less well qualified than many of his subjects because he attended school for three years only. He has been a labour migrant for some years but spent most of his life in his village, and he became headman there many years ago. Having permanently settled in the rural area he began laying a secure economic foundation for his family.

In his youth he trained as a builder. On retirement from European employment he built himself a respectable but not luxurious house. Then he applied himself to agriculture, bought adequate farming equipment, joined a course for progressive farmers and obtained a certificate in farming efficiency. He was offered a purchase area farm, which he declined because he hoped to compete for the sub-chieftainship. Meanwhile he accumulated some capital, opened a small store and placed it in the hands of his younger brother. He took the profit to a bank and never engaged in a conspicuous display of wealth. In fact his clothing is generally threadbare and in no way different from that of other villagers. His living standards are identical with theirs, and much below those of teachers and prosperous businessmen.

When the old sub-chief died Hove competed for office and won it over a senior agnate. This caused some resentment among his relatives but the majority of people respected him because even before assuming office he had shown character qualities which seemed to indicate that he was a born leader. About 60 per cent of his people entirely support him; the rest are unable to decide their attitude towards him.

In spite of his popular acceptance, most people find it difficult to follow his thinking. He is very outspoken and once he has made a statement he does not repeat it; once he has made a decision he does not revoke it. His word stands irrevocably. His foresight and keen understanding give him constant advantages over his slower-thinking neighbours. Consequently he is admired but also feared. People always feel his presence and at times think that he is cunning. His thrift, which prevents him from giving free beer parties and lavishing gifts on his followers, is interpreted as avarice.

The main aims of sub-chief Hove are power and wealth. To achieve these aims he adopted two policies: he tried to gain the approval and esteem of government officials, and he engaged in projects which promised to improve his own and his people's economic conditions. The two policies are interconnected because it is through introducing modern forms of organization that a chief is best able to win government approval. Consequently he experienced no basic opposition between government interests and his people's, as he interpreted them.

Sub-chief Hove is keenly aware of his lack of education and in order to overcome this defect he cultivates the friendship of educated men who can advise him in his dealings with the administration. His first adviser was an extension assistant who resided in his village. This extension assistant was respected by his superiors for his thorough knowledge of agriculture. He informed the sub-chief of modern techniques as soon as they became known, and the sub-chief experimented with them successfully. On the advice of this friend Hove formed the first co-operative society in the tribal trust land in the early 1960s. His area was the only one in which extension staff were welcomed and local people followed the advice given. Consequently the European extension officer took a special interest in this sub-chiefdom and proposed the formation of a farmers' association there. The sub-chief accepted the advice and later also formed a progressive committee, through which an increasing number of people became involved in advanced agriculture and development works. The farmers' association soon drew the attention of neighbouring European farmers. They in turn assisted the villagers with advice and donated £50 to plant a nursery of fruit trees which could later be transplanted to the homes of the peasants.

The progressive committee was concerned with community projects. First of all they built a dam to assure the area of sufficient water in times of drought. Once the co-operative society had been founded and the farmers had produced a considerable surplus for sale, sub-chief

Hove persuaded his men to build a road from their area through nearby farms to the nearest railway station, thereby considerably reducing transport costs. After much discussion his people agreed and the road was built. European farmers gave help on the sections crossing their farms.

As a Roman Catholic in a predominantly Catholic area sub-chief Hove also gained status through church membership and positions on voluntary associations. At religious services he occupied a place of honour next to the missionaries, and negotiated with them as an equal to obtain services for his people. His relationship with the church enabled him to co-operate with missionaries in building a hall for religious purposes, and later he persuaded the missionaries to convert it into a clinic as part of a community project.

These endeavours show that sub-chief Hove used his power not just to dominate his people, but to involve them in collective goals. Because of these efforts the agricultural staff and the district commissioner listened whenever sub-chief Hove came to them for advice and to discuss with them further projects. They were delighted to have an energetic young leader who had the people behind him and who was incorrupt in the eyes of all his followers. Government officials realized that it was only through him that they could develop the area. They consulted him, therefore, whenever they wanted to introduce a new government policy.

Sub-chief Hove had many things in his favour: he was young, lived under ecologically favourable conditions, was not threatened by young educated men, had a strong personality, was admired by the young for his success and feared by the old for his decisive actions; finally he was supported by government. Yet his influence made him slightly high-handed. At meetings he tended to overrule his subjects and often suggested to the district commissioner that their silence meant consent.[1] Gradually some resentment built up.

Open opposition was however kept in check by the obvious advantages sub-chief Hove brought to his people. His close association with government officials aroused some comment, but nobody suspected him of subservience to white officials. His people realized that all chiefs were in an awkward position, and together with their sub-chief they hoped and waited for a turn of events which would enable the British Government to overthrow the post-U.D.I. Government in Rhodesia. Nationalists were welcomed by sub-chief Hove and his people. The people were all

---

[1] When Africans keep silent, their silence indicates opposition. Among Europeans silence is often interpreted as tacit approval. The different meaning attached to silence leads to many misunderstandings between Africans and Europeans.

fully informed of national events. They owned more radiograms than ploughs and switched them on to listen almost exclusively to political broadcasts. In addition to European government support, therefore, the sub-chief was supported by the young educated men who favoured African majority rule. He had convinced them that his tactics were best suited to gain them economic advantages.

By the late 1960s, however, sub-chief Hove had expended too large an amount of his accumulated authority, for as Blau writes, power, like capital, is expended in use:

> If an individual has much power over others, which means that they are obligated to and depend on him for greatly needed benefits, they will be eager to do his bidding and anticipate his wishes in order to maintain his goodwill.... [But] the power of accumulated obligations is depleted by asking others to repay their debts, because doing so transforms, at least in part, the power relations into exchange relations, which presume relative equality of status.[1]

This happened to sub-chief Hove. A final demand for money to erect a gate at the new road separating the tribal trust land from the European farms strained the willingness of his subjects and only after many debates and much cajoling was the task completed.

Then events tested his power. His trusted friend and adviser, the extension assistant, was promoted and transferred to another area. Without his guidance sub-chief Hove realized that agricultural development would come to a halt. He looked for another educated friend and chose a teacher who was distantly related to him. At the same time a new district commissioner took over the administration of the tribal trust land, a man very keen on community development. He informed the sub-chief that his progressive committee had to be renamed 'community board',[2] and become part of the structure of community development. As soon as the progressive committee was brought into association with new government policy the people's subdued resentment turned into open opposition. This opposition was strengthened by the support they received from their chief, who had outlawed community development in his chiefdom. Sub-chief Hove had long realized that his progressive committee was doing the work of a community board, but

[1] Blau (1964), p. 135.
[2] A 'community board' area is smaller than a 'council' area under community development. It includes a number of villages or even a sub-chiefdom. The government encourages the establishment of community boards in the hope that their successful projects will incline Africans in neighbouring areas to follow the example and finally establish a council embracing a whole chiefdom.

had ignored the disapproval of his chief, to whom he owed allegience. When his committee was officially renamed he could no longer ignore criticism. All the activities he had initiated through this committee came to a halt.

With the decline of his influence other powers asserted themselves. The man who had always tried to please European officials was now challenged by traditional forces and obliged to placate them. These traditional forces imposed themselves on him in the form of the traditional high god cult which centres in the Matopo hills near Bulawayo.

Local traditions[1] in the six tribal-trust-land communities confirm the studies of Ranger, Robinson and others[2] that the high god cult still unifies a large area of Rhodesia over which in past centuries a branch of the Mutapa empire held away. The total area of the old kingdom is still today divided into provinces, each of which is linked through a messenger of the high god to the cult centre. Every chiefdom and sub-chiefdom in a province has its own land-shrine, whose spirit medium claims to be in direct contact with the high god. Cult leaders had organized the Shona rebellion of 1896, and during the years of active African

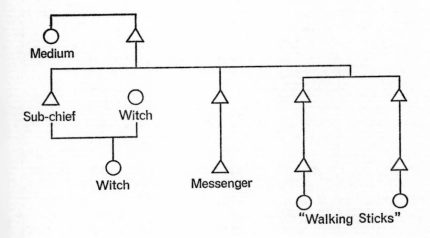

Fig. 5. Genealogy 1 : Genealogy of Subchief Hove

nationalism in the 1950s and 1960s the cult centre had once again become a bank of information to which messengers brought news from

[1] Aquina, Sister Mary, O.P. (1968), pp. 146–155.
[2] Cf. Stokes and Brown, eds. (1966).

all over Karangaland. This information was placed at the disposal of the nationalist leaders. Thus the high god cult combined two elements— the most traditional and the most modern aspects of the indigenous culture—which emphasize opposition to Europeans.

As soon as sub-chief Hove's power began to wane he was forced through cult leaders to withdraw his support from European ad- ministrators. In the late 1960s several messages reached him from the Matopos through the provincial messenger, who was his own brother's son, that the spirits were angry with him for co-operating with Europeans and that they demanded his presence at the cult centre. As one of the messages was delivered a young boy in the village fell possessed. This frightened sub-chief Hove and he set out for the Matopos. There he was told that the high god threatened his area with drought and cattle disease because he had put his confidence in Europeans and not in the beliefs of his ancestors: he had built a dam to provide his people with water but had neglected the rain ceremonies; his people had become rich but they had used their riches for excessive beer-drinking and prostitution. Sub-chief Hove was ordered to go home, to forbid beer parties, to instruct his people to observe strict sexual morality, and to cease co-operating with Europeans. If these instructions were obeyed rain would fall in his area.

On his return sub-chief Hove announced to his people the decrees of the cult officials, and the rain ceremony was held the following week under his auspices.

This ceremony was a great success because heavy rain fell before the ritual was completed. During the celebration the medium became possessed and declared that the high god at the Matopos had chosen two local girls related to the sub-chief to become her 'walking sticks', that is companions and assistants, and that these had to be sent to the Matopos for training. The girls and their parents, who were all Catholics, pro- tested violently, but the medium insisted and threatened that if the children disobeyed the spirits' orders they would die. The children were handed over to the medium. Sub-chief Hove then asked the medium whether the spirits would allow him to divorce his wife and marry another.[1] He was told that the spirits raised no objection.

Soon after these events the spirit messenger from the Matopos became possessed and announced that sub-chief Hove's wife and daughter were possessed by witch spirits. According to custom this enabled the sub-chief to send his wife away without repaying her bride-wealth and to marry another. Not even Catholic neighbours expect a man to live

[1] As a Catholic the sub-chief was not allowed to divorce his wife.

with a wife who is thought to be a witch. Soon afterwards the district commissioner was informed by a missionary about the abduction of the girls, but he decided not to interfere because the government wanted to restore the traditional life of the people. Hence the administration made no difficulties for the sub-chief. All he had endangered was his church membership, which his decision to remarry would in any case have called into question. The people's support for sub-chief Hove reached a new height when the rains fell steadily throughout the season and their crops promised a bumper harvest. Rainfall in Karangaland is often patchy, and it so happened that this sub-chiefdom received more rain than the rest of the chiefdom. Its maize stood twice as high as in the surrounding areas, including the mission fields where good agricultural techniques had been employed. The people attributed the uneven rainfall to the spirits' approval of their sub-chief.

CONCLUSION

This case history presents a sub-chief who skilfully balanced the demands of both the European and the traditional social systems. When his former co-operation with government officials called down on him the disapproval of the guardians of the past he bowed to their pressure and submitted to their demands. As a result he was confirmed in his office. His compliance with traditional religious sanctions proved that he did not reject the traditional value-system, and the district commissioner's acquiescence guaranteed him well-timed government support.

It is difficult to determine how far the substitution of a teacher for an extension assistant as adviser was responsible for the sub-chief's shift of emphasis from European to traditionalist policies. Extension assistants are generally loyal to government, whereas teachers tend to sympathize with African nationalism, and nationalists used to co-operate closely with agents of the high god cult. Sub-chief Hove's success lies in the fact that although he deviated at times from the expectations of both government and his people, at critical moments he was able to retrace his steps quickly enough not to offend his superiors or his subjects too strongly. Instead of satisfying neither side, he succeeded in giving both a measure of satisfaction, which kept him in power. It is difficult to foresee for how long he will be able to balance conflicting interests, and a subsequent replication study of the area should prove useful.

Like chief Mhofu, sub-chief Hove ruled in a fertile district and the land was able to support his people. Poverty caused no unrest in his area. Though his subjects were better educated than those of chief Mhofu their more permanent stay in urban areas reduced their influence in the chiefdom. His own concern for progress won the younger people to his side, and his old and more conservative followers obeyed out of fear. Contact with European culture, therefore, did not threaten his position. Both his people and government recognized him as the legitimate local ruler.

(c) *Case History 3: Compulsive Conformity*[1]

The third alternative open to pro-government chiefs is that of conforming compulsively with government instructions. It differs greatly from the options chosen by the chiefs in the two preceding case histories because it involved the failure of a chief to reconcile conflicting demands.

Chief Shoko ruled in an area of marginal rainfall. Rainfall records show that every fourth year tends to be a year of drought and famine. Consequently the people have to rely frequently on government subsidies for food. Schooling facilities are very poor; no school in the chiefdom provides full primary education. This prevents local labour migrants from qualifying for work in well-paid urban occupations. The labour-migration rate of 56 per cent is above average for Karangaland, but most men work on surrounding European farms. Since farm labourers are paid between £2 10s. and £3 a month, most men do not earn enough to support their families. Only through combined labour migration and peasant cultivation can they procure sufficient food for their dependants. Employment in the neighbourhood enables them to be in frequent contact with their families and the events of their chiefdom. Few modern influences penetrate the area and nationalism is outlawed by chief and people alike. They cannot afford to antagonize the European farmers and government on whom their subsistence depends. These difficult ecological and social conditions form the background against which the actions of the insecure chief of Shoko chiefdom have to be assessed.

Shoko chiefdom consists of two communities, Shoko Murewa and Shoko Museamwa. Each community represents a warring house of the chieftainship. The last chief died in 1944, and ever since the two houses have fought for the office.[2] When in 1951 their chieftainship was reduced

[1] Holleman gives an excellent example of compulsive conformity in his analysis of the action of a chief appointed by government to take the place of a chief government had deposed. See Holleman (1968), p. 234.

[2] A detailed analysis of the succession dispute is given in chapters 6–8. This chapter presents a summary of the conflict, so as to provide an understanding of chief Shoko's compulsive conformity to government orders.

to a sub-chieftainship, members of the Shoko Murewa community approached a nearby European farmer whom they often supplied with cheap labour during harvesting time. They hoped he would draw the government's attention to their plight. The farmer contacted the local member of parliament, who brought the case before the legislative assembly,[1] and the chieftainship was restored in 1956. But it was only in 1964 that the office was filled by a candidate of the Shoko Murewa community. They had hired a lawyer and enjoyed the support of European farmers. The candidate of the Shoko Museamwa community was supported by the traditional chief-makers and many local people.

The new chief, acting for his aged father, failed to win the support of the Shoko Museamwa community. He also alienated his own supporters by allocating land to Africans from surrounding European farms and depriving his own people of grazing land. He knew he could demand more money from outsiders for cultivation rights than from his own people and he hoped, moreover, to win their support against his local opponents. He received large amounts of money, built himself a four-roomed house, and bought a car. To keep his people content he promised the traditional heads of houses sub-chieftainships, but later refused to honour his promise. Consequently he lost the support of both his commoners and local leaders. The newcomers were too few in number to outweigh traditional opposition.

Three years after his accession to the chieftainship, chief Shoko further alienated his subjects by taking from his opponents several fields which had been allocated to them under the Land Husbandry Act, giving them to his supporters. His people complained to the district commissioner, who refused to interfere in the internal disputes of the chiefdom. The chief insisted on his right to allocate land as he pleased and the people had no redress. One delegation complained violently to the district commissioner about the arbitrary action of their chief, but was warned not to oppose a traditional leader; this could earn them the suspicion of being nationalist agitators and lead to their restriction. Finding no help in the official of the ministry of Internal Affairs, the people brought a major land dispute to the magistrates' court. They lost their case because the chief's party had hired a lawyer for their defence and the peasants were unable to argue against him. The Tribal Trust Land Act had given chiefs legal control over the land in their chiefdoms.[2]

[1] The *Hansard* has been checked for accuracy, but the reference is suppressed to safeguard the anonymity of the people involved.

[2] The Land Husbandry Act has not been revoked, but no government official still refers to it.

At the time of rising resentment and bitterness, the district commissioner approached the chief to implement community development.
The chief called his people together, informed them of the district commissioner's wish and ordered them to form a council.[1] When the people
objected he dismissed the dissenters and with a handful of loyal supporters went to the district commissioner's office to report full local
support. The district commissioner congratulated the chief on his
efficiency and the council was established. Once the council was formed
the chief assumed full control over proceedings and silenced all opposition from his councillors. When the people saw that they were impotent
to assert themselves because their chief was constantly supported by
government, they submitted sullenly.

Chief Shoko's self-interest and disregard for his subjects' wishes led
to a conspiracy against him. Village headmen who had lost part of their
land to strangers rallied behind the leaders who had been promised
sub-chieftainships. Secret meetings were held to decide how the chief's
actions could be controlled. At one such meeting the district commissioner's messenger passed by on his patrol. He was asked to deliver a
report of the meeting to his superior. Again, however, the district commissioner backed the chief and informed the headmen that they should
inform the chief, not him, of their complaints. The chief too heard of the
meeting and asked the district commissioner to punish his subjects for
gathering together without his knowledge and consent. This request
however showed that the chief misinterpreted the district commissioner's
role. As a civil servant the district commissioner refused to become
involved in local disputes, and ordered the chief to settle the dispute
himself.

At this point the chief's close agnates, who had supported him in the
succession dispute, turned against him and invited all who had a grudge
against the chief to join them. This brought about the chief's downfall.
They informed the Secretary for Internal Affairs of their chief's mal-
practices, and the local district commissioner received a letter from
head office asking him to replace the chief by a more suitable candidate.

To escape the ever-growing criticism and opposition, chief Shoko
took refuge in drink, gambling and sexual promiscuity. His diary,
which records his activities hour by hour during a whole month of the
rainy season, shows how his personality disintegrated. The main entries
fall under three headings. (1) On Thursdays and Sundays the chief
tried court cases for about two hours, then visited either a multiracial

---

[1] Full details about the establishment of this council are given in chapter 9, *infra*,
pp. 191–197.

hotel at Zimbabwe or the African township of Fort Victoria to have a drink and gamble for some five to nine hours. (2) He repeatedly visited the district commissioner to inform him of local events in his chiefdom. (3) Several days each week he visited the Shoko Museamwa community in order to inform himself of local discontent through women friends. These visits took place on weekdays when labour migrants were absent from their villages and the chief was sure not to meet his friends' husbands. These women were strategically placed in various villages so that no local opposition could escape his attention. He repaid his informers generously and was always welcomed by them. Fellow villagers reported the chief's visits to the women's husbands, but the men were frightened to sue their chief for adultery. A few entries in the diary, finally, refer to agricultural activities, but the hours spent on ploughing and weeding are far fewer than the average peasant would spend during this month of the year.

CONCLUSION

This case history records the failure of a pro-government chief. Unlike the successful pro-government chiefs discussed earlier, chief Shoko lived in an ecologically infertile area. Frequent droughts made his people economically dependent on both government and European neighbours. This dependence discouraged involvement with nationalism. Lack of education, and employment on European farms, further reduced the people's contacts with modern ideas. Like the people of Mhofu chiefdom, therefore, they showed great interest in their past and local customs.

In constrast to chief Mhofu, chief Shoko lacked local support. He had no traditional claim to the chieftainship and had risen to power through the help of Europeans who benefited from his accession. Just as the chiefdom as a whole was economically dependent on European assistance, so the chief was politically dependent on European support and protection. As soon as government withdrew its support, he fell. His disdain for traditional legitimacy, therefore, cost him his legitimacy in the modern bureaucratic system because government could not afford to keep in office indefinitely a chief who had been rejected by his people. Bureaucracy demands efficient administration.

Chief Shoko failed as patriarch, by forcing on his people government policies which they rejected and by ignoring their legitimate claims for justice, and he also failed as a bureaucrat by allowing the administration of his chiefdom to disintegrate. The disintegration of his personality, moreover, which showed itself in his recourse to sexual promiscuity, drinking and gambling, was a direct result of his insecurity. Chief Shoko was a pro-government chief who failed to satisfy the demands of both his subjects and his superiors.

2. ANTI-GOVERNMENT CHIEFS

Personality disintegration is much more frequent among anti-government than among pro-government chiefs, because the latter may at times succeed in harmonizing or balancing conflicting expectations; anti-government chiefs, on the other hand, are frequently forced to compromise, and any compromise causes them serious distress. This is borne out by the following three case histories.

(a) *Case History 4: Passive Conformity*

Chief Shiri, who administered Shiri chiefdom during the interregnum following his brother's death, was during the time of fieldwork in a very insecure position. He was addressed as chief, but knew that he had no guarantee of being finally appointed. In addition to personal insecurity he was faced with a dissatisfied peasant population.

Shiri chiefdom has poor sandy soils and the very high population density of 148 people per square mile. Scarcity of land forces 40 to 50 per cent of the men to seek work as labour migrants. Fairly good schooling facilities have enabled many to become skilled artisans and white-collar workers, both in towns and in their own villages. Mobility between town and country is high and many new influences from urban areas are cultivated by locally employed teachers and businessmen. Consequently many new avenues of prestige have been opened up. Nationalism is widely accepted by most of the people. In spite of these

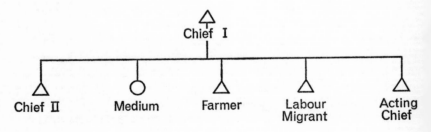

Fig. 6. Genealogy 2 : Genealogy of Chief Ngara

modernizing influences traditional prestige has not lost its attraction, and even some members of the new élite are willing to compete for traditional status. These forces constituted a threat to the weak local chief.

Shiri chieftainship is comparatively young, having been founded in the 1890s. Its first chief died as recently as 1956. The old chief was succeeded by his son,[1] but his son survived him by only six years. The fieldwork coincided with the interregnum following the second chief's death.

Chief Shiri became acting chief through intrigue. He had fought with his elder brother during his lifetime and settled at a distance from him in the chiefdom. At the second chief's death people expected that another son of the first chief would act during the interregnum. The eldest surviving son, however, had bought a purchase area farm, and the government was not willing to let him act for his deceased brother. Another was a labour migrant and unable to return home. At this point a concubine of the late chief deserted his family, took with her his money and the chiefly insignia, and went to the youngest brother who had quarrelled with the chief. This man accepted her favourably and offered her land in his village. The transfer of the insignia was contested by the chief's relatives and needed ratification by the district commissioner. The youngest brother, therefore, wooed a powerful and educated businessman whose family was distantly related to the chieftainship to help him to office. The businessman supported his claim before the district commissioner and the insignia were officially granted to him for the time of the interregnum.

Chief Shiri found himself in a similar position to chief Shoko. Like the former he had gained office through illegitimate means. Further developments show that like chief Shoko he alienated one section of his people after another. But there were significant differences between the two: chief Shiri ruled a people reasonably well educated, most of whom were nationalists. Through the businessman, himself a fervent supporter of nationalism, chief Shiri was introduced to leaders of the Zimbabwe African People's Union and occasionally accompanied party members to the capital. People thought that the chief shared their anti-government sentiments. As long as he remained under the businessman's influence, the chief did nothing to alter this impression.

Chief Shiri's recognition as acting chief deprived him of his relatives' support and increased his dependence on the businessman. He needed him both to advise him on the administration of his chiefdom and the treatment of government officials, and also to supply him with goods

[1] For succession rules see *supra*, p. 61 and *infra*, pp. 107–110.

H

on credit from his store. Chief Shiri's illiteracy, and the higher education of the businessman, therefore, as well as the chief's initial poverty and the businessman's wealth, put chief Shiri in a difficult position, for, as Blau observes:

> People who become indebted to a person for essential benefits are obligated to accede to his wishes lest he cease to furnish these benefits. An individual who distributes gifts and services to others makes a claim to superiority over them. If they properly repay him or possibly even make excessive returns, they challenge his claim and invite him to enter into a peer relation of mutual exchange. If they are unable to reciprocate, however, they validate his claim to superiority.[1]

This happened to chief Shiri.

Meanwhile the acting chief antagonized not only his relatives but also the ordinary people of his chiefdom, especially the teachers, by charging very high court fees. He was soon able to replace his round wattle-and-daub hut by a brick house with corrugated iron roof, glass windows and door-frames, and fenced off his property, as some prosperous tribal trust land farmers had begun to do. His economic dependence on the businessman decreased. But by looking only for his personal advantage and disregarding his followers, he roused his people to rebellion. At a beer drink a village headman once threatened him with violence. Chief Shiri instigated court action against his insubordinate subject, and the local magistrate fined the headman a small sum of money. The judgment stated that the village headman had been provoked by the chief, who was under the influence of alcohol.

At this stage chief Shiri also antagonized the businessman. This deprived him of a reliable adviser, on whom his efficiency depended. The businessman had become village headman with the chief's support by evicting two elder brothers. Later, when a delineation officer visited the tribal trust land to define 'community board areas', the businessman and five other local leaders asked to be appointed as sub-chiefs. Chief Shiri promised to support their claims for government recognition. As soon as the promise was made the businessman announced publicly that as sub-chief he would compete for the chieftainship. Chief Shiri took fright and reported to the district commissioner that his authority was being undermined, and asked that none of his subjects be officially recognized as sub-chiefs. The district commissioner agreed to the chief's request. Chief Shiri had begun to look for government support.

From this moment onward the businessman intensified his opposition

---

[1] Blau (1964), pp. 321–322. Cf. also Kuper (1965), p. 286.

to the acting chief. He fostered local discontent against his administration. Realizing that his own chances for chieftainship were slender, because he was only distantly related to the chiefly family, he threw his support behind a candidate of a senior house, who finally became chief.[1] When chief Shiri saw that he had lost all local support he indirectly began backing government policies, though he still stressed that he shared his people's hope for majority rule.

Once chief Shiri attended a meeting organized by the businessman to inform people of new government policies regarding land conservation. At the end of the meeting young nationalists appeared and asked the people to join their party and so help to bring about an African government; they promised more land and higher wages as soon as the white government had been overthrown. The businessman seemed to enjoy their visit, though he did not associate himself with them. Chief Shiri, on the other hand, left the gathering to join a beer drink. The nationalists followed him and respectfully asked for permission to address his people, but he replied: 'If you want to address the people, you must first ask the district commissioner's permission. I cannot give it to you.' The ordinary people began to gather round the young men and an old commoner praised them: 'Look at these men. They will bring us life. At present we are dying. I have six children but only two acres of land and one ox. When they rule the country, all will be well.' The chief grumbled: 'These men are bad.' Seeing that he could do nothing chief Shiri left the village and went home.

The next day both African and European police visited the people who had attended the gathering. The rumour spread that chief Shiri had called them to embarrass the businessman. The businessman proved that he had no connection with the nationalists and later told the people: 'Our chief is not a good leader. He supports government because he gets money from it; but he knows that our claims are right.'

People became convinced that chief Shiri had changed his loyalty. When he attended the chiefs' meeting in Salisbury in 1964, at which the government asked the traditional leaders' opinion on independence, a rumour spread that chief Shiri had backed the government against his own people. The content of the proceedings, published in a white paper,[2] differs widely from the stories which circulated in Shiri chiefdom. The people of Shiri chiefdom told each other that the chiefs had been asked to choose between a European and an African government; those who

[1] This is contrary to Karanga custom, which holds that the founder of a chieftainship is succeeded by his own descendants. Cf. *infra*, pp. 107–110.

[2] 1964, *The Demand for Independence*.

desired no change should choose money, those who wanted majority rule should pick up soil, the symbol of African independence. People said that chief Shiri, like most other chiefs, had chosen money. This story enraged the local people, and a fortnight after his return the chief's homestead was guarded by European police. Physically protected by Europeans against his own people, chief Shiri had no choice but to become a pro-government chief.

When the ministry of Internal Affairs launched its community development campaign in his chiefdom, the chief allowed himself to be manipulated by a government official, though he did not force his people to accept a council as chief Shoko had done. Chapter nine analyses in detail the chief's passive acquiescence.[1]

Faced with this dilemma, chief Shiri began to drink heavily. He was never sober except when he expected the visit of a government official. When the final election for a new chief took place, he stood stripped of all supporters and the chieftainship went to a senior house. Once again the government could not support a man who was incompetent by both European and African standards.

CONCLUSION

Like case history three, case history four shows the breakdown of an insecure chief. The difference between the options chosen by chiefs Shoko and Shiri lies in the fact that whereas Shoko chiefdom consisted of poor peasants who were economically dependent on the goodwill of Europeans, and therefore unwilling to co-operate with nationalists, chief Shiri's people were used to a highly diversified economy, were open to modern ideas, and nationalism was their fully accepted creed. Consequently chief Shiri could not but start off as an anti-government chief, whereas chief Shoko was forced to co-operate with Europeans. Chief Shiri's change of loyalty became necessary as he lost his people's support. He not only alienated one group of his supporters after another, as chief Shoko had done, but he also departed from his people's political conviction. Finally there remained no further bond between chief and people. They refused to accept him as their legitimate ruler, and their rejection caused him to seek escape in drink.

(b) *Case History 5: Withdrawal*

No compromise and role-change need occur among anti-government chiefs who opt for withdrawal, though they too tend to break down under

[1] *infra,* pp. 173–180.

the strain. But whereas chiefs who submit passively to conflicting pressures break down under them, chiefs who withdraw from or overtly oppose government policies break down under the uncompromising attitude of government. This is shown in case histories five and six.

Ngara chiefdom, whose leader sought escape from his intercalary position through withdrawal, shares most ecological and social characteristics with Shiri chiefdom. Chief Ngara is a very old man and lives in an area where education is available to a higher level and on a larger scale than usual. Most of his subjects are therefore fervent nationalists.[1] The chief's own family has a deep seated aversion to the European government because as early as 1914 his father's younger brother was deposed by a local commissioner when he failed to report a cattle theft by two of his subjects from a nearby European farm.[2] Chief Ngara and his people frequently quote this deposition to show that Europeans must be treated with suspicion.

Chief Ngara is in a structurally weak position because he was appointed in preference to a candidate who had stronger traditional claims and was very popular, but who was unacceptable to government because he was a leading nationalist. The old chief himself, though not a party member, does not oppose nationalism. He lives in the past and opposes social changes in general. The modern world confuses him and he pretends not to understand what goes on around him. Unlike many other old chiefs, chief Ngara has not fully abdicated the government of his chiefdom to his sons. On certain occasions he allows a son to act for him, especially when he has to deal directly with European administrators. But even then he is often present. Hence his sons can do nothing of which the old chief does not approve. Many people respect him as a venerable old man and ignore all government instructions unless he has authorized them. This gives chief Ngara greater power than most chiefs possess.

Chief Ngara has certain advantages over other chiefs. He is deaf, and if he does not agree with what the district commissioner tells him, he pleads inability to understand what is said. He is too old to walk far, and although he has a car he often pleads that old age or ill health prevent him from coming to a meeting if he disagrees with the agenda. In his absence government officials can deliver long speeches, to which the people listen quietly and nod their heads, but they conclude that

---

[1] There seems to be a consistent correlation between upper primary and lower secondary education and African nationalism.

[2] Checked in the National Archives. Reference suppressed to preserve the anonymity of the chief.

though the talks interest them they cannot comment without the chief's consent.

The reason for the strong support enjoyed by chief Ngara in his opposition to government policies is that although his own and his people's motives differ, their aim is identical: they do not want to grant Europeans any influence in their area if they can possibly prevent it. To the old chief Europeans represent a modern and alien power which he is unwilling to recognize; they did not exist in his childhood and he cannot square their presence with the values taught him by his ancestors. The people led by teachers and businessmen desire an African government elected on a general adult franchise. By the absence of their chief at government meetings and their own inactivity they hope to prevent the implementation of government policies. They are therefore willing to invoke traditional custom and refuse to deal with outsiders if their chief is absent. This means that even young nationalists claim to be loyal to the customs of their ancestors if this furthers their nationalist aims.

Chief Ngara's opposition to government showed itself most clearly when he opposed the introduction of community development. He did this through simply absenting himself from all meetings called by Internal Affairs officials. Once however he was caught when the district commissioner ordered him to come for a meeting without giving him the reason. His presence ended in a family tragedy.

When the chief arrived at the meeting-place he found that not the district commissioner but his deputy, the district officer, was present. The district officer addressed the meeting, consisting of chiefs and their councillors, in a manner offensive to Karanga etiquette. He sat in front of his audience on a table, dangled his legs, smoked a pipe, and in between his puffs spoke a few words in English, which his interpreter translated into the African language. He began by announcing that the dip fees for cattle had to be increased from 2s. 6d. per beast to 3s. 0d. in order to make the service self-supporting;[1] the government was no longer able to subsidize cattle dipping. He continued: 'However, you do not need to pay the increased dip fees if you form a council and start community development. Your council might be able to run the service much cheaper and so you can save money.' Then he explained in detail the function of community development. Chief Ngara sat silently through the meeting. When the district officer finally asked him

---

[1] Cattle dipping is compulsory throughout Rhodesia to prevent cattle epidemics. Cattle-owners made a contribution of 2s. 6d. per beast. This contribution, however, was insufficient to cover the·expenses of the service.

personally what he thought about the new policy the chief said slowly: 'I and my people want no change. Write to head office that I and my people want no council and we refuse to pay increased dip fees.' With these words the chief sat down, applauded by all the Karanga. The district officer replied cynically that he would forward his reply to the Secretary for Internal Affairs, but assured him that he knew the answer in advance.

Several months later, when chief Ngara sent one of his sons to the district commissioner's office to collect his salary, the district commissioner informed the son that he had received a reply from head office stating that the chief's refusal to pay increased dip fees was unacceptable, and that it was his duty as acting chief to convince his people of their duty to pay. A long argument ensued between the two men, but the chief's son was powerless. The district commissioner stressed that as chief he had merely to command his people and they would obey him.

When the chief's son passed on the district commissioner's message to the people, they declared that he had been bribed and had accepted money from government for selling his people. They reminded him of his weak submission in the 1950s to the implementation of the Land Husbandry Act, which village headmen in Shiri chiefdom had successfully arrested.[1] They claimed that the Act had deprived them of land and cattle, and that the increased dip fees were a further act of government exploitation. After this meeting rumours spread that the people had decided to kill the acting chief.

Caught between a clear order from the government and rebellion from his people, the chief's son was driven to despair. He imagined assassins behind every tree and surrounded himself with a bodyguard. A week after his interview with the district commissioner he committed suicide.

His suicide startled everybody, for suicide is very rare among the Karanga. Tensions in the chiefdom abated. Chief Ngara withdrew still more into utter non-co-operation. By the late 1960s he was staying permanently in his village; he refused to give any European access to his people and firmly resisted the introduction of community development. His people stood solidly behind him. The district commissioner ascribed the boycott to nationalist influences and claimed that agitators had used the old chief as a tool to prevent efficient administration.

---

[1] The Land Husbandry Act was implemented in Ngara chiefdom without much local opposition. In neighbouring areas, however, people had resorted to violence in some instances and had succeeded in preventing the full implementation of the Act.

CONCLUSION

Case history five shows that opposition to government policies is likely to expose chiefs to great suffering because of the government's power to impose its will on chiefs. But it need not deprive a chief of his people's support.

Chief Ngara, who because of his old age lived in a different world from most of his people, nevertheless remained closely united with them. He resented government policies because they introduced alien elements into his chiefdom; his people resented them because they were imposed on them by Europeans. Consequently, although the chief's and the people's motives differed, their aim was identical.

In this respect chief Ngara differed from chief Shiri, who had broken all bonds uniting him with his people. Though the district commissioner frowned on chief Ngara's lack of co-operation, he was reluctant to ask for his deposition because of the strong support that the people gave their chief. He expected, moreover, that the chief would soon die, and hoped that he would be succeeded by a more co-operative ruler.

This case history would seem to indicate that it is less serious for a chief, once he has been officially appointed, to risk the disapproval of administrators than to alienate his own people. Though chief Ngara suffered greatly through the suicide of his son, he remained in power because he kept the support of his people.

(c) *Case History 6: Overt Opposition*[1]

The last alternative open to anti-government chiefs is overt opposition. This alternative was chosen by chief Nzou. Nzou chiefdom has identical ecological and educational characteristics to the Shiri and Ngara chiefdoms, though its land is slightly more fertile. Frequent movement of fairly educated labour migrants brings new ideas and money into the area. The chief himself had undergone twelve years of schooling and was headmaster of an upper primary school before he was appointed chief. He therefore shared the values of his educated subjects.

Chief Nzou was relatively young when he was appointed chief. His father's brothers were still alive and should have taken the office. But the government at the time was endeavouring to appoint younger and more educated chiefs who seemed capable of modernizing their areas. Consequently on assuming office the young chief had to overcome opposition from his older agnates, who complained: 'Why did you

---

[1] The classical example of a Rhodesian chief's overt opposition to government is the case of Mangwende. See Holleman (1968), chapters 3 to 6, especially p. 235.

make friends with Europeans and take our name from us? You are only our son; how can we, your fathers, obey you?'

In spite of this initial difficulty, however, the chief soon won acceptance. He increased his herd of cattle and distributed it for herding purposes among his people. They were allowed to milk them and to use them for ploughing. He also won renown as a skilful and fair judge, but severely reprimanded those who brought their cases to the district commissioner.[1] He insisted that African affairs had to be settled by Africans, and that Europeans ought not to be given more influence than they already possessed. This gained him the support of the young educated men.

In his own tribal trust land he rose to a high position when all the other chiefs were made his sub-chiefs. His own people were proud of him. The district commissioner too was proud to have a progressive chief in his area who understood administration and kept order in his chiefdom. His fame spread beyond the province, and when in 1962 the Council of Chiefs was founded he became its first president. He also served on the Board of Trustees for tribal areas and was one of the first members of the Constitutional Council founded in 1962. In the early 1960s, therefore, chief Nzou was one of the most important chiefs in Rhodesia. In 1963, six years before the African Law and Tribal Courts Act was passed, he stated his determination to work with his fellow chiefs for the return of civil and criminal jurisdiction to chiefs. He added: 'We want to regain all powers which were traditionally possessed by chiefs, and we shall fight to obtain them. We do not yet know the attitude of the new government towards Africans.[2] We do not know the future, only the present. But we shall go on pressing our claims. No one should expect evil things before they have happened.' Chief Nzou therefore kept an open mind when many Africans were already critical of the new government.

His openness towards government however did not make him a compliant tool. Years earlier, when the Land Husbandry Act was implemented in his chiefdom, his men had fought government officials with sticks, and at one stage had overturned an extension officer's car. Throughout the period of fieldwork, chief Nzou was known as a firm supporter of African nationalism. He was the close friend of the founder of a local African independent church, who had opened the first all-African school in the tribal trust land. This man was the father

[1] At that time district commissioners had the right to try all African civil cases.
[2] The party which had ruled Rhodesia throughout its history was replaced in 1962 by a right-wing party. Cf. *supra*, p. 19.

of the later vice-president of the Zimbabwe African National Union, and his school the meeting place where like-minded people gathered. Chief Nzou often visited the school. During those days chief Nzou was a great man, respected throughout Rhodesia, admired by his people, and befriended by African nationalists. He was welcomed in all villages and enjoyed many a good beer drink with his subjects; but he was no drunkard. Missionaries of the Dutch Reformed church were proud that the most important chief in the area was one of their people.

Chief Nzou was a man of conviction and did not shift sides as his own interests demanded. Consequently he became involved in political events, which caused his downfall. When the African nationalist party split into the Zimbabwe African People's Union and the Zimbabwe African National Union, chief Nzou supported the latter because this party appealed especially to educated Africans and his friend, the founder of the independent church, strengthened his link with the party through his son. Chief Nzou supported the party's activities, and when its members collected signatures for the British Government in protest against the Rhodesian Government's demand for independence under minority rule, he signed his name.[1] Members of the Chiefs' Council who were loyal to the government objected to chief Nzou's open opposition and forced him to resign as president.[2] At the same time chief Nzou lost his membership of the Board of Trustees for tribal areas and of the Constitutional Council. His support for a national cause, therefore, deprived him of country-wide leadership positions.

His exclusion from all prestige positions outside his chiefdom crushed chief Nzou. By 1964 he had begun to drink heavily. He said in an interview: 'I must now be neutral in politics in order to save myself. I have spoken up too much. At present I just forward my people's wishes to government without indicating my support or opposition. Last week some Zimbabwe African National Union leaders came to me with a request. I just forwarded it to the district commissioner, who turned the application down. I no longer care. I must at least remain a chief. I have lost enough.'

By this time the other chiefs in the tribal trust land whose chieftainships were down-graded in 1951 had had them restored. This cost chief Nzou prestige. His salary, which was based on the number of his taxpayers, was reduced.

When all African nationalist parties were banned and the nationalist

---

[1] Cf. for similar activities of chiefs in former Northern Rhodesia and Nyasaland: Rotberg (1966), pp. 192–194 *et alia*.

[2] Cf. *supra*, p. 21; S.I.A., 1963, p. 5; S.I.A., 1964, p. 5.

leaders restricted or detained without trial, chief Nzou became apathetic. He frequently met with friendly chiefs who shared his political views, but he sought to forget his frustration in drink. By 1968 his health was so undermined by alcohol that European doctors diagnosed an advanced stage of cirrhosis of the liver and dismissed him as incurable. By 1969 chief Nzou was unable to leave his home and had almost lost his voice. At 53 years of age he was an invalid who had to hand over the administration of his chiefdom to his son.

Even in his degradation, however, chief Nzou preserved elements of his dignity. No district commissioner ever treated him disrespectfully. His people obeyed him even when he was an invalid. When chiefs were given back the power to allocate land in grazing areas and many chiefs took the opportunity to amass personal wealth through giving out land for money, chief Nzou resisted all petitions from both his subjects and outsiders to reduce the chiefdom's pastures. He convinced his people that the Land Husbandry Act, which they had once fought, had proved useful, and he decided to preserve it intact. By 1969 Nzou chiefdom was the only chiefdom in its tribal trust land which did not suffer from overstocking.

Chief Nzou could not confine his interests to his own chiefdom. Unlike pro-government chiefs his interests were nation-wide. In 1969 he strongly objected to a parliament consisting of an equal number of Ndebele and Shona delegates, openly declared his loyalty to the British Queen, and approved the British Prime Minister's policies towards the Rhodesian Government.[1]

CONCLUSION

This case history shows that a chief's overt opposition to government is impossible to sustain indefinitely. Chief Nzou's nationalism caused his political downfall, but he was spared the humiliation experienced by some chiefs conforming to government demands who are rejected by Africans and Europeans alike. Like chiefs actively or passively conforming to government, therefore, chiefs who seek to escape through withdrawal or overt opposition also break down under the strain of conflicting demands.

[1] Cf. the faith of Northern Rhodesian chiefs in the British Government: Rotberg (1966), pp. 202, 210, 251, *et alia*. For Rhodesian African attitudes towards the Queen cf. *The Rhodesia Herald*, 2.7.1969.

GENERAL CONCLUSION

The six case histories show that both pro- and anti-government chiefs can retain the loyalty of their people if they act out of conviction and share to some extent the political ideology of their people. Only those who depend exclusively on European support because they lack legitimacy in the eyes of their followers are likely to lose their position. Those to whom government refuses recognition, such as the unsuccessful competitor of chief Ngara,[1] cannot even take up the office of chief. Government legitimization is therefore of prime importance. But once they are appointed, government support is not enough. Popular support is then essential. This is the reason for the Karanga chief's dilemma: he needs the recognition of his patriarchal following as well as of his superiors in the bureaucratic administration of Rhodesia.

Once in office the strain is greater on anti-government than on pro-government chiefs because they have to be constantly on the alert to attack a new policy or to defend their own and their people's position. Consequently personality disintegration is much more frequent among the latter group than among pro-government chiefs.

The case histories indicate further that a chief is seldom free to adopt a pro- or anti-government stand, for a significant factor determining his major role, that is, whether he will be a government servant or representative of his people, seems to be the general social environment of his chiefdom. The case histories have shown that all anti-government chiefs ruled people who were better educated and were therefore more nationalistic than people ruled by pro-government chiefs who had little access to schooling and less contact with European culture. Chiefs are therefore to a considerable degree one with their people and express their basic sentiments. Individualists, like the sub-chief in case history two, are an exception.

Fallers concludes that by locating structural conflicts in the social personalities of individuals rather than between discrete groups, the unity and stability of the system of chieftainship can be maintained.[2] The case histories show that the present administrative system in tribal trust lands can be preserved as long as chiefs are willing to serve as shock-absorbers. Many chiefs are willing to serve in this capacity because the position of chief still carries prestige in the eyes of many Africans and guarantees wealth. The unanimity with which chieftainship is accepted by the people shows that it still performs essential services to the Karanga. Yet the failure of many incumbents to solve the tensions

[1] *supra*, p. 97.
[2] Fallers (1955), p. 304.

inherent in their office tends to bring modern chieftainship into disrepute. Even educated Karanga would regret such a development, because many of them share the sentiment of the South African chief and nationalist, Luthuli, who wrote that 'the institution of chieftainship will die out in the course of time, but it would be a pity if its end is ignominy'.[1]

[1] Luthuli (1966), p. 122.

CHAPTER 6

Karanga Succession: the Opening of a Social Drama[1]

INTRODUCTION

The succession dispute of the Shoko chiefdom analysed in this and the following two chapters is characterized in the following observation: 'the political world is a world of conflict that, however changing its superficial forms, can never be quieted. It is a world in which competing interests try continually to grasp its privileges and riches and in which struggle for power is dominant.'[2] This succession dispute which lasted for over twenty years is not typical of Karanga succession in general because most succession disputes are settled within two or three years. The present case has nevertheless been chosen because those concerned availed themselves of all the techniques at their disposal. Competitors in other recorded succession disputes selected only a few of the many possibilities open to them. Mitchell writes:

> The typicality of the material is irrelevant since the regularities are set out in the description of the over-all social structure. In a sense the more atypical the actions and events described in the case history, the more instructive they are, since the anthropologist uses case material to show how variations can be contained within the structure.[3]

The succession dispute of Shoko chiefdom derives its complexity from the interplay of African and European social institutions. In the context of Rhodesia's plural society, traditional chief-makers compete with European employers, lawyers, civil servants and members of parliament to install their candidate as chief. Situations of competition in which rivals strive for identical aims are often complicated by conflicts in which competitors ignore institutionalized means to resolve the contest. They

---

[1] The term 'Social Drama' is taken from Turner's book *Schism and Continuity in an African Society*. But because of fundamental differences in Turner's and the present field data, especially differences in scale and complexity and the absence of a 'processional' form in Karanga succession disputes, Turner's analytical approach is not adopted.

[2] Gray (1968), p. 46.

Mitchell (1964), p. xiii.

appeal to structurally opposed models of interaction, and the succession dispute widens like a spiral, drawing within its orbit large segments of Rhodesian society. In such situations traditional norms and values are steadily undermined and lose their hold on the actors in the social drama. Simultaneously, however, the people's sustained interest in the on-going conflict conveys the impression that the succession dispute has become a value in itself, a focus of attention that breaks the monotony of the uneventful life of a peasant community.

The first part of this chapter outlines the general succession rules of Karanga chieftainships and so provides the conceptual model against which individual succession disputes can be judged. The second part of chapter six, together with chapters seven and eight, analyse how people manipulate this structural model and show 'how exceptions and variations ignored in the process of delineating a structure are accommodated within it in reality'.[1]

1. THE PRINCIPLES OF KARANGA SUCCESSION

Chapter three[2] stated that many Karanga chiefdoms were established in their present territory in the nineteenth century. It may therefore be assumed that their genealogies are accurate, and not telescoped to fit into a structural model. Historical evidence corroborates local tradition.[3] Most recorded genealogies fall into nine or ten generations and are subdivided into three phases. Many tribal histories are characterized by a tripartite division, even in cases where a much greater time-depth is involved than in Karanga genealogies. Vansina, for example, writes of a Congo tribe that its 'past consisted of three periods: a period of origin, a period of migration and a static period during which no fundamental changes occurred'.[4]

Tribal historians, that is, the spirit mediums of Karanga chieftainships, relate why and how the groups' ancestors split off from older chiefdoms in other parts of the country and migrated to their present territory. They sometimes attribute the break-up to land shortage, but more often to a struggle for leadership. Frequently one section of an expanding chieftainship, despairing of its chances to provide a leader, secedes and goes in search of a new territory. It establishes its own political unit. During its migration it changes its praise-name in order to

---

[1] Mitchell (1964), p. x.
[2] *supra*, p. 44.
[3] Abraham, oral information.
[4] Vansina (1965), p. 101.

distinguish itself from the old chieftainship, but it retains its old clan affiliation, through which it claims distant kinship with its parent body. This process seems to have occurred approximately every six generations, and by that time the population of a chiefdom had sufficiently increased to create an intense competition for leadership. The intensity with which succession disputes are at present fought among the Karanga is due to European settlement in Rhodesia, a factor that prevents tribal migrations. Instead of splitting into two groups, Karanga chiefdoms have to settle their leadership problems through internal compromise.

The first three or four generations of chiefly genealogies refer to distant ancestors who lived in the country of a group's origin and did not migrate with them. Their history provides a charter affiliating the new political unit with a well-established senior group. Only the names, not the deeds, of these distant ancestors are remembered.

The next three generations are the most crucial in the history of a chiefdom. They relate how the group moved into its new territory and how the present power-balance was established. The leader of the migrating group, often accompanied by his brothers and their families, belongs to the first generation of the second phase. He is not necessarily the oldest man; often his elder brothers become ritual experts and renounce political office. After settling down the descendants of such elder brothers become the chief-makers of the new chiefdom.[1]

Since migrating groups tend to be very small, often not larger than extended families, their first leaders seldom claim the title of chief. Their sons, however, assume this title if, by the time they succeed, their groups have sufficiently increased to constitute independent political units. Relations with neighbouring chiefs are then fixed, either through conquest or through intermarriage.

Since the Karanga idea is that rulers ought to be polygynists, chiefs tend to have many sons. At a first chief's death his eldest son succeeds him in office and is followed by his younger surviving brothers until all have held office in turn. In the third generation of phase two these brothers establish the houses of the chieftainship among which the office of chief is expected to circulate in the future. There exists no limit to the number of houses that may be established.[2] During this phase a chieftainship reaches its highest vitality. Succession disputes seldom arise because the succession rule applicable to this stage of a chieftain-

---

[1] Shiri chiefdom is an exception to this rule. Cf. *supra*, pp. 93, 96.

[2] In other parts of Rhodesia, especially among older chieftainships, there seems to be a tendency to confine the chiefly office to three houses. This is not the case among the Karanga.

Land shrine (above) in the Ngara chiefdom. 2. Picture shows a court case being tried at a homestead in the Guruuswa Purchase area.

3. Typical village (above) in a tribal trust land.

4. Three young nationalists canvassing for followers in the Shara chiefdom. They are holding up membership cards of the Zimbabwe African People's Union showing their leader J. Nkomo demanding 'one man one vote'.

5. Chief Shoko's
new house
(above).
6. Chiefs and their
followers attend a
meeting of a
government
minister
announcing
community
development.

7. Installation ceremony of Chief Shoko (above). While the chief's relatives deliver speeches, the chief waits inside the car. 8. Picture shows European guests of honour at Chief Shoko's installation ceremony.

ship is clear and generally accepted. Case history one in chapter five[1] records the secure position of a chief who still belongs to this generation. By the end of the second phase, a new chieftainship is firmly established and the houses which in the future may provide chiefs are fixed.

The third phase opens with the death of the last son of the first chief. The office of chief should ideally go to the eldest son of the first chief in the third generation of phase two. This man, however, as well as most or all of his brothers, is very often already dead, because if the founder of the chieftainship was a polygynist with many wives his eldest son is likely to have been well advanced in years before his youngest son was born. Consequently his grandchildren by his eldest son may be older than his younger sons. If this happens the senior house of the chieftainship is permanently excluded from succession because one Karanga succession rule states that no man may become chief unless his 'father' had been chief. During the third phase this 'father' may be a classificatory father of the same house of the chieftainship. If a house thus loses its claim to the chiefly office, the chieftainship passes to the next senior house. In this way houses are constantly eliminated from competition. Under no circumstances should a man of a junior generation become chief while members of a senior generation are still alive, because 'sons' ought not to rule their 'fathers'.[2]

It seems that at this stage in the past a split usually occurred in the chieftainship: if a house saw itself permanently excluded from office though it had many descendants, it tended to migrate and establish itself as an independent political unit. The inability to secede during the twentieth century intensifies succession disputes among candidates for chieftainships. Conflicts are further complicated because by this time competing candidates can appeal to different succession rules practised in their own chiefdom.

Firstly, candidates can argue that a father ought to be succeeded by his son; this happens during the first part of the second phase of the chieftainship. Secondly, candidates can argue that the eldest by birth should succeed, because this rule operates in the third generation of phase two, when each of the sons of the first chief establish his own house of the chieftainship. Thirdly, candidates can argue that the office of chief should rotate between the various houses established by the chiefs of phase two; this is the general Karanga custom. These three principles are likely to come into conflict when the eldest man of the chieftainship belongs to a junior house, or when a very old chief

---

[1] Cf. *supra*, p. 78.

[2] Chief Nzou's elders objected to obeying their 'son'. *Supra*, pp. 100–101

I

dies whose son had administered the chiefdom for many years. If a
acting chief is himself old and much respected by his people, he may b
unwilling to let the office pass to another house. In such a situation eacl
competing group claims the office for different reasons, and all thei
conflicting claims are based on traditional principles. Phase three
therefore, is characterized by intense competition and structural con
flicts.

These structural conflicts affect the local power-balance in three way:
Firstly, there is a constant drift of office towards junior houses and a:
exclusion of senior houses. Secondly, sons fight hard for their fathers t
become chiefs, because if their fathers, often too old to administer th
chiefdoms effectively, were to be passed over they and their childre
would later be disqualified from office. Thirdly, senior sons of senic
houses who have little chance of holding office tend to shift thei
allegiance from their own to junior houses, in the hope that the winnin
candidates will reward them with subchieftainships. Segmentatio
which in the past caused fission at chieftainship level, now turns inwar
and produces new alliances within individual chiefdoms. This proces
operates at all levels of the Karanga political system. It subdivide
chiefdoms, subchiefdoms and villages into opposing factions. Barne
observation that tribal history can be reduced to fission and segment
tion[1] is therefore relevant to Karanga political processes.

This outline of Karanga succession principles is derived from a larg
number of genealogies. Several genealogies deviate from this model
one point or another, but these deviations do not invalidate it because,
Turner observes, 'before one can study breach one must be aware (
regularity'.[2]

The history of Shoko chiefdom, which has passed through all thre
phases of its genealogical development and now undergoes segmentar
processes at subchiefdom and village levels, illustrates how the
principles work themselves out in concrete situations.

2. APPLICATION OF THE KARANGA SUCCESSION MODEL TO SHOKO CHIEFDOM

The social drama of the succession dispute in Shoko chiefdom
intimately linked to the early history of the chiefdom. The ancestors
the group arrived in Karangaland in the middle of the nineteen
century. Local tradition has preserved an account of the split from

[1] Barnes, 1955.
[2] Turner (1957), p. xvii.

parent group some three hundred miles to the north-east of their present settlement. The local spirit medium Homam (H11) recite on ritual occasions the names of distant ancestors in the stereotyped phrase:

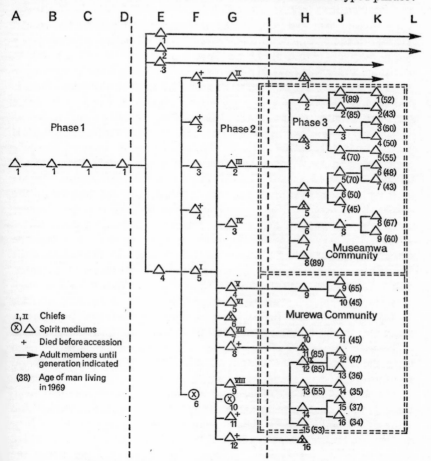

Fig. 7. Genealogy 3: skeleton genealogy of Shoko chiefdom[1]

'Abraham (A1) is the father of Benjamin (B1); Benjamin (B1) is the father of Caleb (C1); Caleb (C1) is the father of David (D1). These men, who never left their homeland, are remembered because they link the young chiefdom to one of the most important clans of the Shona-speaking people.

The sons of David (D1), namely Eber (E1), Enoch (E2), Ephraim

[1] See Appendix B, pp. 238–239.

(E3) and Esau (E4), arrived near Zimbabwe in the middle of the nineteenth century after fleeing from their relatives, whose cattle they had
stolen. They were invited by a local chief to settle with him and help
him fight an invading group, which threatened to annex his territory.
The refugees accepted the invitation and conquered the newcomers.
Already in the next generation, however, they outnumbered their hosts
and became a chieftainship in their own right. Their hosts formed a sub-
chiefdom under their jurisdiction.

When the question of leadership arose, all members of generation E
and several of generation F had already died. Feleg (F3), the oldest
surviving member of the group, was therefore unanimously chosen as
chief. The descendants of Eber (E1), Enoch (E2) and Ephraim (E3)
were permanently excluded from office but were compensated for their
exclusion with the right to nominate the new chiefs. They assumed
the ritual office of *magwee*, 'nominators'. It seems that the descendants
of these houses have filled this office throughout the history of the
chieftainship because the people remember the nominators of every
chief. The nominators, belonging to the senior houses, consider themselves as 'fathers' of the chieftainship because the first chief was the
classificatory son of the founders of their houses. As chief-makers the
senior houses exert a strong influence over the political life of the chiefdom. Their genealogical seniority and ritual authority confer high
prestige on them. They are regarded as 'the owners of the soil' because
during the traditional investiture ceremony of chiefs the nominators
place soil in the hands of the successful candidate and install him in
office with the words: 'receive your soil'.[1] The descendants of Esau
(E4), therefore, respect the descendants of Eber (E1), Enoch (E2) and
Ephraim (E3).

The drift of political office towards junior members operated from
the beginning of the chieftainship. Feleg (F3) never ruled as a chief, and
none of his children ever held the chiefly office. A legend relates how
at his installation ceremony the spirit medium Dinah (F6) was delayed,
and how in his impatience to assume office Feleg (F3) performed the
function assigned to the medium: he drank the blood sacrificed to the
ancestors. On arrival the medium Dinah (F6) learned of the sacrilege;
she fell possessed and declared that the ancestors had rejected Feleg
(F3) as chief. The nominators met and appointed Finon (F5), Esau's
(E4's) youngest son, as chief.

---

[1] In older chieftainships, whose founders had become vassals of the Rozvi kings,
these words were traditionally spoken by representatives of the king at each new
accession ceremony.

Finon (F5) ruled for many years and made his chieftainship famous among his neighbours. He had 36 sons, seven of whom became chiefs in turn after his death, namely Gad (G1), Gamaliel (G2), Gatam (G3), Gazer (G4), Gerar (G5), Gothan (G7) and Gilead (G9). Gether (G8), Gideoni (G11) and Gomer (G12) died before their turn of office and their descendants therefore have no claim to the chieftainship. Gershom (G6) who might have become chief, became a spirit medium. He was possessed by Esau (E4) and was therefore ineligible for political office because the Karanga generally hold that political and ritual offices should be kept apart.

The office of spirit medium carries prestige in a chiefdom but it is inferior to that of a chief. It seems that those who for structural reasons are disqualified from becoming a chief tend to fill this ritual office. The structural positions of spirit mediums in the third phase of the chief's genealogy bear this out. In this phase competition for the chieftainship had become acute, and those men who became spirit mediums had little chance of becoming chief: Hadad (H1) belonged to the senior house and was older than his classificatory fathers of junior houses; it was highly improbable therefore that he would become chief. The same applies to Ham (H3). The fathers of Homam (H11) and Hushim (H16) had not been chiefs and so they could not expect to become chiefs themselves. As men struggled for prestige positions no more women claimed to be possessed by ancestral spirits. It was only during phase two that female mediums, such as Dinah (F6) and Tamar (G10), operated in the chiefdom.

Spirit mediums constitute the second category of men who, because disqualified from political office, are recompensed with ritual leadership. The medium does not choose the next chief but confirms or rejects the decision of the nominators. He differs structurally from the nominators in that he is a voice from within the chiefly family and not an outsider. As such he is viewed as less impartial than they and it is believed that the medium's residence, if not his affiliation to a particular house, tends to influence his pronouncements. Medium Homam (H11) lives among the people of the house founded by Gilead (G9), and is thought to favour a candidate of that house for the chieftainship; Hushim (H16), who until his death lived with the people of Gamaliel (G2), was regarded as the medium favouring a leader from that house.

The nominators live along the southern fringe of the chiefdom. Shoko chiefdom is divided into two communities, Shoko Murewa and Shoko Museamwa. Community Shoko Museamwa consists of the house of Gamaliel (G2) and its allies in the western part of the chiefdom;

Eber's (E1's) descendants live with them. The Shoko Murewa community, incorporating the houses of Gazer (G4) to Gershom (G7), lives in the eastern part of the chiefdom, and the descendants of Enoch (E2) and Ephraim (E3) live with them. The people of Shoko chiefdom are unable to record any occasion on which the nominators disagreed on a candidate for the chieftainship. They are considered unaligned.

The early history of Shoko chiefdom shows that between generations F and G succession followed from father to son, and within generation G brothers succeeded each other as chiefs. Many people expected that from generation H onwards the chiefly office would rotate between the seven houses established in generation G. No longer would candidates contest as individuals for office, but as members of houses. Each house forms a corporate personality, replacing its founder.

By the time chief Gilead (G9) died the major houses provided their own followings. It seems that in generation H each of these houses was approximately as strong as were all the people of Shoko chiefdom in generation F, when the first chief was appointed. The hypothesis put forward in the first part of this chapter[1] is that at this stage in the past fission might have occurred. If the houses that have lost their claim to office could move away and start their own political unit, they would retain two things in their new genealogy: the names of the key ancestors Esau (E4) and Finon (F5), to prove their descent from the Shoko chieftainship; also the name of the founder of their own house in generation G. The first cycle of the Shoko chieftainship would thus be concluded. With the departure of one section, either the Shoko Murewa or the Shoko Museamwa community, Shoko chiefdom would become a senior chiefdom, to which the new chiefdom would refer to fix its status in wider Karanga power-politics.

The impossibility of fission and migration at chieftainship level during the twentieth century eliminates the traditional channel of tension relief discussed above. Instead the struggle is turned inward and confined to a small territorial unit. The age composition and segmentation of various houses give rise to an internal reorganization of the chiefdom.

The age composition of contenders for the chieftainship is a vital factor. Owing to the polygyny of leaders, the junior houses of a chieftainship have more younger men alive in each generation than the senior houses. The genealogy of the Shoko chiefdom shows that in generation H, apart from the spirit medium Homam (H11), only the two houses Gamaliel (G2) and Gilead (G9) have any survivors. Of these

[1] Cf. *supra*, p. 109.

Gamaliel (G2) has one man alive and Gilead (G9) three, two of whom are only in their fifties and therefore likely to live for many years. This shows that as a generation dies out the chiefly office tends to drift from senior to junior houses. Should Haran (H6), the only survivor of generation H in the house of Gamaliel (G2) die, then Gilead (G9) is the only house in the chiefdom which has a right to provide a chief. Hence Havilah (H8) and Hul (H12) are bound to compete fiercely for the chieftainship.

The segmentary nature of Karanga chiefdoms causes further complications. The genealogy shows that most active adults of the house of Gamaliel (G2) who provide the leadership of the Shoko Museamwa community belong to generation K, while in the Shoko Murewa community, dominated by the house of Gilead (G9), active adults belong to generations H and J; its men are therefore genealogically senior to those of the Shoko Museamwa community, but younger in age. This gives the Shoko Murewa community a structurally leading position and further increases its tensions with the Shoko Museamwa community.

In addition the house of Gamaliel (G2), which has adults spread over three generations, is subdivided into opposing sections: the descendants of Hadoram (H2) realize that if the chieftainship should come to their house it would go to the younger members of Hamul's (H4's) family. They have therefore deserted their own house and supported Gilead's (G9's) descendants, hoping to be rewarded with a subchieftainship over the Shoko Museamwa community. Japheth (J7) who fights for his classificatory father Havilah (H8) is therefore attacked on two sides: by the combined opposition of the house of Gilead (G9) and by the section of his own house that is descended from his father's brother Hadoram (H2).

The principle of segmentation splits support even at village level. On the death of Hamul (H4), the most important village headman of the Shoko Museamwa community, his position was taken by his eldest son Jalam (J5). During the 1950s Jalam (J5) migrated to a resettlement area and Japheth (J7) expected to take over the village headmanship. Instead, Jalam (J5) appointed his own son Keturah (K6). This roused Japheth's (J7's) anger, and in order to have a village of his own and not to be ruled by a 'son' he split the village. From this moment onward the descendants of Jalam (J5) deserted the cause of their own house and together with the descendants of Hadoram (H2) supported the house of Gilead (G9) for the chieftainship. This left Havilah (H8), the candidate for the house of Gamaliel (G2), with the support of the descendants of Ham (H3), Hanoch (H5), Haran (H6), Hareph (H7) and Jamin (J6) and

Japheth (J7). Even with these defections, however, the remaining group constituted a strong following capable of effectively challenging the candidates from the house of Gilead (G9).

This structural analysis of the history of Shoko chiefdom shows that the principles of Karanga succession and segmentation apply fully to this chieftainship. There is no structural deviation from the model. The stage is set for intense competition between the houses of Gamaliel (G2) and Gilead (G9). The ensuing social drama analyses how competition changes into conflict as different factions apply to different institutions to press their claim for office.

3. THE SOCIAL DRAMA

'The historical approach may be seen as the most tightly controlled type of comparative analysis . . . History affords the social anthropologist a much neglected laboratory for testing the validity of structural assumptions and social mechanisms.'[1]

The social drama of the succession dispute in Shoko chiefdom now to be related provides the kind of material of which Lewis spoke, permitting us to test the validity of the structural principles outlined in the model of Karanga succession and of the social mechanisms and techniques offered to the people by diverse institutions in Rhodesia's plural society.

The social drama falls into five parts, here referred to as 'acts'. Act one opens in 1943 with the death of the last chief in generation G and stretches to the demotion of the chieftainship in 1951. Act two begins in 1951 and ends in 1961, when the people succeeded in regaining the chiefly status for their group. Act three lasts from 1961 to 1964 and records the intense competition and conflict between the houses of Gamaliel (G2) and Gilead (G9) for the chieftainship. Act four occurs in 1964 and describes the success of Gilead's (G9's) house. It highlights the various forces that had operated in the chiefdom during the preceding years and foreshadows future events. Act five covers the years 1964 to 1969 and shows how the maladministration of the chiefdom leads to the deposition and replacement of the acting chief; it presents no solution of the conflict. The struggle for power still goes on.

The atypicality of this case history is brought about by the demotion of the chieftainship by the government and the ensuing intervention of Europeans in the people's competition for political office.

Earlier historical events are relevant to an understanding of the

[1] Lewis (1968), p. xx.

intensity with which the succession dispute of Shoko chiefdom is fought, for the structure of a present situation is 'not fully revealed without reference to its development over time'.[1]

PROLOGUE

Gilead (G9), the youngest of Finon's (F5's) surviving sons, had left Shoko chiefdom in his youth and settled in Ndebeleland, because he did not expect to survive his elder brothers and become chief. To win favour with his hosts, he informed the Ndebele king and his warriors of a cave in which the people of the house of Gamaliel (G2) took refuge during raids. On one occasion he led a warrior band to the cave; the Ndebele collected wet branches, lighted them in front of the cave, and drove the suffocating people and cattle out of their hiding place. They captured the cattle and took the men as slaves to their own country. The descendants of Gamaliel (G2) preserve the memory of this treason and quote it as the cause of perpetual enmity between the houses of Gilead (G2) and Gamaliel (G9).

In 1920 Gothan (G7), a full brother of Gamaliel (G2), died and left the chieftainship vacant. Gilead (G9) returned from Ndebeleland and claimed the office. Gamaliel's (G2's) descendants objected to a traitor becoming chief, but the spirit medium pleaded that no son of the first chief be passed over. Gilead (G9) became chief, and ruled until 1943.

The long reign of Gilead (G9) had important consequences for the power balance in the chiefdom. Neighbouring European farmers came to view him and his family as the only legitimate rulers of the chiefdom and were little aware of the claims of other houses. Gilead (G9) lived so long that the senior houses of Gad (G1) and Gatam (G3) had no more surviving sons at his death. Moreover, owing to the government's insistence that sons act for their old fathers, Hul (H12) had acted for Gilead (G9) for many years, and even Joab (J12), Gilead's grandson, had served as his messenger. This concentration of political offices in one family consolidated their power and when Gilead (G9) died his family felt strong enough to retain the chieftainship.

ACT 1: THE EARLY SUCCESSION DISPUTE

Scene 1

At the death of Gilead (G9) in 1943 the following candidates competed

[1] Lewis (1968), p. xviii.

for the office of chief: Hareph (H7) of the house of Gamaliel (G2) presented the claim of the Shoko Museamwa community; Helon (H9), son of Gazer (G4), put in a claim for his house and Hirah (H10) claimed the office for the descendants of Gothan (G7). The most vocal competitor was Hul (H12), the son of the last chief, Gilead (G9). Hareph (H7), Hirah (H10) and Hul (H12) were living in the chiefdom, but Helon (H9) had migrated to another tribal trust land[1] and was recalled when the succession was discussed. Havilah (H8), an old man from the house of Gamaliel (G2), also moved back into the chiefdom. He had lived on land formally allocated to Europeans under the Land Apportionment Act but not occupied by them until the 1940s. He returned to his relatives at the time of the succession dispute and supported his elder brother Hareph (H7).

Of the four candidates for the chieftainship, each put forward a different justification for his claim. Hareph (H7) quoted the common Karanga succession rule that he belonged to the senior house and that, as the chieftainship should now circulate among the houses founded by the last chiefs, it was his turn to succeed to office. Helon (H9) claimed that he was the oldest by age and pointed out that in Shoko chiefdom the office of chief had always gone to the oldest man. He thereby quoted a rule which regulates succession in phase two of Karanga genealogies, but which no longer applies to phase three. Hul (H12) had no other claim than that his family had held the office for many years and that he was unwilling to let it pass to another house. His followers supported his endeavour to retain the office permanently in their hands. All the other candidates objected to this argument and claimed that it was contrary to Karanga custom. Hirah (H10) urged his claim less strongly than the other candidates because he had no special reason for claiming the office; he competed because he was one of the few survivors of his generation and knew that if he failed to become chief his descendants would be excluded from the chieftainship for ever.

At this point an outsider intervened. A young district officer showed interest in the succession dispute, listened to all the claims, and came out in support of the oldest candidate Helon (H9). Hareph (H7) and his followers strongly objected to the choice, but Hul (H12) and his family protested weakly. The nominators saw in the district officer's suggestion a compromise solution, because Helon (H9) was very old and not expected to live long. They therefore seconded the civil servant's

[1] Throughout this account the terminology used by government departments since 1962 is used in order to avoid confusing the reader with alternate terms for the same institutions and offices. Cf. *supra*, p. 21 footnote.

proposal and the district commissioner sent a letter to the Governor recommending Helon's appointment as chief. But before the letter of appointment was received Helon (H9) had died; his son Jehu (J9) acted for three years.

Scene 2
Meanwhile Hareph (H7), Hirah (H10) and Hul (H12) continued to compete with each other for the chief's office. One day Hul, with his followers, invaded Jehu's village and forced the acting chief to surrender the chiefly emblems. Jehu (J9) feared Hul's powerful family and offered no resistance. Enraged at this submission Hareph (H7) and Hirah (H10) went to the district commissioner, followed by Hul (H12) and his family, and each party accused the other of intrigue. Soon afterwards Hareph (H7) and Hirah (H10) died. Their relatives suspected Hul (H12) of sorcery, but because such an accusation is a criminal offence under Rhodesian law they dared not state their suspicion openly. Instead they rumoured that the son of a traitor was as evil as his father and had killed his relatives through sorcery.

Scene 3
After Hareph's (H7) funeral his younger brother Havilah (H8) competed for Gamaliel s (G2's) house. Havilah (H8), however, was an unsuitable candidate for the chieftainship: he was an old bachelor who had never married. People of Gilead's (G9's) house claimed that he was sterile and therefore unfit to rule the chiefdom. The Karanga believe that the health and virility of a ruler guarantee the well-being of his chiefdom. They further stressed that his long residence outside the chiefdom on European farmland disqualified him from office, since a chief should be a man of his people, not an adventurer who came home when it suited his interests.

Scene 4
Mutual accusations continued. In 1951 the two competitors appealed again to the district commissioner to settle their dispute, but were told that government had streamlined African chieftainships, had reduced many to subchieftainships, and had demoted their own chieftainship. The reason was that the relatively small number of taxpayers in their chiefdom did not warrant an independent political unit. The district commissioner concluded that their succession dispute had become redundant; they were fighting for something which no longer existed.

ANALYSIS

The reduction of Shoko chieftainship to a subchieftainship concludes act one of the social drama. The act introduces some of the main characters of the succession dispute: Havilah (H8), Hul (H12) and civil servants. In the first scene of this act, where four candidates fight for the chieftainship, a solution is brought about through the intervention of a European government official. Frankenberg's observation[1] that close-knit communities call on outsiders and strangers to solve internal disputes seems applicable to the Karanga case. The traditional chiefmakers accepted the district officer's decision as a compromise although they knew that he had picked on the weakest succession rule, one which was no longer valid in the third phase of Karanga chieftainships. The candidates' appeals to conflicting succession rules and the people's inability to decide whether to back one of the competitors rather than another prevented the nominators from making a decision that would be universally acceptable. The Karanga lay great emphasis on consensus. Because of the nominators' hesitation the spirit medium Hushim (H16) could not speak either, since his function was to confirm or reject the decision reached by the other ritual experts. The ease with which decisions are made depends, therefore, on an actor's detachment from the competition. The spirit medium, himself a member of the chiefly family, though disqualified from office, cannot speak. The nominators who belong to the chiefdom but stand outside the chiefly family have greater freedom, but still stand too close to the issue to solve it. European civil servants, finally, who are complete outsiders or strangers,[2] and not members of the traditional social system, can regulate its processes from the outside. They can intervene and decide an issue which no spirit medium or nominator could solve. Power to settle a controversy seems therefore to increase with social distance.

The strong objection of Hareph (H7) and his followers to the introduction of a new rule in phase three, and the acquiescence of Hul (H12) and his family to Helon's (H9) appointment, mark the first clear distinction between the methods employed in the struggle for power by the contending houses. Members of Gamaliel's (G2's) house insisted on generally accepted Karanga customs, and their claims were in agreement with these. Members of Gilead's (G9's) house, on the other hand, could not do this because they had no traditional claim. They therefore accepted any procedure which was likely to work to their advantage. They

[1] Cf. Frankenberg (1957), pp. 4, 5, 12, 17, 18.
[2] Frankenberg (1957), pp. 18–19.

realized that Helon's (H9's) appointment was only a temporary solution and would enable them to press their own claim in the near future.

Scene two reveals the compromise character of the solution, which led to a head-on collision between the two leading protagonists, Hareph (H7) and Hul (H12). The unsuccessful appeal to another outsider, a district commissioner, threw the competitors back on their own resources. Throughout the succession dispute district commissioners tried to remain outside judges and to avoid involvement. They represented bureaucratic administration in its ideal form.

The deaths of Hareph (H7) and Hirah (H10), both very old men who may have died of natural causes, played into Hul's (H12's) hands. The Karanga belief in sorcery serves as a safety valve in intricate social situations. Members of Gamaliel's (G2's) house found in it the moral support for righteous indignation against Hul (H12) and his family, and they could now wage their succession dispute in terms of 'good' and 'evil'.

This scene shows some of the consequences deriving from the structural principles involved in Karanga succession. The competition of the old men reveals that they are only symbols for their houses. They are obliged to join in the competition whether they are personally interested in the chiefly office or not, because their position imposes on them the duty to compete. This is especially evident in the case of Hirah (H10), who merely put up a claim to save the honour of his house. Moreover, the real contestants are not the old men, but their sons or classificatory sons, Japheth (J7) and Joab (J12), who will rule during their fathers' lifetime; for while the old men win the prestige for their houses, their sons wield the actual power.[1]

Scene three opened with a new power balance. Only two candidates were left. Through the elimination of fringe candidates the two communities of Shoko Museamwa represented by Havilah (H8), and Shoko Murewa, represented by Hul (H12), became starkly opposed to each other. The composition of these communities varied: whereas almost all members of the Shoko Museamwa community belonged to the house of Gamaliel (G2) and to the descendants of the nominator Eber (E1), the Shoko Murewa community consisted of the descendants of all the other houses of the chieftainship and was therefore less homogeneous than the Shoko Museamwa community. Both communities had an approximately equal number of taxpayers, but Havilah (H8) enjoyed more active support than Hul (H12). Many supported Hul (H12) only

---

[1] Cf. *supra*, p. 59. Most Karanga chiefdoms are ruled by the chiefs' sons.

because they had been used to obeying his orders when he acted for his father Gilead (G9).

With an even number of supporters the two rivals tried to undermine each other's claim through rumours and propaganda. The real charges were made in terms of Karanga values: one faction accused the other of sorcery, and the other accused its rival candidate of sterility.

The tactics chosen in scene three differ therefore from those in scene one. At the beginning of the dispute the competitors laid emphasis on their structural positions. Moral considerations were only added as the competition became more intense.

Scene four shifted back to the district commissioner's office. Whenever the internal mechanisms failed to reach a compromise, the district commissioner who stood outside the community was asked to exercise his overriding powers. Should the people reject his decision they could blame him for aggravating the internal division. The district commissioner was therefore put into the classical role of Frankenberg's 'stranger':[1] he was requested to sort out internal difficulties and then bear the blame for alienating one section of the community. The district commissioner performed his task to perfection when he announced that their chieftainship had ceased to exist by a decision of the European government. This announcement enabled the people to unite temporarily against a common outside enemy. Act one then ends with a truce.

---

[1] Frankenberg (1957), p. 5. *et alia.*

CHAPTER 7

The Struggle for the Chieftainship

ACT 2: THE STRUGGLE FOR THE RESTORATION OF THE CHIEFTAINSHIP

Scene 1

The Government's demotion of Shoko chiefdom to a subchiefdom greatly disturbed the people. For a time they forgot about their rivalries and combined their efforts to regain their chiefly status. Hul's (H12's) family was in a better position to help than the descendants of Gamaliel's (G2) because it had close connections with a number of influential Europeans. A wealthy European farmer, Mr Thomson, owned an estate of many thousand acres adjoining the chiefdom. To satisfy his need for seasonal labour he had established a friendly relationship with Hul (H12), and for decades had employed many men and women from the Shoko Murewa community on his farm. Most of them worked for very low wages. In return the tribesmen could rely on farmer Thomson's advice whenever they encountered unfamiliar situations. A personal relationship existed between Hul's family and the farmer, because Mr Thomson employed Husham (H15), Hul's younger brother, as a shop assistant near the tribal trust land; also Joshua (J16), Hul's classificatory son, had worked since his early childhood as a domestic servant in farmer Thomson's family. Husham (H15) and Joshua (J16) informed farmer Thomson of major events in the chiefdom. A mutual indebtedness grew up between the European farmer and the people.

Farmer Thomson is an extraordinary European. Son of a pioneer, he grew up on the farm and speaks the indigenous language as well as the Karanga. As a young man he often used to accompany his African employees on hunts and to beer parties, and came to understand their customs better than most Europeans. Occasionally he identifies himself with the people in half-serious amusement when he states that like any *mutorwa*, 'stranger', he received his land from chief Shoko. He is loved by many Karanga, even by men of other chiefdoms in the tribal trust land, who consider him their friend.

Yet farmer Thomson is also a demanding employer, a very sharp businessman, and proud of getting Africans to work for him at minimum wages. Occasionally he asks the chief for men to harvest a field and in return pays him a lump sum of money for a community project, such as the development of a school; this comes cheaper to him than if he paid each individual worker.

The chief's family appreciate this economic exchange as well as the farmer. During the interregnum and the reduction of the chieftainship, farmer Thomson was at a slight disadvantage because Hul (H12) had less authority over his people than in the past and found it more difficult to provide the farmer with cheap labour. Hence the chiefly family knew that farmer Thomson had an interest in their case and that they could turn to him for help.

In addition to their ties with the European farmer, Hul's family had a connection with the Internal Affairs department. Joshua's (J16's) elder brother, Joseph (J15), was a messenger of the district commissioner and was able to give his family easy access to this civil servant.

The house of Gamaliel (G2) was less fortunately placed. Its leader Japheth (J7), who championed the case of the old man Havilah (H8), was the most prosperous peasant in the whole tribal trust land. Modern farming techniques won him the esteem of the government's agricultural staff, but because agriculturalists were uninfluential with the Internal Affairs' personnel[1] and not responsible for African administration, they could not help Japheth (J7) in the succession dispute.

Japheth (J7) also established friendly ties with a European farmer, Mr Williams, who lived near his border of the tribal trust land. But his relationship with farmer Williams was very different from Hul's relationship with farmer Thomson. Farmer Williams too is well known and prosperous and a large employer of labour, but he has a permanent labour force living on his farm and many of his workers were born there. Consequently he does not recruit local men and is independent of labour supply from the chiefdom. Moreover, the stretch of tribal trust land near his farm is exceptionally fertile and its people do not look for work on European farms. Farmer Williams is personally interested in the economic life of the Karanga and during droughts he supported Japheth's applications to the district commissioners for boreholes and dams. Whenever the Internal Affairs department failed to help, he allowed the

[1] Until 1962 the agricultural staff working in African areas was subject to control by Internal Affairs' personnel. Between 1962 and 1969 they came under the Department of Agriculture. Constant friction characterizes the relations between civil servants of the two government departments. Cf. *The Rhodesia Herald*, 28.3.1969, 31.3.1969, 3.4.1969, 1.5.1969, 8.5.1969, 29.5.1969. *The Sunday Mail*, 6.4.1969, 20.4.1969, 11.5.1969, *et alia*.

Karanga to drive their cattle to his farm to drink at his dam.

Farmer Williams' wife too has played a role in the lives of the people. She initiated African women's clubs in the chiefdom and Japheth's wife was the first African club leader. The closest associates of Japheth's wife were wives of other successful farmers, generally village headmen and relatives of her husband who supported him in his struggle for the chieftainship. They formed an affluent social circle not only because of their husband's good returns from agriculture, but also because farmer Williams' wife taught the women modern housekeeping, cooking, sewing, and hygiene. Their living standards rose above those of other peasants.

The Shoko Museamwa community could therefore count on economic assistance and advice from farmer Williams and his wife; but unlike farmer Thomson this couple showed no interest in the political processes of the chiefdom. Farmers Thomson and Williams were acquaintances.

As soon as the chieftainship had been demoted, Hul (H12) sent farmer Thomson a message through Husham (H15) and Joshua (J16) and asked him for assistance. Farmer Thomson listened sympathetically and called a large gathering of over a hundred men on his farm. Members of all houses of the chieftainship were present. He inquired carefully into their history and finally came to the conclusion that they were traditionally entitled to a chieftainship. At Japheth's request he approached farmer Williams and then headed a delegation consisting of the two European farmers, Hul (H12), and the shop assistant Husham (H15), to the headquarters of Internal Affairs in the capital.

Farmer Thomson expected to be received cordially and respectfully by the Secretary for Internal Affairs, because as chairman of the largest European farmers' association and committee member of many other statutory bodies he was one of the leading farmers in his province. In the capital, however, he was unknown; the Secretary for Internal Affairs treated him politely but made no promises. He assured him that the tribesmen's complaint would be examined and that meanwhile the European farming community should see that the people refrained from violence.[1] Farmer Thomson was hurt at the inconsequential reception and summarized the outcome of the interview in the words: 'We received little satisfaction from our visit.' Farmer Williams, who had accompanied the group at farmer Thomson's request, never intervened again in the chieftainship issue.

---

[1] At this time the Federation of Rhodesia and Nyasaland was being discussed and African nationalists began to win followers in African areas.

K

Scene 2
For years the people heard nothing. Farmer Thomson repeatedly phoned
the district commissioner and was told that head office was doing nothing to restore the chieftainship. Then he thought of another approach:
he drew the people's attention to a leading local lawyer and recommended that they ask him for legal advice. Joab (J12), acting for his
ageing father Hul (H12), approached the lawyer on behalf of his group.
At farmer Thomson's recommendation every man in the chiefdom
contributed five shillings and every woman two shillings and sixpence to
pay the lawyer's fee. Again years passed and nothing was heard about
the lawyer's actions. Meanwhile, however, Hul (H12) and Joseph (J15)
had acquired cars. When Joab (J12) announced a new collection to
obtain more money for the lawyer the people of the house of Gamaliel
(G2) demanded an account of the money which had been collected some
years previously. Joab (J12) refused to give the account and the people
of the house of Gamaliel (G2) refused to contribute further money.
By this time Joab (J12) had taken over the leadership of the Shoko
Murewa community. He was angry at the Shoko Museamwa community's unwillingness to contribute and declared that members of
the house of Gamaliel (G2) proved through their refusal that they were
no longer interested in the chieftainship; further negotiations would be
undertaken by the house of Gilead (G9) only.

Scene 3
Members of the house of Gamaliel (G2) retired in sullen opposition and
concentrated their efforts on increasing their agricultural production.
Japheth (J7) built up a strong economic leadership in the Shoko
Museamwa community and the leading village headmen Kemuel (K3),
Kendon (K4), Kenovz (K5), Kohath (K8) and Korah (K9) followed his
example. They formed a close-knit group, bound together by common
political and agricultural interests. They tried to live as independently
as possible from the acting leader Joab (J12) and brought their court
cases to Japheth (J7).
    In 1956 external intervention played into their hands. A new district
commissioner saw that the official administration of the Shoko Museamwa community was deteriorating because the people did not recognize
Joab (J12). He therefore called a meeting of the Shoko Museamwa
community and suggested that the people select their own subchief.
The meeting was attended by the local people, by a leading chief of the
same tribal trust land who was officially responsible for the administration of Shoko chiefdom, by Joab (J12) deputizing for his old father, and

by Husham (H15), the younger brother of Hul (H12). All the men who were in any way connected with the administration of the Shoko Museamwa community were therefore present. The district commissioner advised the people to elect a young leader, because the government wanted progressive men to administer tribal areas.[1] The local villagers put forward three candidates: Jabeth (J1), an old man whose son Kedar (K1) hoped to take over the leadership of the community; Jahleel (J4), a respected village headman, and Japheth (J7) the unofficial but effective leader of the community. The voters were asked to queue up behind the candidate of their choice. Ninety-two men voted: Jabeth (J1) received twenty votes, Jahleel (J4) thirty and Japheth (J7) forty-two. The district commissioner declared the election valid and decisive and promised that as soon as the chieftainship had been restored Japheth (J7) would receive the emblems of subchief. Meanwhile he allowed Japheth (J7) to try court cases and to perform all other functions normally performed by subchiefs. Kedar (K1) was very disappointed with the election results and began to befriend members of the house of Gilead (G9).

Japheth (J7) acted as subchief until 1962, when Joab (J12) complained to a new district commissioner that Japheth's leadership undermined his status as acting chief. Since no records by the former commissioner about Japheth's (J7's) appointment could be found, the new commissioner forbade Japheth (J7) to try court cases.

Scene 4

Simultaneously with these developments, the struggle to regain the chieftainship continued. In 1960 farmer Thomson suggested to Hul's (H12's) family yet another approach which might regain them their chieftainship. He approached his friend and neighbouring farmer, Mr Smith, who was member of parliament for the European community. Farmer Thomson asked Mr Smith to meet the Karanga on his farm, but the member of parliament did not favour a large African gathering. He consented however to meet the leaders, Hul (H12), Huppim (H13), Husham (H15), Joab (J12) and Joseph (J15), but no members from the house of Gamaliel (G2), were present at the meeting. The politician listened to their arguments and promised to take the case to parliament. Where the farmer and lawyer had failed the politician succeeded. In 1961 the people were notified that their chieftainship had been restored and that they could proceed to elect their new chief.[2]

[1] Cf. C.N.C., 1947.

[2] Information checked in the *Hansard*; the reference is suppressed to safeguard the anonymity of those concerned.

ANALYSIS

Act two introduces new actors into the social drama. European farmers, a lawyer, a member of parliament and the head of the Internal Affairs department are all drawn into the people's struggle for power. This lifts a traditional issue onto a national level. The reason for the involvement of the wider European society into the affairs of this patriarchal community lay in the demotion of the chiefdom by an external bureaucracy. In such a situation no traditional mechanisms existed to restore the earlier state. It was an atypical situation complicating the succession dispute. Since these outside agents succeeded in returning the chieftainship to the people, it was likely that one faction would call on them at a later stage to assist them when the struggle was no longer with outsiders but among their own people.

Like act one, act two falls into four scenes. The first scene introduces a neighbouring European farmer, who offered to mediate between the Karanga and government. He was suited for this task because he was sympathetic to both sides. He was influential among Europeans and popular with Africans. As a leading farmer and public figure in a very small European community he closely identified himself with government. In his social circle it was assumed that government was the affair of the white élite, most of whom knew each other personally. In the rural European community in which farmer Thomson lived he was well known and respected. His local prestige, however, did not extend to the capital and so he miscalculated his influence at the national level. In a sense his position in the European farming community resembled that of an African patriarch in a tribal trust land. When he confronted the leading bureaucrat of the Internal Affairs department he was received as an ordinary farmer, not as a local leader.

The Secretary for Internal Affairs saw himself as an administrator and refused to be involved in the political machinations of private individuals. His conception of his role differed from the idea the former had of a civil servant. The farmer saw only pride and aloofness where the administrator considered non-involvement a professional duty imposed on all bureaucrats.

On the African side farmer Thomson's move to visit the capital reinforced the division between the houses of Gamaliel (G2) and Gilead (G9). Once the initiative to approach European outsiders had been taken by the house of Gilead (G9), it was relatively easy for them to exclude members of the house of Gamaliel (G2) from further negotiations.

In scene two farmer Thomson provided another link between the tribal community and the wider one of Rhodesia as a whole. He introduced the Karanga to a European lawyer. Up to that time people of Shoko chiefdom met European law in the district commissioner's or magistrate's courts, but none of them had ever engaged a lawyer. It was an exciting experience to gain access to a European institution, which was presented to them as very powerful.

In spite of repeated questioning of all parties, no instance could be discovered in which the lawyer helped the people to regain their chieftainship. Whether Joab (J12) used the money to buy cars or not, the people's suspicion of misappropriation of funds was aroused when they saw no tangible results. The Karanga, who possess very little money, are concerned about every penny they contribute to a common enterprise. Since the members of the house of Gamaliel (G2) had already accused members of the house of Gilead (G9) of immoral behaviour,[1] the new suspicion confirmed their image of that house. Since the house of Gilead (G9) controlled the channels of communication they were in a position to eliminate the house of Gamaliel (G2) from further negotiations. Recourse to a lawyer, therefore, though ineffective in itself, ended the truce between the rivals and proved that the temporary unity *vis-à-vis* an outside threat was not strong enough to overcome internal division.[2]

Scene three shows that exclusion from the political arena may lead to withdrawal and a concentration on non-political activities. In redirecting his energies into agriculture, Japheth (J7) succeeded in building up a strong economic leadership which had political consequences. It created in the Shoko Museamwa community a new sense of unity with the leader. It provided an economic basis which could later be used for political purposes. Japheth (J7) moved into the centre of the power struggle just as Joab (J12) had done in the house of Gilead (G9). By this time both Havilah (H8) and Hul (H12) had moved into the background and their descendants had taken over their position as protagonists.

The result of this partial withdrawal of the Shoko Museamwa community from politics illustrates the contention that every action has consequences that the actors are unable to anticipate. The disaffection of the Shoko Museamwa community with the leadership in the Shoko Murewa community restricted the effective administration of the whole chiefdom. As a complete outsider and stranger, but as a man of authority,

---

[1] *supra*, p. 121.

[2] Cf. Evans-Pritchard (1947), pp. 143–144. Evans-Pritchard argues that internal disputes are submerged when an attack from the outside threatens the in-group.

the district commissioner could legalize an already existing situation by recognizing Japheth's (J7's) leadership. It was a compromise just as the district officer's decision had been in 1943. Like the former it did not solve the problem; it increased it. At a later date it had to be resolved when Joab's (J12's) position had become more secure.

One result of this compromise was that people in the Shoko Museamwa community began to look upon themselves as a distinct subchiefdom within the larger unit of Shoko chiefdom. This increased the distance between themselves and the house of Gilead (G9), and laid the seed for further divisions among themselves. For when the voting indicated that a descendant of Hamul (H4), not Hadad (H1), was likely to be subchief there was a faster internal segmentation. Act four will show that the drift of office to the junior section alienated the descendants of Hadad (H1) and created antagonism between Kedar (K1), who fought for his father Jabeth (J1), and Japheth (J7). Through outside intervention, therefore, the unity of the house of Gamaliel (G2) was disrupted. Frankenberg's hypothesis of the 'stranger' must therefore be refined: an unpopular decision by a complete outsider may temporarily unite internal factions; but a decision that favours one section of a previously united group may lead to the group's disintegration.[1]

Scene four, like scenes one and two, sees the initiative back with farmer Thomson. By introducing the people to yet another European institution, that of parliament, farmer Thomson by-passed the administration and appealed to the legislative assembly. He had tried the bureaucratic and legal approach; both had failed. He succeeded through an influential politician. The chieftainship dispute of a relatively small Rhodesian chiefdom had become a national concern through the intervention of European supporters. Micro-politics became macro-politics.

This extension in scale of a local issue accented internal rivalries. By the time the final negotiations took place, the two communities had lived apart for so long that members of the house of Gilead (G9) felt under no obligation to consult members of the house of Gamaliel (G2). This enabled members of the house of Gilead (G9) to attribute the member of parliament's success to their own exertions and accuse the senior house of Gamaliel (G2) of apathy. The structural principle by which chieftainships usually drift to the junior houses was seen clearly in the junior house's success in activating European institutions.

Act two highlights certain traditional principles, such as the drift of

[1] Given that structural principles of segmentation are at work, which would in any case have brought about this disintegration in the future. The outsider's decision therefore speeds up internal fission, but does not cause it.

office to junior houses. It also proves that a Rhodesian chieftainship is not only the concern of African people. Since European neighbours and government officials provide tribesmen with new methods and channels for solving their disputes they give the conflict a new direction. They force Africans to grapple with social institutions that are alien to their culture. This is an important characteristic of the political system in modern Karangaland.

ACT 3: COMPETITION BETWEEN HOUSES FOR THE CHIEFTAINSHIP

Scene 1

As soon as the local district commissioner was informed by head office that the chiefly status had been restored to the people of Shoko chiefdom, he called a meeting. The house of Gilead (G9) had been informed of the reason for the meeting by friends of their son Joseph (J15), employed by the Internal Affairs department. Consequently Hul (H12) and his supporters came fully prepared. They had consulted farmer Thomson and had been advised to ask for an election by vote. When the people were therefore asked by the district commissioner to appoint their chief, Hul (H12) and his family asked that he be chosen by vote. Havilah (H8) and his followers objected and demanded that the nominators appoint the new chief according to the custom of their chiefdom. The district commissioner was in favour of the traditional procedure and ordered the nominators to proceed. Members of the house of Gilead (G9) declared that they would not consider themselves bound by a decision of the nominators. They insisted on a modern election procedure.

The nominators met and unanimously elected Havilah (H8) as chief because he belonged to the senior house.

Scene 2

Hul's (H12's) family refused to recognize the result of the nomination and again turned to farmer Thomson for advice. Farmer Thomson contacted the Secretary for Internal Affairs and recommended that an election be held to assure the new chief the widest popular support. The Secretary for Internal Affairs agreed and phoned the district commissioner, asking him to hold the election. The district commissioner passed the order on to his assistant district officer. The district officer delayed the voting. This gave Joab (J12) a chance to canvass. The delay brought the district officer a rebuke from his superior, and the Secretary for Internal Affairs came in person to Shoko chiefdom to supervise the election.

The election took place at a local school. Three candidates competed for the chieftainship: Havilah (H8), Hul (H12) and Jehu (J9), son of Helon (H9), who had died before he received his letter of appointment. Three tins were placed inside a classroom and each village headman was asked to drop a piece of paper in his candidate's tin. The tins were marked by their owners' hats. A teacher, unrelated to the candidates, guarded the entrance and later counted the votes. Of seventy-six votes cast, thirty-eight votes went to Havilah (H8), thirty-six to Hul (H12) and two to Jehu (J9). The Secretary declared the meeting closed and instructed Havilah (H8) to come the next day to the district commissioner's office to be registered as chief.

The voting result surprised farmer Thomson and distressed Hul (H12) and his family. Hul (H12) approached Jehu (J9) and asked him for his two votes because he clearly had no chance of becoming chief. In return he promised to reward him with a subchieftainship once he had been installed. Jehu (J9) consented. Immediately Joab (J12) drove to town to consult his lawyer. The lawyer informed the district commissioner of the transfer of votes, which cancelled Havilah's (H8's) majority. When Havilah (H8) arrived at the district commissioner's office to be registered as chief, he was told to wait for an answer from head office.

Scene 3

Having waited for four months without hearing of further developments Japheth (J7) went with Havilah (H8), Kenaz (K5) and the nominator from the house of Eber (E1) to the capital to see the Secretary for Internal Affairs. The Secretary promised to attend to their case immediately. He corresponded with the local district commissioner, who strongly recommended that the new chief be chosen by the nominators. After some weeks the people were instructed to elect their chief in the traditional way.

The house of Gamaliel (G2) was pleased with the new decision, but the house of Gilead (G9) was most apprehensive, because they had lost a previous nomination. They discredited the nominator of Enoch's (E2's) house and appointed a young man who did not qualify for the task because neither his father nor his grandfather had been nominators before him. Nobody apart from Hul's (H12's) family recognized him.

Next Joab (J12) tried to win favour with the nominator of Eber's

(E1's) house. He offered him money if he would appoint his father. This nominator however was afraid of Joab's lawyer and declared that he would nominate in the same way as his father had nominated before him. He added: 'Even if lawyers are bought with money, nominators are not.'

When the nomination took place Havilah (H8) was again unanimously elected. The nominators placed their hands on his head to confer on him the authority of chief and the protection of his ancestors. Members of the house of Gilead (G9) had arrived at the meeting by car. They listened to the decision of the nominators and then drove to the district commissioner accusing the house of Gamaliel (G2) of bribery, alleging that they had been driven away from the meeting-place with sticks. Consequently when Havilah (H8) arrived with the nominators at the district commissioner's office to inform him of his nomination, the district commissioner refused to accept him. The nominators were very angry and the senior nominator of Eber's (E1's) house declared that since the district commissioner usurped the nominators' right to appoint a chief the nominators would no longer intervene in succession disputes.

Scene 4

In 1963, a year after the unsuccessful nomination, Havilah (H8) received unexpected support from the spirit medium Homam (H11), who lived near Hul's (H12's) village and was believed to favour the candidate of the house of Gilead (G9). During a beer drink the medium became possessed and cried out: 'The chieftainship should go to Havilah (H8) because it is his rightful turn. We are wrong in trying to keep it for Hul (H12).' The teacher who had supervised the election was present and hastily took notes of what the medium said. When Joab (J12) saw the teacher writing he exclaimed: 'C.I.D.[1] are present; let the medium stop.' But the medium cried out still louder: 'Do no harm to the teacher; he is our great friend.' But a fight had already broken out, and only after a long struggle did the teacher and his friends escape.

Scene 5

Members of the house of Gilead (G9) again consulted farmer Thomson, who was surprised at the support for Havilah (H8). He recommended that the people once more consult a member of parliament. As soon as their visit to the European member of parliament became known to the house of Gamaliel (G2), Japheth (J7) visited the African member of

[1] Members of the Criminal Investigation Department.

parliament for the district.[1] The African member of parliament suggested he ask parliament to appoint a commission of inquiry to examine the claims of the competitors and to make the final decision. The European member of parliament supported this motion. Other parliamentarians, however, considered a commission of inquiry too expensive and likely to set a precedent. They decided instead that chiefs from other tribal trust lands be invited to form a court of arbitration.

Scene 6

At the end of 1963 the leaders of Shoko chiefdom were called to the district commissioner's office and told that three chiefs from other tribal trust lands would arbitrate between them. Members of the house of Gilead (G9) declared that they objected to outside intervention; if outsiders were to appoint any person but Hul (H12) they would not submit to their decision. But Japheth (J7) stated that his people would submit to outside arbitration. The district commissioner dismissed the people. Outside the office Huppim (H13) declared: 'We are no longer interested in a settlement because for some weeks we have been paid as if we were chiefs. We have all the authority we ever can have, only the emblems are missing. This dispute has cost us much money with the lawyer and we shall never let the office pass to another house, not even after Hul's death.'

In early 1964 the people were again called to the district commissioner's office. The Secretary for Internal Affairs was present and introduced to them three Karanga chiefs whom the district commissioner had chosen. The district commissioner hung up a genealogy of Shoko chiefdom and explained the history until the death of Helon (H9). He concluded: 'After Helon's death Hul (H12) was appointed by the Governor to act until a successor had been officially appointed.' Jethro (J11) asked when the appointment had been made, because the people knew nothing about it. The district commissioner looked through his papers but could not find the document. Japheth (J7) grew apprehensive and declared: 'It is now very difficult for us to come to an agreement, because the government did wrong in appointing Hul (H12) against the wishes of the people. We feel convinced that government will again make a decision without taking our views into account.'

---

[1] Rhodesia is divided into constituencies and electoral districts; constituencies elect members of parliament by upper-role voters, that is persons with high property qualifications; electoral districts elect members of parliament by lower-roll voters, mainly Africans who are allowed to vote on the basis of education and lower property qualifications.

The European civil servants withdrew and the people discussed the succession with the three visiting chiefs for two days. The arguments reached a climax when one of the visiting chiefs asked who had been the leader in the chiefdom during the years when the chieftainship had been reduced to a subchieftainship. A man from the house of Gilead (G9) said: 'It was Husham (H15), because he introduced us to farmer Thomson, and farmer Thomson has helped us ever since.' As soon as farmer Thomson was mentioned the speaker was shouted down and forbidden to mention the farmer again. The visiting chiefs became alert and wanted to know more about him. But the speaker was frightened and only muttered that the people had held meetings with the farmer and had collected money to regain their chieftainship. The visiting chiefs asked what had happened to the money, but Joab (J12) rebuked the speaker so severely that he did not dare say another word. Even members of the house of Gamaliel (G2) supported Joab (J12) and affirmed: 'We are all black people (*isu vose vanhu vatema*); we are all one. Let us forget about the Europeans because if one of us should be arrested we would all be sorry.'

At the end of the second day the people asked the visitors who should be chief. One of the chiefs answered: 'We are not allowed to make a decision; we have been ordered to write down all you have said and to make suggestions. The final decision will be made by Europeans.' This brought to an end the last public discussion about the chieftainship. The people had no more voice in future developments.

ANALYSIS

Act three is the central act of the social drama and better than any other event described in this book makes explicit the interplay of modern and traditional forces in Karanga succession disputes. It reveals the intensity with which such disputes can be fought when the traditional channels of tension-relief through fission and migration are no longer open. The determination with which each house fought the other shows that both realized each other's strength and so acknowledged each other as equals. It also shows how competition, which follows a common set of rules, gives way to conflict, in which different groups apply different sets of rules. As the conflict accelerated, more and more practices from the European sector of Rhodesian society replaced the traditional approach.

Act three indicates how the effects of the dual economy, the dual political system and the dual social organization of Rhodesia bewilder those who are orientated towards the past and unskilled in European techniques. Through the introduction of new practices, traditional norms become blurred and confusion arises as to the validity of any particular procedure. Lloyd writes that the introduction of new techniques or of new actors necessitates an adjustment of roles in the original structure; if in such situations the deviant behaviour of individuals is unchecked by forces of social control, norms and values may be changed.[1] Act three illustrates this process of social change.[2]

Act three falls into six scenes. Scene one brings together the major actors: members of the two contesting houses, the district commissioner representing the administration, and farmer Thomson, the employer of African labour and friend of the chiefly family. These three groups have different interests in the dispute. The Karanga strive for a traditional political office and power in their own chiefdom. The civil servant is concerned about the smooth administration of the area, and the farmer, a little politician in his own way, promotes his own economic interest by furthering the political aspirations of his neighbours. He is the people's door to the modern world. Those who realize that they have no traditional claim to the chiefly office eagerly accept his suggestion of modern electoral procedures. This raises the question of which rules are valid in the conflict, because the group that has a traditional claim to the chieftainship is unwilling to depart from traditional election procedures. Only the district commissioner remains a relatively neutral outsider. As guardian of traditional customs he favours election by nominators, but remains submissive to the instructions of his superior and reluctant to depart from civil-service norms.

In scene two the structural conflict is intensified by the farmer's appeal to the Secretary for Internal Affairs. The district commissioner is temporarily pushed out of the centre of negotiations through the initiative of a European who has no legal right to intervene in the lives of Karanga tribesmen. Soon the conflict between social structures caused disturbance in both the bureaucratic and the patriarchal systems.

But the intervention of the highest administrator proved as futile as the exertions of local civil servants because one European institution was used to block the working of another. The group which had renounced traditional norms and adopted non-traditional techniques showed itself equally uncommitted to the norms of European institutions. They were

[1] Lloyd (1968), p. 27.
[2] The events described in the act coincided with the first spell of fieldwork. All the actors were personally interviewed and through these interviews the preceding acts were reconstructed.

gamblers, willing to try any method that promised success, and ready to abandon it if it failed.[1]

Scene three restores the hierarchical relations of the administrative hierarchy, but disrupts the traditional system because the constant appeals and delegations to civil servants reveal that the traditional system has become impotent to solve the succession dispute.

Once farmer Thomson ceased to appeal above the head of the district commissioner to a higher administrator, the bureaucratic machinery ran smoothly. The Secretary for Internal Affairs never made a decision without passing it to the people through their district commissioner. This enabled the district commissioner to communicate with the Secretary for Internal Affairs and suggest the solution he thought best. In winning the Secretary's approval for another nomination, he also circumvented the European farmer and so proved that he and no other European had a say in the political processes of the Karanga. The struggle for power therefore went on at two levels: between the two contending houses of the chieftainship and between different segments of the European community.

A third level of conflict came to the surface when the traditional chief-makers realized that their function had been taken over by European bureaucrats. The nominators saw that the real 'nominator' was government, and that they themselves were pushed around so as to appear to appoint the chief. The struggle for power at this level lay between two different institutions. This touched the source of the chief's legitimacy. The failure of the nominators confirmed that chiefs were no longer appointed by traditional institutions.

In addition to structural conflicts scene three reveals a contrast of values. The nominator, the real guardian of tradition, interprets the lawyer's fee as a bribe. In the appointment of a chief he contrasts the alien practice of European law to what he finds the morally superior Karanga practice. For a second time in the social drama moral reasons are given to justify a claim when structural reasons fail. The succession dispute therefore involves ideologies as well as social institutions.

Scene four is the only scene in act three which does not involve Europeans and which is exclusively confined to the tribal trust land. It lasted only a few hours. The spirit medium, whose function it is to confirm or reject the nomination made by the nominators, openly declared his support for their decision even after the district commissioner had invalidated it. The medium's pronouncement is significant for two

---

[1] It may be argued that their opponents gambled as well. The only difference is that it was to their advantage to stick to traditional rules.

reasons: firstly, he lived near Hul (H12) and was thought to support his claim; secondly, he made the pronouncement at a beer drink in the Shoko Murewa community when no member of the Shoko Museamwa community was present. If an outsider had not been present—the teacher who had counted the ballot papers at the election—the pronouncement of the medium might have been hushed up.

The spirit medium set the seal on the nominator's decision. Havilah (H8) now had full traditional support, through he lacked all support from modern institutions. The Europeans who backed Hul (H12) in his struggle for the chieftainship were ignorant of Havilah's traditional strength. The fronts were now clearly marked: Havilah (H8) had traditional custom, the nominators, the medium, and a large number of supporters. Hul (H12) also had a large number of people behind him, but he lacked traditional support; on the other hand, he was backed by a European farmer and a lawyer.

Scenes five and six take place outside the tribal trust land. This indicates that the final decision in the succession dispute is taken not by the people but by outsiders. The second appeal to parliament shows that the Karanga soon learned how to manipulate foreign institutions. Members of the house of Gamaliel (G2) had become alert to the danger of being left out in the competition for modern support. Of their own accord they contacted a member of parliament. The two parliamentarians were not interested in taking sides with either faction, but concerned rather in satisfying the people they represented. They appeared to fight for a common aim and succeeded in remaining perfectly neutral on the issue, more neutral in fact than some of the administrators.

Parliament's recommendation that external chiefs investigate the dispute solved the deadlock in the power struggle. For a second time therefore an appeal to parliament had brought a solution. This appeal from a small chiefdom to the national legislative assembly brought into close association the two most remote poles of Rhodesia's political hierarchy. It did not however undermine the power of the Internal Affairs department, for the chiefs who investigated the issue had no authority to make a decision.

Scene six, dealing with the implementation of the parliamentary recommendation, shows the intransigence of members of the house of Gilead (G9) and the willingness of members of the house of Gamaliel (G2) to submit to an impartial investigation. This willingness rested on their confidence in the justice of their claims. How far the well-known attitude of the house of Gilead (G9) affected the final adjudication is difficult to determine.

The final inquiry by the chiefs was remarkable on three counts: firstly, it was opened by the Secretary for Internal Affairs and the district commissioner; this stressed that the Internal Affairs department was in full control of all proceedings. The people knew that this was a formal and final inquiry. Secondly, farmer Thomson was openly repudiated by members of both houses. Joab (J12) above all felt that the support he had so far received from the farmer weakened his position before an impartial Karanga tribunal. No satisfactory answer could be found for the reaction of members of the house of Gamaliel (G2): instead of cashing in on Joab's embarrassment they joined him in suppressing the information before the visiting chiefs. The reason: 'We are all black people' seems hardly justified in a dispute in which one party constantly looked for European help against their own relatives. Had the house of Gamaliel (G2) exploited this weakness in the members of the house of Gilead (G9), the outcome of the dispute might have been different. Even the prospect of future unity under a common chief seems insufficient to explain the self-abnegating attitude of the house of Gamaliel (G2) for act five shows that division continued unabated. Thirdly, the visiting chiefs stated clearly that a final decision lay with European administrators and that they themselves could only make recommendations. Like the members of parliament, therefore, they remained outside the succession dispute. The decision was made where the real power over Rhodesian chiefs lies: with the department of Internal Affairs.

Act three differs from act two in that the opponent is no longer the government but a group of relatives. The two acts resemble each other in that the techniques employed to win the first conflict are used to settle the second. This introduction of alien institutions causes a breakdown of the traditional techniques of solving a succession dispute. External circumstances had arisen, which the traditional system could not cope with. The most important of these circumstances was the great increase in population after European occupation, and the inability of chiefdoms to split and migrate. Once fission became impossible conflicts were internalized. It is likely that as other chiefdoms experience similar intense competition by ever larger numbers of candidates for the chieftainship, they too will have recourse to European institutions to settle their disputes.[1] As appeals to European institutions become more frequent, the traditional African system will undergo change. Traditional institutions, such as those of nominators and spirit mediums, will become less effective and are likely to be replaced by elections and other

---

[1] Another chief in the sample communities also employed a lawyer to defend his chieftainship.

European political practices. This development puts in question the government's intention to preserve traditional African customs. It seems that the forces of change unleashed by European settlement and administration, and the many situations of culture contact resulting in co-operation between African and European neighbours, militate against the preservation of African chieftainships as they have existed in the past.

Shoko chiefdom is an extreme case of interaction between Europeans and Karanga in a traditional succession dispute. Nevertheless consultation and co-operation between African and European neighbours is frequent in rural areas, especially in the economic field. Chapter five[1] recorded European farmers' interest in the development projects of a subchiefdom. This chapter[2] has shown the economic assistance rendered by two European farmers to the people in Shoko chiefdom. An inquiry by a senior government officer in the Ministry of Agriculture revealed that about one-third of all European intensive conservation area committees in Rhodesia actively assist their African neighbours with advice and material help.[3] The interaction between Africans and Europeans in Shoko chiefdom is therefore not unique in Rhodesia. In many areas the races co-operate across the colour bar, and in doing so European culture is spread to African society. The longer this process continues the more profoundly will the character of African chieftainship be transformed.

[1] *supra*, p. 82.
[2] *supra*, pp. 123–125.
[3] Personal communication.

CHAPTER 8

Achievement and Failure

ACT 4: THE INSTALLATION OF CHIEF SHOKO

Scene 1

A month after the inquiry by the visiting chiefs the people were again called to the district commissioner's office. The house of Gilead (G9) had learned through Joseph (J15) and his friends in the Internal Affairs department that the Governor had appointed Hul (H12) as chief. The house of Gamaliel (G2) did not even know the reason for the meeting. Consequently members of the house of Gilead (G9) came with several cars and a hired bus carrying their supporters whereas members of the house of Gamaliel (G2) came by bicycle or on regular buses.

The district commissioner came out to meet the people, waving the letter of appointment, announcing that the long succession dispute had come to an end and that the government had appointed Hul (H12). Hul was still sitting in his car. He was led out by his jubilant supporters. The district commissioner clad him in the chiefly red robe, placed the white helmet on his head and the chain of chieftainship round his neck. Then he exclaimed: 'Here is your chief.' The women of the house of Gilead (G9) ullulated and the men clapped their hands. Young men carried Hul on their shoulders into the car and the procession moved slowly out of town while the people of the house of Gilead (G9) sang the traditional praise-songs of their chieftainship.

Scene 2

When the procession reached the chief's village Joab (J12) made an important speech: 'I know that in the past we have been fighting and nobody was eating food in a hut of our rivals. But now I ask you to work together and to accept each other's food. I beg you all not to use hurting words. I am now like government. If you go on fighting I shall punish you. If you have a complaint against the people of the house of Gamaliel (G2) I shall judge justly and not favour you simply because you are of my house. We shall soon hold a big feast to which the people of all the houses will be invited, as well as the three chiefs who have helped us, and also the district commissioner. We shall invite all our

L

relatives wherever they are working and put an announcement into the African newspaper.' Huppim (H13), who had strongly supported his brother in the struggle, added: 'The chieftainship has been given to us by God. I know that some of us are already thinking how we can hurt the losing house. But remember: if we do evil the chieftainship will leave us. We must live together in peace.'

Scene 3

Members of the house of Gamaliel (G2) were amazed at the government's decision. They had been so confident in the legitimacy of their claim that they never doubted that an impartial inquiry would support them. As soon as the victors' procession had left the town Japheth (J7) and his followers asked to see the district commissioner. The African corporal however refused to admit them. Now that they could not talk to the local administrator Japheth (J7), accompanied by Havilah (H8) and the descendant of Eber (E1), went once more to see the Secretary for Internal Affairs. Each of the three men put forward another reason, reinforcing his companions: Havilah (H8) pointed out that he was a more important man than Hul (H12) because his father's mother was the second wife of Finon (F5), the founder of the chieftainship, whereas Hul's (H12's) mother was merely a junior wife. The nominator of Eber's (E1's) house complained that his advice on the appointment of the chief had been ignored by government although as senior nominator he was the 'father' of all the people in the chiefdom. Japheth (J7) expressed fear that in the future the chieftainship would never leave the house of Gilead (G9) because since Hul (H12) had succeeded his father Gilead (G9), Joab (J12) might claim a new succession rule and insist on succeeding his father. The Secretary for Internal Affairs assured him that government would never permit the introduction of primogeniture into their chieftainship and suggested that the people return home and register Havilah (H8) as the next chief.

Havilah (H8), the descendant of Eber (E1) and Japheth (J7) unanimously rejected the Secretary's proposal, because it would have been a tacit recognition of Hul's lawful appointment. Furthermore they stressed that a preparation for the installation of a future chief during the lifetime of another implied the desire for the present chief's death and could therefore be interpreted as an act of sorcery. The Secretary for Internal Affairs had nothing to say to this and dismissed them.

Scene 4

Realizing that traditional support was no longer sufficient to claim a patriarchal office, members of the house of Gamaliel (G2) also began to look for European support. Japheth (J7) engaged a lawyer to investigate how his family could regain the chieftainship, but he received no positive help. He then joined a society called 'Mutual Aid', consisting of retired higher police officers; it promised lifelong legal advice to those who paid a monthly subscription of ten shillings for three years. Japheth (J7) persuaded five of his staunch supporters to join, and by the time the fieldwork was completed all were paid-up members.

Scene 5

Meanwhile the house of Gilead (G9) prepared for Hul's (H12's) solemn installation ceremony. The feast was fixed for Rhodes and Founders, a public holiday in Rhodesia, which gave an opportunity for members of the chieftainship who were in European employment to come home for the feast.

Early on the morning of the feast, the people killed an ox donated by farmer Thomson. At 10 a.m. farmer Thomson arrived with Mr Smith, the member of parliament. Shortly afterwards Joab's (J12's) lawyer drove up together with the family of a European businessman, from whom Joab had ordered two dozen chairs to seat his guests. Because the preparations were not yet complete, the Europeans were led into a nearby house belonging to a teacher and were served with bottled beer and whisky. Over the drink they discussed the weather and their crops. The district commissioner had not come.

By noon some 800 Africans had arrived. Apart from the local subchief whose ancestors had accepted the people of Shoko chiefdom into the area, no chief was present. None of the three chiefs who had inquired into the succession dispute accepted the invitation. African constables who had arrived the night before at the special request of Hul's family to maintain law and order were the only government officials present.

The ceremony took place in the open. A square had been cleared in the village, and on one side, in the shade of some huts, stood a row of chairs for the Europeans. Opposite these stood a row for the chief's family. Behind these and on both sides stood the African people. At noon the new chief drove up in Joseph's (J15's) car from a nearby hut, to the blowing of a traditional horn and the ullulating of the women. He was accompanied by the spirit medium Homam (H11). A scarf was hoisted as a flag on a long pole and fastened to the car, which remained parked behind the chief's family. The chief and the spirit medium remained inside the car. The Europeans were asked to sit on their reserved seats and waiters in white uniforms carried their drinks to them.

Joseph (J15), the civil servant, greeted the guests in a well-delivered English speech, which his younger brother translated into the African language. He invited the people to join in a 'hip, hip, hurray' to welcome the European guests. Then he greeted individually about a dozen chiefs, none of whom was present; yet he did not mention the subchief who was sitting next to him. He concluded his speech with the words: 'We thank the Europeans who are sitting in front of us for their help, because they have done more for us than I can recount. When we were fighting among ourselves they fought for our side; when we could not understand why government delayed the appointment of our chief they made us understand. In many places where Africans are not allowed to speak these men spoke for us. Through them we have found salvation.'

The next speaker, Husham (H15), less fluent in English than Joseph (J15), praised the Europeans in the African language but had his speech translated into English. Only one speaker, Huppim (H13), briefly addressed the Karanga when he thanked the village headmen for their contribution to the feast; but then he too turned towards the Europeans and stressed the good relations existing between the people of Shoko chiefdom and the surrounding European farming community. Before he sat down he invited the Europeans to address the people.

Farmer Thomson spoke first. Whereas the Karanga tried to speak in English, farmer Thomson spoke fluently in the African language and nobody translated his words into English. He excused certain invited guests who had not come for the ceremony, especially the district commissioner, farmer Williams and the African member of parliament. He concluded: 'Nobody is happier than myself that the chieftainship has been returned to you. Today you are born again. The future will be very hard; this is only a beginning. Poverty must be ended, hatred must cease. You must work together as one family and try to make your chiefdom happy. I want you to be happy and to be rich.' The member of parliament too spoke in the African language, but he was not very fluent and people found it difficult to understand him. He drew special attention to the villagers' children and their right to a happy future under a just chief.

After the speeches the spirit medium suddenly emerged, dancing, from the car, and the women ululated. To general applause Hul (H12), the old chief, climbed out of the car and sat in the middle of his relatives. The Europeans were invited to bring their gifts, and each came forward to lay a pound note on the table in front of the chief. The names of all the donors and the amount they contributed were called out and written in a book. Soon after this the Europeans left.

Then the village headmen of Shoko chiefdom were summoned to

name to come forward with their gifts. All headmen from the Shoko Murewa community were present, but of the thirty-one village headmen of the Shoko Museamwa community only six attended. Among these were the descendant of Eber (E1) and Kedar (K1), Keturah (K6), and Kiriath (K7). Kedar (K1), Keturah (K6) and Kiriath (K7) had shifted their allegiance to the house of Gilead (G9) because as senior members of the house of Gamaliel (G2) they had lost the leadership to the junior section headed by Japheth (J7). Eber's descendant was present to report to Japheth (J7) the happenings at the feast. Japheth's name was called out several times but nobody of his village had come; nor had any of his close supporters, such as Kemuel (K3), Kenan (K4), Kenaz (K5), Kohath (K8) and Korah (K9).

Japheth (J7) later declared that he had not attended the feast for three reasons: firstly, because his presence would have been interpreted as a tacit approval of Hul's appointment; secondly, because the chieftainship had not been given to the lawful house; and thirdly, because the nominators had had no say in it. The present chief was therefore not the chief of the people. He concluded: 'The chieftainship was given by the district commissioner. We have all seen it with our own eyes. There was no need for a feast because the office was not given to Hul by the people. Hul and his family constantly invent new customs. We want our old customs.'

The total money collection amounted to £32.

The presentation of gifts was followed by eating and drinking. The people had expected a feast, but not much food and drink had been provided and the Karanga grumbled at their hosts' stinginess. By 6 p.m. the chief's village lay deserted. A few people returned the next day and complained loudly about the inadequacy of the food and drink. In the afternoon of that day Hul's family decided to kill a small bony ox to satisfy the clamour of the people, and Husham (H15) was sent to town to buy soft drinks because no beer was left.

Not only the people but also the African constables complained about the lack of food, and threatened to return to their station before their period of duty had expired. They were given a pot of beer to themselves and retired to their sleeping hut. Thus ended the installation of the new chief.

ANALYSIS

The installation ceremony, which could have been used to bring the succession dispute to a close and to reconcile the contending houses,

laid the seeds for further estrangement between the chiefly family and
the people. It served as a warning that the house of Gilead (G9), which
had won the chieftainship through European support, would use the
office for its own personal needs and advantages irrespective of the
people's welfare, verifying the observation that 'it is always a dangerous
moment when something for which men have fought long and hard
has been won'.[1] As act four progresses the actors reveal ever more
strongly that none of them desired a reconciliation, but only a victory.

Scene one shows the official installation of the chief by the Internal
Affairs Department and demonstrates the dependence of the winning
house on government support. It can be said that the victory was a
victory won by Europeans. The district commissioner, not the traditional chief-makers, clad the new chief in his regalia and presented him
to his people. It was a victory for the district commissioner as well as
for the chief's family, because he could expect that phone calls from
farmer Thomson and the lawyer would cease. Above all he looked forward to a time when Shoko chiefdom would be efficiently administered
by an officially recognized chief. His African assistant therefore interpreted his attitude rightly when he prevented Japheth (J7) from
approaching him. Competition had to cease. The government had
settled the issue.

Scene two in the village of the new chief is the only scene of unity in
the act. Joab (J12), who from that moment onward officially acted for
his father, emphasized in a public speech the need for unity in the
chiefdom, and his relatives re-emphasized the need. To lend solemnity
to his pledge of impartiality the acting chief declared: 'I am now like
government.' By this statement he promised to act as objectively in his
decisions as do civil servants. Later developments will reveal a further
meaning: the new chief also believed himself to be as powerful as
government.[2]

In spite of these words, however, all knew that the struggle had not
yet ceased. In act three Huppim (H13) had stressed that no decision
of an outsider would be acceptable unless it meant victory for the house
of Gilead (G9). Consequently they could not expect less determination
from members of the house of Gamaliel (G2).

Scene three expresses the doubts of the losing house in the government's impartiality. The house of Gamaliel (G2), which had relied on
the justice of its claim, began to realize that a traditional right alone is
insufficient to counter European support. Even a junior official in the

[1] Kaegi (1968), p. 226.
[2] Cf. *infra*, pp. 158–159.

bureaucratic hierarchy could block their access to the district commissioner.

Many competitors in the succession dispute found it easier to gain access to the Secretary for Internal Affairs than to the district commissioner. The reason was that tension and insistence on superiority are greater in situations where social distance is small than where social distance is great. The Secretary for Internal Affairs is so far removed from the day-to-day occurrences in an African chiefdom that he can afford to listen to people without causing himself any inconvenience. On the contrary, easy accessibility strengthened his control over local situations. Japheth (J7) recognized better than the Secretary for Internal Affairs the constant drift of office to the junior house. The Secretary's suggestion that Havilah (H8) should be registered as the next chief however proved that this high-ranking civil servant was unfamiliar with Karanga customs. Consequently the losing party came to the conclusion that government officials could not be relied upon to protect their rights. They felt betrayed and alienated. The Shoko Museamwa community had been law-abiding throughout its history; now the law had deserted it. The appeal to the senior administrator proved as useless as it had been on earlier occasions. Political success lay outside the bureaucratic hierarchy.

Scene four shows how disillusionment with government impartiality drove the leader of the Shoko Museamwa community to try the same techniques which brought victory to the house of Gilead (G9). But because these people lacked a knowledgeable European friend to introduce them to the legal profession, they haphazardly approached men less efficient than those engaged by the house of Gilead (G9). This shows that inexperienced Africans can only hope to make the best use of a European institution when they are guided by a well-intentioned European who is fully familiar with that institution.

Scene five records the climax of the victory won by the house of Gilead (G9): the feast in the tribal trust land at which the new chief was solemnly presented to his European supporters and, in a very secondary sense, to his own people.

Guests of honour were farmer Thomson, the lawyer and the European member of parliament. Absent were farmer Williams, the district commissioner, and the African member of parliament. The African member of parliament and farmer Williams were prevented by business, but no reason was given for the district commissioner's absence. Consequently only those outsiders attended who had personally supported the house of Gilead (G9). The African member of parliament and far-

mer Williams, who were impartial or who supported the house of
Gamaliel (G2), sent an excuse. The district commissioner remained a
complete outsider. Had he attended the ceremony members of
the house of Gamaliel (G2) would have accused him of open
partiality.

Attendance at the installation ceremony became therefore a sign of
support for the new chief. This was equally clear on the African side.
As the gift-presentation ceremony revealed, hardly any people from
the Shoko Museamwa community had arrived. Some 800 men, women
and children represented a small proportion of the inhabitants of the
chiefdom. The absence of neighbouring chiefs, especially of the three
chiefs who had submitted their report to the administration, was interpreted by the house of Gamaliel (G2) as a disagreement with govern-
men's decision. The presence of Hul's supporters and the absence of his
opponents proved that the struggle between the two houses would
continue. The European-sponsored and government-appointed chief
lacked the support of a large section of his people, and seemed intent
on alienating what little support he had. Joseph's (J15's) welcome to
absent chiefs and his disregard for the local subchief estranged the only
high-ranking Karanga leader in the community.

An evaluation of the importance which the chiefly family attached
to the European and African supporters was expressed in the enter-
tainment of guests. The honour shown to Europeans and the careless-
ness with which Karanga supporters were treated proved that the
chiefly family realized it had won the chieftainship exclusively through
European friends, and that the ceremony was held in thanksgiving for
their assistance.

This attitude was stated explicitly in the speeches. The speeches
delivered by members of the house of Gilead (G9) summarize their
conviction that the chieftainship had been conferred on them by
Europeans. All the Karanga tried to speak English and, if they were
unable, had their speeches translated. This showed that their main
audience consisted of the European guests. They expressed no debt
to their own people.

Whereas the Karanga spoke in English, the Europeans spoke in the
African language. This showed that there had been no need for the
Karanga to speak in English because the European visitors understood
their language. It only mystified their own followers, who could not
understand their leaders and needed an interpreter. The content of the
European speeches too differed from those of the Karanga. Farmer
Thomson and the European member of parliament exhorted the people

to unity and hard work and so transcended the sectional interests of the house of Gilead (G9) in their recommendations.

The spirit medium's dance was the only remnant of traditional custom that survived at the installation ceremony, and even this was blurred by conscious adoption of European culture items when the medium emerged from a car on which an imitation flag had been hoisted. Hence this small relic of the past looked out of place in its surroundings and was appreciated almost exclusively by the Europeans, who now witnessed the only esoteric event which they had been looking forward to.

The money collection aimed at covering the costs of the feast. A large part of the contribution was made by the Europeans. The gifts brought by the local people were very small. The total sum of £32 was comparable with the amounts collected at most Karanga marriages, and therefore proves a great lack of support for the new chief.

More significant than the low contribution was the fact that all the supporters of Japheth (J7) were absent, except the descendant of Eber (E1), who stated that he had merely come as an observer. The only people from the Shoko Museamwa community who attended the feast were those village headmen who had deserted the cause of their own house and thrown in their lot with Hul (H12), because their genealogical position had made it impossible for them to assume leadership in the house of Gamaliel (G2). Consequently their presence indicated an internal split in the senior house. Social structure once again determined allegiance.

Long ago Hobbes observed: 'Riches joined with liberality is power; because it procureth friends, and servants: without liberality, not so; because in this case they defend not.'[1] Karanga culture is well aware of this principle, and lavish feasts have always been among the chief means by which leaders held their followings together. At an accession ceremony, which ought to unite a divided chiefdom, feasting might have won many people for their chief. Instead the insufficient supply of meat and beer—the only beast killed on the first day was that donated by farmer Thomson—proved that the chiefly family was unconcerned about local support. When as early as 6 p.m. the Karanga dispersed they knew that the feast had been given only for the Europeans. The open discontent about food shortage on the second day was fomented by the very constables whom the chiefly family had called for protection against possible violence. The feast therefore ended with an almost total alienation of all the people. Hul (H12) and his family were rejected

[1] Hobbes, p. 56.

because of their inhospitality. The chief was seen as the chief of the Europeans. Europeans had created him and Europeans expected to benefit from his rule. The people realized that they could expect nothing from him. In this way the feast endorsed the public opinion that the chief was nothing more than a government chief. No chief of the people had yet been found.

The absence of a modern élite in Shoko chiefdom[1] and the lack of a central mission station deprived the people of a nationalistic leadership and forced them to seek their spokesmen among European farmers. The use of a leading farmer rather than a missionary or member of the indigenous élite confined the people's attention to their own tribal trust land. Europeans knew that in helping their neighbours to fight for their chieftainship they protected their own positions. The more Africans are concerned with traditional issues the less they are interested in those of national significance. Hence the interdependence of Europeans and Africans in this area is not merely economic, as pointed out above,[2] but also political. The succession dispute of Shoko chiefdom coincided with the period of African nationalism in Rhodesia and completely immunized the tribesmen against this modern ideology.

ACT 5: THE RULE AND DEPOSITION OF THE ACTING CHIEF

Scene 1

With the installation of the new chief farmer Thomson considered his task done. He was pleased that the man who had always provided him with cheap labour had become chief. He thought that from now on his Karanga neighbours ought to settle their internal differences among themselves, and so withdrew from further political involvement in the chiefdom.

Since Hul (H12) was too old to rule his people he officially appointed his son Joab (J12) as acting chief, and the district commissioner recognized this appointment. Joab (J12) inherited a position full of unresolved conflicts. The two houses of Gamaliel (G2) and Gilead (G9) were still unreconciled, though a split had occurred in the house of Gamaliel (G2) which Joab (J12) actively exploited to his advantage by promising Kedar (K1) a subchieftainship over the Shoko Museamwa community. This widened the gulf between Kedar (K1) and Japheth (J7). In addition

[1] There are far fewer teachers employed in Shoko chiefdom than in the Shiri and Ngara chiefdoms. Joseph (J15) is a civil servant and therefore unlikely to organize local opinion in opposition to European interests.

[2] *supra*, pp. 123–125.

to tensions about local leadership in the Shoko Museamwa community, Japheth (J7) and his supporters began to suffer agriculturally when Joab (J12) allocated land in their grazing areas to alien Africans from European farms. They brought several cases before the magistrate, but because Joab's (J12's) lawyer was more efficient than the assistance received by Japheth (J7) and his friends from the Mutual Aid society, the people always lost.

Two cases especially roused the indignation of the Shoko Museamwa community. Kenan (K4), one of Japheth's (J7's) staunch supporters, had built a four-bedroomed house with corrugated iron roof, door-frames and glass windows on a little hill near his fields. His cattle grazed on the slopes of this hill and rested in the cattle byre built at the bottom of the hill. One day Joab (J12) allocated the slope to a stranger from a nearby European farm, and the man began ploughing up and down the hill. Kenan (K4) protested against this allocation because the stranger was ploughing the land on which his homestead stood and where his cattle grazed. As a progressive farmer he also objected that ploughing up and down hill caused soil erosion and ruined the land of his ancestors. But the chief declared that his allocation was final and that the stranger was to continue ploughing the slope. When the first shoots sprang up Kenan's (K4's) cattle strayed into the field and destroyed the crop. Kenan (K4) was fined in the chief's court for negligent herding. This happened several times. To add to the irritation, the stranger ploughed all round the little hill without leaving an access road by which Kenan (K4) could reach his home by cart. After two seasons Kenan (K4) saw himself forced to abandon his well-built house, and began to erect some wattle-and-daub huts near his fields. By the end of the fieldwork the house built on the top of the hill was derelict.

On another occasion Joab (J12) allocated land in the grazing area belonging to Kohath (K8), a supporter of Japheth (J7), to people of Kedar (K1), who supported the chief. Since the people of Kohath (K8) knew that they would not receive a fair hearing in Joab's (J12's) court they appealed to the district commissioner, but the district commissioner told them to present their case to the chief. In their frustration they decided on self-help, and when the crops grew eight men ploughed them in. The case was brought to the magistrate's court, and Japheth's followers were each fined £5 or a fortnight's imprisonment for wilfully destroying property. The judge ruled that the chief had the right to allocate land to whom he thought fit. Japheth (J7) drew money from his bank account to pay his supporters' fines. He himself had not taken part in the ploughing.

As more and more grazing was allocated as fields to strangers, cattle starved and the local peasants saw their livelihood threatened. Many cattle strayed on European farmland and many cattle-owners had to pay fines for cattle trespasses. Japheth (J7) appealed to farmer Williams for help. Farmer Williams appealed to the district commissioner for a more rational land-use in the Shoko Museamwa community, but was told that the events in the tribal trust land did not concern him, since he was a European farmer. Several years of drought finally ruined the farmland of the Shoko Museamwa community, and in 1968 the Department of Conservation and Extension declared the land a reclamation area. Within less than four years land at one time the most fertile in the tribal trust land had become unproductive. In despair Japheth (J7) applied for a loan, drew all his money from the bank, and opened a mill to earn a non-agricultural income for his family. The land had ceased to feed the people.

Scene 2

Meanwhile people of the Shoko Murewa community and supporters of the house of Gilead (G9) in the Shoko Museamwa community also began to reject Joab's leadership. Those who had been promised a subchieftainship in previous years, especially Jehu (J9) and Kedar (K1), demanded that the promises made to them be fulfilled. To have appointed subchiefs, however, would have reduced Joab's power to allocate land.

People also complained that they had to pay too much money to obtain a field. Officially Karanga do not pay for land. In practice those who receive land may make a gift to their chief. Joab (J12) decided the size of this gift, and unless he was paid a certain amount of money he made no allocation. The people concluded that by demanding a high and fixed amount of money Joab (J12) was bringing land into the market just as Europeans had done.

Another contention arose over the way court cases were tried. Close relatives and supporters of Joab (J12) always won their cases, whether their actions had been right or wrong. Finally even Joachim (J13) Joab's younger brother and court assessor, expressed concern at the injustices which took place. People also objected to the high fees charged by Joab to try their cases.

By 1967 Joab lived in greater affluence than ever before and had built himself a large house, superior to any in the tribal trust land. But his people regarded him as an exploiter.

Scene 3

The only people who could stop corruption in the tribal court were members of Hul's (H12's) own extended family. Traditionally corruption was stopped by replacing a 'bad' chief by a 'good' one. When Husham (H15) saw how his brother's son alienated all their supporters he began to plan a conspiracy. He tried to befriend Japheth (J7) and suggested that Joab (J12) be overthrown. But Japheth (J7) was unwilling to co-operate with Husham (H15): he reckoned that as long as Joab (J12) acted for his old father Hul (H12), there was some hope that Hul (H12) might die and be succeeded by Havilah (H8); if Husham (H15) became chief, a man not much older than himself though of a senior generation, then his own house would be permanently excluded from the chieftainship. Though opposed to Joab (J12), therefore, Japheth (J7) did not accept Husham's friendship.

Husham's first supporter was his elder brother Huppim (H13). Huppim could not make a bid for the chieftainship itself because he was not a real son of Gilead (G9). When his mother had married Gilead (G9) she was already pregnant from a former marriage. Huppim (H13) had a strong character and was a born leader. On various occasions, both during court cases and at beer drinks, Husham (H15) and Huppim (H13) openly disagreed with Joab (J12). Once they told him: 'You are nothing but a name in this chieftainship. You are our son. Do not boast if we, your elders, address you by the name of our chieftainship.' Repeatedly they threatened to report his unjust judgements and open favouritism to the district commissioner. To counteract the opposition of his own family Joab (J12) tried to befriend Japheth (J7) by consulting him on general policies such as the introduction of community development.[1]

In 1967 a large number of village headmen of the Shoko Murewa community met under Jehu's (J9's) leadership and discussed how to guard their interests against the chief. They invited Japheth (J7) from the Shoko Museamwa community, but Japheth refused to attend. While they were meeting, a messenger from the district commissioner passed by on his routine patrol and they approached him to inform the district commissioner of their grievances. The district commissioner sent them word to bring their complaints to the chief. As soon as the chief heard about their meeting he asked the district commissioner to punish his subjects for holding a meeting without his knowledge and consent; but the district commissioner answered that it was a chief's task to settle internal disputes.

[1] *infra*, pp. 191–192.

To strengthen his position, Joab (J12) asked both Japheth (J7) and Husham (H15) to judge between him and the unruly village headmen. He hoped that this show of confidence would win them to his side. Japheth (J7) suggested that since all the disputants were related to each other it was wisest to forget what had happened and to work together in the future. Joab (J12) angrily rejected the advice and called Japheth (J7) a 'wolf in sheep's clothing' who had no regard for the injury done to his chief. Husham (H15) proposed a communal meal during which peace could be restored, and suggested that each of the conspirators contribute ten shillings to buy goats for the meal. His advice was accepted.

But after the meeting Husham (H15) dissuaded the conspirators from paying their fine. The men realized that Husham (H15) was planning to oust Joab (J12) from the chieftainship, and they waited. Both Husham (H15) and Huppim (H13) doubled their efforts. They visited the people and told them how angry members of the chiefly family were with the unfair court trials, the selling of land to outsiders, and the broken promises about giving subchieftainships to former supporters. They pointed out too that the chief was establishing himself as an absolute ruler: not only had government greatly increased his powers, but he was vice-president of the new community development council, head of the *dare*, that is, the chief's traditional council, and chairman and treasurer of the school committee.

Japheth (J7) and his supporters remained neutral in the new conflict. They were glad to see the division in the chiefly family and concluded that 'the soil has refused them' (*ivu rakaramba*). This means that the ancestors were displeased with the house of Gilead (G9) because it had illegally usurped the chieftainship.

When Joab (J12) was warned by some of his friends that his classificatory fathers were plotting to depose him he answered: 'With the new powers government has given to chiefs nobody can lay hands on me. I am untouchable. The conspirators waste their time.'

Scene 4

Husham (H15) planned his strategy carefully. First he sent a delegation to his elder brother Hul (H12) and suggested that since his son Joab (J12) had administered the chiefdom so badly he ought to be replaced by a younger son. But the old man remained silent. He loved Joab and informed him of the delegation. Joab at once visited the district commissioner and was assured that an investigation would be made. The district commissioner called some neighbouring chiefs from the same tribal trust land and asked their opinion. One of these chiefs, who had

had jurisdiction over Shoko chiefdom during the 1950s, remembered how actively Husham (H15) had fought for the restoration of the chieftainship. He recalled that his own position had consequently been weakened. He therefore declared that Husham (H15) was a power-hungry man. The district commissioner was pleased with this assessment. He had been placed in a delicate position when he received the many complaints about Joab (J12). He had seen the agricultural deterioration in the chiefdom on the one hand, and on the other was instructed by his superiors to support chiefs. The outside chief's condemnation of Husham (H15) therefore helped him to make up his own mind, and when he heard Husham in his evidence refer to Joab as his 'son' he reprimanded him and ordered him to address him as 'Chief Shoko'. When Husham claimed that Joab belonged to a junior generation the district commissioner shouted: 'You stubborn man, the other chiefs have witnessed that you are a trouble-maker. I do not believe anything you say.' The district commissioner then asked Joab whether he wanted him to pass the case to the magistrate's court. But Joab, at the request of his relatives, who urged him not to incriminate his 'father' before Europeans, suggested that the case be tried in his own court in the tribal trust land. This closed the issue. Husham (H15) concluded that the new government policy favoured the chiefs in whatever they did. He stressed that in the past no unjust chief would have held his office for a long time.

The rebellion had some positive effects in that during the succeeding months Joab allocated less land to strangers, charged lower court fees, and tried cases more justly. Yet the improvement did not last long. Soon he again accepted bribes, and although Husham (H15) tried repeatedly to visit the district commissioner, the district commissioner did not admit him. This increased Joab's confidence, and he exclaimed: 'You can try as hard as you like; you will never depose me. I am the real chief of this area and after my death my son will inherit this office. Government has recognized me.' Yet Husham swore: 'As truly as I live, one day you will be an ordinary villager.'

Scene 5
Husham (H15) made another attempt to unseat Joab (J12). He headed a delegation to the Secretary for Internal Affairs, and he presented the same complaints that he had put before the local district commissioner. The Secretary for Internal Affairs listened, but told the people to go home. He answered that he would correspond with the local district commissioner, and he did so. The district commissioner was displeased that an appeal had been made to his superior, and told the people: 'I

am not a Karanga and do not belong to your chiefdom. Solve your own problems.' But the administration in Shoko chiefdom was running down. Complaints against Joab multiplied in the district commissioner's office. Those who felt that their court cases had been settled unjustly continued to report them to the district commissioner. The department of Conservation and Extension also informed the district commissioner of the appalling condition of the land in the chiefdom. He realized that he was backing an unsuitable man.

Meanwhile Husham (H15) called a meeting in the tribal trust land, but Joab (J12) refused to attend. His old father Hul (H12), the chief, crawled to the meeting. The people told him that they had nothing against him; it was his son Joab (J12) who had offended them. In Joab's absence, however, they could do nothing.

At last, at the request of the Secretary for Internal Affairs, the district commissioner stepped in. He called the old man Hul (H12) to his office and instructed him to replace Joab by another son. He threatened that if he once more saw Joab wearing the emblems of chieftainship he would arrest him.

Joab sought help from African civil servants at the district commissioner's office and invited them to free drinks at the beer hall of the local African township; but they could do nothing for him. He then asked a neighbouring chief to bring up his case at the national Council of Chiefs. His colleague did him the favour, but reported back that Internal Affairs had already deposed him as acting chief and that nothing could be done. Joab laid down the emblems of chieftainship. The people rejoiced and many commented: 'We knew that this would happen to a chief who judges so unjustly.'

Scene 6

The last stage of the observed succession dispute occurred when the district commissioner held a meeting in Shoko chiefdom to appoint Joab's successor. He announced: 'I have been ordered by government to tell you that Joachim (J13), Joab's younger brother, is now your acting chief. This is an order from government and none of you has the right to question the appointment. Anyone who goes against Joachim goes against me, and anyone who goes against me goes against the government.' He then invited the new acting chief to address his people Joachim (J13) said: 'I am happy to be your chief. I will try to work together with all of you. I will hate nobody. I will try to help all and to punish evil.'

Husham (H15) then sprang up and wanted to argue with the distric commissioner about Joachim's appointment, but the district commissioner ruled his speech out of order. He warned that the government would take action against all who grumbled at the appointment. When Husham later appealed to a higher-ranking civil servant his appeal was abruptly dismissed.

EPILOGUE

The fieldwork was concluded in 1969, but the succession dispute still continues. The factions have multiplied. Joab (J12) has been replaced by Joachim (J13), but the split in the house of Gilead (G9) has not been healed. In addition to the split of the chiefdom into two communities represented by two warring houses, each of these major houses has split into opposing factions. Japheth (J7) still fights for his classificatory father Havilah (H8), but is more afraid of Husham (H15) than of a younger acting son of Hul (H12). Husham (H15) wants the office for himself and might have succeeded if Japheth (J7) had backed him. The senior branch of the house of Gamaliel (G2) is still loyal to Hul (H12) and still hopes for a subchieftainship in the Shoko Museamwa community. Hence none of the structural problems have been solved. In fact, a solution is unlikely under present social conditions in Rhodesia. The essential conditions under which a patriarchal system can work have been abolished by a bureaucratic administration, and the new chiefs are neither fully patriarchs nor fully bureaucrats.

ANALYSIS

Act five, covering the years 1964 to 1969, falls into six scenes, in which Joab's (J12's) power is severely tested. Each succeeding scene shows how the acting chief has alienated one group after another.

Scene one shows the alienation of the Shoko Museamwa community from chief Shoko. Instead of fostering unity to strengthen his chiefdom, Joab (J12) actively encourages division, first by intensifying the split in the house of Gamaliel (G2) by promising Kedar (K1) a subchieftainship, and then by widening the gulf separating the Shoko Murewa and Shoko Museamwa communities by irresponsibly allocating land to strangers.

In addition, scene one, like the other scenes of this act, focuses on the role of the district commissioner in the life of the chiefdom. He, rather than the chief, was the centre around which events revolved, even if he pushed the chief into the forefront. Such an attitude temporarily

M

strengthened the chief's position but over time created a gulf between him and his people. Not until another government department drew attention to the destruction of natural resources in the area did the district commissioner instruct the chief to be more conscientious in land-allocation. The Department of Conservation and Extension was already drawing up a reclamation scheme, and on its implementation the Ministry of Internal Affairs stood to lose some control in the area. Hence internal conflicts in the chiefdom again caused divisions among European outsiders. All sections of the community were too closely linked to be unaffected by each other's actions.

The outcome of all legal struggles between Joab (J12) and the Shoko Museamwa community proved that the chief would always win. The only attempt of the Shoko Museamwa community to manipulate a European institution, the Mutual Aid society, failed. The people of this community realized that their strength lay exclusively in traditional institutions. Again therefore they withdrew from the political dispute and concentrated on economic pursuits. The same patterns established in the earlier acts of the social drama constantly repeat themselves.

Scene two highlights the same issues in the Shoko Murewa community. Joab (J12) alienated the people of his own community through injustices and extortion, so that his support dwindled to nothing. He did not realize that if people had nothing to gain from his leadership they would cease to follow him; and that only through providing them with new services could he keep them under an obligation.[1] He saw himself as a government chief, not a chief of the people, and failed to realize the intercalary position of Rhodesian chiefs. In despising the support of his people he ignored the strongest foundation of every rule: the power of public opinion.

Scene three traces the increasing alienation still further when his closest relatives, who had fought with him for the chieftainship in the past, rose in rebellion. The division of the house of Gilead (G9) followed the natural cleavages of the genealogy and paralleled the development in the house of Gamaliel (G2). With Hul (H12) as chief, and Joab (J12) acting for his old father, Husham (H15), the leader of the rebellion, saw himself permanently excluded from the chieftainship. His elder brother Huppim (H13), who was not a fully legitimate son of Gilead (G9), was no threat to him, and since Huppim had to play a minor role under Joab (J12) he became Husham's natural ally. If Husham had succeeded in winning the support of the Shoko Museamwa community, he could easily have displaced Joab. Japheth (J7) was keenly aware of the struc

---

[1] An observation made by Blau (1964), pp. 136, 322.

tural implications of Husham's conspiracy. He also knew that Husham would be a better chief than Joab. However, a bad chief from the house of Gilead (G9) was more advantageous for his house than a good chief. For this reason he also consented to assist Joab in policy decisions and to mediate between him and his people.

Scene three therefore witnesses a complete shift of allegiances, without in the least altering the basic competition between the two houses. The split in the house of Gilead (G9) promised a distant victory to the house of Gamaliel (G2); hence they concluded: 'The soil has refused them.'

This scene, like the preceding one, ends with the acting chief's confidence in government support, irrespective of the attitude of his own people. Again therefore the claim is made that a successful chief is one whom government protects. Joab's disregard of the conspirator derives from his confidence for, as Blau writes:

> By tolerating an opposition movement, and probably even laughing it off, people demonstrate that their own strength is immune to it, and this social evidence that the opposition does not have to be taken seriously undermines its strength by discouraging potential supporters from joining such a movement presumably doomed to failure.[1]

Scene four is dominated by the rebel leader, who skilfully planned his moves. Husham (H15) did not immediately fight for himself, but merely asked the old chief to appoint a more worthy son as acting chief. This screened his personal motives, and presented him as a man acting for the welfare of the people. It was a challenge expressed in moral values and therefore marked a new intensity in the conflict. Joab realized the threat and sought government protection.

Joab (J12) had never experienced divided loyalties because he never cared to be accepted by his people. He had identified himself with government and expressed this identification not only in his actions but also in words when he said: 'I am now like government.'[2] Yet whenever two opposed systems meet, one position must bear the brunt of conflicting demands. If the chief escaped from this intercalary position, the district commissioner was forced into it. As a complete outsider to the traditional system,[3] and fully committed to government's bureaucracy, he was unwilling to fill this role. Consequently he tried to avoid it by calling on other chiefs to make the decision. The outside chief's partiality

[1] Blau (1964), p. 327.
[2] *supra*, p. 146.
[3] He stressed that he was not a Karanga and did not belong to their chiefdom. *Supra*, pp. 155–156.

suited the district commissioner because it enabled him to stress his role
as protector of government chiefs. The deterioration of administration
and agricultural production in the chiefdom, however, as well as the
shift in the power balance within the traditional system, placed opposing
pressures on the civil servant. His major duty was to guarantee the
smooth administration of his district. The conflict forced him to change
his support. Similar reactions to conflicting demands by a district commissioner and African leaders[1] show that structural positions determine
actions to a very large extent. Yet the bureaucrat's total commitment
to government and his independence of the African people greatly
decreased the intensity of his conflict.

The fall of the acting chief Joab (J12) reinforces the conclusions of
chapter five[2] that government support alone is not enough. No chief
can rule without at least a minimal support from his people. A chief who
relies exclusively on government support is like a man who tries to stand
on one leg.

When, stripped both of his followers and of European support, Joab
(J12) appealed to African civil servants for assistance, these acted according to civil service norms: they refused to take sides. Yet in fact they
were refusing to side with a man who lacked powerful support. The
fellow chief who tried to assist Joab (J12) found that the Council of
Chiefs was powerless to reinstate a man once the administration had
made a decision. Their authority was subject to that of the Ministry of
Internal Affairs. This shows that the only viable sources of support are
either Europeans or a strong following; that in the long run the support
of a following counts, but for many years government support alone can
maintain in office a chief who consistently breaks the norms of his own
community.

Scene six records the installation of Joab's successor, and closes the
social drama as far as it could be observed during the fieldwork period.
The installation ceremony, though on a much smaller scale than the
installation of Hul (H12), shares two common characteristics with the
former. Firstly, the new acting chief appealed for unity among all his
people and promised them a just rule. But just as in act four the division
between the warring houses was in no way overcome by this appeal for
unity, so in act five Joachim's (J13's) appeal for unity did not reconcile
Husham (H15) to the rest of his family. Like Japheth (J7) in act four,
Husham swore to continue fighting Hul's sons, so that eventually the

[1] In this he resembled the subchief in case history two, chapter five, who skilfully
balanced the demands made on him by opposing interests. *Supra*, pp. 80–87.
[2] *supra*, pp. 103–105.

chieftainship should come to him. The house of Gilead (G9) had become as deeply divided as the chiefdom itself.

Secondly, the official installation was made by the district commissioner because a chief is chief by order of government. As in all the preceding acts, the only unifying bond was the administrator's authority. The district commissioner's speech: 'This is an order from government and no one has the right to question it. Anyone who goes against Joachim (J13) goes against me, and anyone who goes against me goes against government', restored the general belief that government backs chiefs. This backing is only withdrawn if a chief becomes blatantly unfit for office. In all normal circumstances, therefore, the chief and government are one.

One fact has not been stressed in the narration of this social drama: between 1943 and 1969, over which period the history of Shoko chiefdom has been traced, many district commissioners served in the area. The exact number could not be ascertained, because the National Archives do not allow the public access to records covering the current period, and the district secretary only had records covering the period from 1964 onwards. Between 1964 and 1969 six district commissioners worked at the station from which Shoko chiefdom is administered. Consequently many district commissioners were involved in the succession disputes, and the competitors for the chieftainship had to address themselves to several strangers filling the same role. In spite of this constant shift of personnel, the consistency of the civil servants' decisions and actions give the impression that 'the district commissioner' is one social person.

CONCLUSION

Turner writes of a social drama that:

> It reflects different aspects of the same structural conflicts. It may be objected that such factors as innate psycho-biological constitution and personality variations determined by differential training in the early years of childhood take precedence over sociological factors in shaping the events to be described. But it is clear that the different personalities involved occupy social positions that must inevitably come into conflict, and each occupant of a position must present his case in terms of generally accepted norms. A person can avoid disputes over succession only by renouncing the claim to office vested in his position. In a society governed by rules of kinship, he cannot abrogate his position, into which he is born and by virtue of which he is a member of the village community. Personality may influence

the form and intensity of the dispute, it cannot abolish the situation in which conflict must arise.[1]

This analysis of the social drama in Shoko chiefdom has demonstrated that the conflicts between houses and within houses were determined by the structural positions of individuals. The competition between Helon (H9) and Hirah (H10) in act one, especially showed that these men had to compete for their houses even if, like Hirah (H10), they were not personally interested in the chieftainship. Japheth (J7) was likewise cast in a leadership role by his structural position. His character, however, made him a most suitable leader. Structural and personal advantages thus combined to consolidate his position. Joab (J12) differed from Japheth (J7) in that he lacked the latter's leadership qualities but not his ambition. It is doubtful however whether a more capable leader could have avoided the split within the house of Gilead (G9), because segmentation is built into the structure of Karanga chieftainships. Unless those conditions are restored which in the past century allowed Karanga succession rules to function, the traditional system cannot reproduce itself. Population pressure and restriction to narrow stretches of land are bound to create a situation in which internal conflicts cause the traditional society to change its character.

This change is hastened by the interplay of European and Karanga social institutions. Economically European and Karanga communities are interdependent. Economic interdependence leads to social bonds. These bonds can be manipulated for political aims, both at the national and local level. When traditional chief-makers are supplanted by lawyers, parliamentarians and civil servants, and when the patriarchal system of chieftainship is subordinated to a modern bureaucracy, traditional life atrophies. This is true even in a community that is strongly orientated towards the past, that is interested exclusively in traditional politics and completely immune to national aspirations.

Every Karanga community is inexorably drawn into the modern life of Rhodesia. The chieftainship has ceased to be as self-sufficient as it was in the past. Every chiefdom has become a section of a much larger political unit, and it is in the context of this larger social unit that the individual power-struggles of chiefdoms gain their meaning.

Ndabaninge Sithole has summed up another changing aspect of the position of chiefs in European-controlled African countries:

Before the coming of the white people, African . . . chiefs and other native authorities were ultimately responsible to the people, not to a foreign

[1] Turner (1957), p. 94.

power as now is the case. The present African chiefs no longer represent the will of the people, but that of a foreign power. In other words, European powers, while preserving the shell of African . . . chieftainship, have emptied African . . . chieftainship of its real content.[1]

To this must be added that not only European administration but also the European public at large has contributed to a transformation of African chieftainship. The succession dispute of Shoko chiefdom shows that European economic and social systems too have had their effect on African chieftainship, and transformed it into a new entity peculiar to twentieth-century Rhodesia.

Since 1943, the history of Shoko chiefdom has been a long-drawn-out struggle for power. Chapters six to eight have analysed the structural implications of this power struggle, first between different houses of the chieftainship and later between subsections of these houses. Two major elements of power have been used in the contest: physical force and moral values.

Weber defines power in terms of physical force, as 'the chance of a man or of a number of men to realise their will in a communal action even against the resistance of others, who participate in the action'.[2] All contenders here strove for the command of physical force. Chieftainship was for them a symbol of the power to impose their will on others. Joab (J12) controlled the access to powerful Europeans. In identifying himself with powerful outsiders and enjoying their protection, he could use their power to impose his will on his people. His power therefore did not rest in himself but was conferred on him by 'strangers'.[3] Consequently his authority lacked authenticity and a firm foundation. It crumbled when the strangers lost interest in him.

Yet the concept of physical force does not exhaust the concept of power. Louch writes that there are other aspects of power, less tangible, but equally potent, which determine events, such as 'powers to persuade, powers of tradition, and powers of authority itself, the willingness of people to follow the lead of one whom they recognize as making demands on them'.[4] It is in these senses that Japheth (J7), and later Husham (H15), had power in Shoko chiefdom. These men lacked the means of control which the district commissioner put at Joab's (J12's) disposal, but they had influence: Husham (H15) could persuade the people to follow

---

[1] Sithole (1959), p. 99.
[2] Gerth and Mills, eds. (1961), p. 180.
[3] Frankenberg (1957), pp. 18–19.
[4] Louch (1966), p. 187.

him rather than a decadent chief, and Japheth (J7) was backed by the whole traditional system and the people's willingness to recognize his claim.

The analysis of the social drama, moreover, has shown that 'moral suasion, or value-judgements'[1] are involved whenever structural arguments lose their effect. They therefore characterize moments of high tension and often precede, justify or intensify internal cleavages. For example, accusations of immoral behaviour in act one scene two[2] justify the antagonism between the structurally opposed houses of Gamaliel (G2) and Gilead (G9); the accusation of financial dishonesty in act two scene two[3] formally excludes one house from negotiations with Europeans and intensifies the cleavage. In the central act[4] European and Karanga institutions are contrasted in moral terms and actors reject as immoral one aspect of the alien institution of European law. The final opposition between Husham (H15) and Joab (J12) is fought entirely on moral issues.[5] Though Joab (J12) is finally deposed by government for administrative inefficiency, the rebel leader fought him on moral grounds and defended the internal split of the house of Gilead (G9) by pointing to the injustices of the acting chief.

The actors in the social drama therefore evaluate office-bearers in moral and not in purely structural terms. They do this because they are deeply committed to the normative system; they have internalized the norms of society and accept them without question. An analysis of social structure must therefore be supplemented by an analysis of the actors' moral values, for, as Morton-Williams writes: 'A social structure is not merely an organized system of relationships but a moral order, especially to those individuals who contribute to change through the exercise of their free will.'[6]

Tillich adds that 'every political system requires authority, not only in terms of possessing instruments of force but also in terms of the silent or expressed consent of the people. Such consent is possible only if the group in power stands for an idea that is powerful and significant.'[7]

Chieftainship is an institution highly valued by the people of Shoko chiefdom, but the family which finally acquired the office of chief was

[1] Louch (1966), p. 188.
[2] *supra*, pp. 119, 121.
[3] *supra*, pp. 126, 129.
[4] *supra*, pp. 132–133, 137.
[5] *supra*, pp. 150–160.
[6] Morton-Williams (1968), p. 4.
[7] Tillich (1967), p. 43.

rejected by the people. Though the acting chief therefore stood for an idea that was 'powerful and significant' for all, he failed because he did not live up to the expectation which people attached to his role. Not the legitimacy of the institution of chieftainship but the legitimacy of Joab's rule was questioned.

Government too is an institution accepted by people of Shoko chiefdom because it possesses the instrument of force and so embodies ultimate authority. Their constant appeals to officials of the Ministry of Internal Affairs are a silent recognition of the legitimacy they ascribe to government. Yet these appeals also witness to the powerlessness of their patriarchal institutions *vis-à-vis* the powerful alien bureaucracy. The social drama of the chiefdom's succession dispute shows that the real rulers of tribal trust lands are not chiefs but European bureaucrats.

The succession dispute of Shoko chiefdom illustrates that modern Karanga are confronted with a great variety of often conflicting social values. This normative heterogeneity results from the increase in scale of their political, economic and social environment. In a small, homogeneous society norms are very powerful because they are accepted by all. As a small-scale society becomes part of a larger unit, that is, as its scale is extended, heterogeneous ideas are introduced. Because new and often conflicting values are held out to the people, individuals no longer know by which standards to judge what is right and wrong. In such circumstances their social interaction often assumes the appearance of a game, and the individual actors in a social drama appear as gamblers.

CHAPTER 9

Community Development, its Failure and Rejection

1. COMMUNITY DEVELOPMENT

(a) *General Policy*

Previous chapters have analysed the tensions inherent in two contrasted political structures, a traditional patriarchal society and a modern bureaucracy. Community development intensifies these structural inconsistencies by introducing a further element into the patriarchal system which is contrary to its nature: democratically elected councils. Weber saw an inherent contradiction between democracy and bureaucracy because the former strives to shorten the term of office by election and to level the governed in opposition to the ruling group.[1] This conflict is still greater between democracy and a patriarchal system in which men obtain a political office by right of birth, where no two men hold an identical social position, but where everybody is either superordinated or subordinated to his neighbours. Ideally men who serve on community development councils are elected from among all the people of a local community. Hence achieved and not ascribed status determines leadership on these local government bodies.

To understand community development in Rhodesia a distinction must be made between the government policy that became the basis of district administration in 1962[2] and was publicly announced by the Prime Minister in 1965 and the internationally accepted philosophy of community development, which has had a long history in America, the United Kingdom and elsewhere. It has recently been given great emphasis in the independent states of Africa and has been used by African leaders to create a national consciousness, particularly in Ghana and Tanzania.

Community development aims at mobilizing local resources through the initiative of the people and so raise their living standards and aspirations. Batten, an international authority on community development, described it like this: 'a process of increasing people's satisfactions

[1] Gerth and Mills, eds. (1961), p. 226.
[2] Green (1963), p. 11.

by helping them to satisfy their existing wants, or to learn new wants and ways of satisfying them, or to make more satisfying choices from a widening range of possible alternatives.'[1] Batten argues that the economic stagnation of many countries is due to the frustration of peasants who do not know how to adjust themselves to changing social conditions. They therefore react with apathy.[2]

In Rhodesia the situation is more complicated than in other African countries that are attempting to implement community development, because Rhodesian Africans are ruled by a white minority. The land is legally divided into African and European areas. When community development first became a government policy many people, especially missionaries and African nationalists, realized that the emphasis on the development of individual communities would intensify the division between Africans and Europeans. From its inception therefore community development acquired racialist overtones. It was seen as the thin edge of the wedge of separate development in Rhodesia.

It is doubtful, however, that the original intention of the Rhodesian Government was to use community development as a means to introduce separate development. The administration of African rural areas had been over-centralized and all powers had been concentrated in the hands of commissioners. This over-centralization had removed initiative from the people and accustomed them to accept what they needed from European outsiders. Several commissions[3] called for a reorganization of the administrative department, a decentralization of functions, and a degree of autonomy for local communities. The government invited an international consultant on community development to study local conditions. This specialist came to the conclusion that 'Rhodesians have the need for and the capability of carrying out community development'.[4]

The awareness that community development would lead to separate development became stronger after a general election in 1962. The moderate government party was replaced by a right-wing government party, which abandoned the policy of partnership and led Rhodesia to a unilateral declaration of independence from Great Britain. The new government intensified the training programme for community-development workers and hastened to implement the new policy. Leading politicians and civil servants proclaimed it as 'the corner stone of government

[1] Batten (1965a), p. 229.
[2] ibid., p. 222.
[3] Mangwende, Patterson and Robinson Commissions.
[4] Green (1963), p. 11.

policy'[1] and tried to prove that it had always been practised in the administration of African areas in Rhodesia. In 1969 the deputy secretary for Internal Affairs wrote:

> Community Development is nothing new. It would be easy to trace the idea back to our outstanding early Native Commissioners who called it 'good administration'. After all it is simply uncommon common sense based on insight, and, throughout the eras of development . . . there ran a thread of such thinking. The thread was submerged in the drive for economic development, it emerged again in the 1960s. Of course it has been analysed, refined and decked out in new jargon, including a label which has passed into international currency, but this is no justification for looking upon it as some mysterious theory imported from outside.[2]

By making community development an explicit policy and by implementing this policy through indirect pressure, the Rhodesian government eliminated an essential element of the philosophy: its voluntary character. Batten and Green had insisted that community development must be voluntarily accepted by the people. Chapter one indicated the extreme reluctance with which Rhodesian Africans have accepted councils throughout this century.[3] The acceptance of councils in the late 1960s was not due to direct force by administrators but rather to indirect pressure, such as the withdrawal of public services and the elimination of outside help. Christian missions, for example, were asked to hand over their schools to community councils and were forbidden to expand primary education. The intention was to stimulate African self-help.[4] A Catholic African newspaper reports a typical example of indirect compulsion: at the beginning of the 1969 school year two to three times as many children registered in one school for the first class than there were places for them. The school manager approached the district commissioner for an additional classroom but was told that no expansion was permitted unless the people formed a council and took over the school from the mission.[5] The people, bitterly opposed to community development, were given the choice of depriving their children of education or of submitting to a government policy they resented.

Soon public opinion grew strong against community development. Chiefs feared that elected councillors would undermine their authority. Missionaries were reluctant to hand over schools to councils because

[1] Wrathall, Minister of Finance, 1969, p. 96.
[2] Howman (1969), p. 5.
[3] *supra*, pp. 14–15, 18–19, 23–26.
[4] Cf. Howman (1969), p. 7.
[5] *Moto*, March 1969, p. 7.

they feared a lessening of Christian influence in African education, a dropping of academic standards, and a great reduction in further expansion of schools.[1] Roman Catholic missionaries were investing large sums of money in schools and knew that without their contribution the people would not be able to keep pace with the increasing demand for education. Teachers feared interference from illiterate elders in the running of schools. Peasants appreciated the benefits they received from missionaries and were unwilling to take over the schools. Moreover, parents of schoolchildren already exerted as much influence over the schools as they desired through the local school committees. They did not want to lose their control to community development councils, which would reduce local autonomy. Chapter three[2] showed that the effective social units in Karangaland are school communities, which are identical with communities centring around land-shrines and the residences of senior village headmen or subchiefs. These neighbourhood clusters are too small to form independent sections under local government. Peasants in general objected to community development because they saw in it a new means of taxation; nationalists encouraged these fears by emphasizing that community development today means *apartheid* tomorrow.[3] Consequently the government policy of community development acquired many unfavourable overtones.

(b) *The Structural Position of Civil Servants in Community Development*
The decision to make community development the cornerstone of government policy[4] required that key positions be filled by civil servants. The district commissioner became the spearhead of the new policy.[5] The Prime Minister's directive on community development in 1965 outlined the functions of the various officials. It stressed that 'the district commissioner is the guardian of the process of community development and is charged with the task of fostering and supporting local government'.[6] The district commissioner is the president of every African council, but he may depute his assistant district officer to take his place. Consequently the commissioner is fully informed of all council proceedings. Though most district commissioners have handed over to elected Africans the position of chairman, which they filled in the past,[7]

[1] Cf. Appendix C.
[2] *supra*, pp. 48–51.
[3] *supra*, p. 23.
[4] *supra*, pp. 167–168
[5] *supra*, p. 23. S.I.A., 1963, p. 8.
[6] Prime Minister, 1965, para. 24.
[7] *supra*, p. 25.

their presidency enables them to influence proceedings and to direct council activities.

The district commissioner is not only a key figure on individual councils but he also co-ordinates the activities of all the councils in his district. At monthly district conferences all civil servants, under the presidency of the commissioner, discuss local community development projects, and the technical staff is told where their services are most urgently required. The district commissioner's first-hand information of local plans increases his influence among his fellow civil servants.

Through the district commissioner local development is also co-ordinated with provincial and national development plans. European civil servants and politicians form provincial conferences and a cabinet co-ordinating committee respectively to watch and direct the implementation of the new policy.[1] No African is involved in community development at these levels of policy and planning.

African civil servants do play a part however in the lower echelons of community development. Government-trained 'community advisers' assist people 'through organized communal self-help' to define their needs and achieve their goals. It is the task of community advisers 'to teach people to help themselves and to make their own decisions and plans'.[2] Community advisers 'are simply there to find out what the people want, within the law, and help them to achieve their aspirations within the "local good" '.[3] Most community advisers have been civil servants in another government ministry[4] and have accepted transfers to the ministry of Internal Affairs because it offers them higher salaries.

Batten writes: 'It goes without saying that the success of a community development agency will be affected by the community's attitude towards it. Unless this attitude is favourable it is unlikely that the community will act on the agency's advice or even listen to it.'[5]

Since government is the agency concerned, and in particular the Ministry of Internal Affairs, the success or failure of community development is likely to depend on the people's attitude towards the administration. Antagonism towards government is likely to block the implementation of community development in areas strongly influenced by African nationalism, but in areas where the government's legitimacy is accepted by the people less opposition is likely to occur. To a lesser

[1] Prime Minister, 1965, para. 17.
[2] ibid., para. 30.
[3] ibid., para. 31.
[4] *supra*, p. 24.
[5] Batten (1965a), p. 8.

degree the personalities of civil servants may influence local readiness to experiment with councils. Frequent transfers of civil servants however make this factor less important than the roles they fill.

(c) *The Effects of Community Development on Traditional Leaders*

Chapters two and three[1] drew attention to the different social structures and economic conditions of tribal trust lands and purchase areas. Purchase area farmers are more affluent than tribal trust land peasants and therefore likely to have more cash available for community projects. Furthermore, purchase areas are administered by democratically elected committees, and no chiefs have influence in these communities. Consequently community development might be expected to be more welcomed by progressive farmers than by people living at subsistence level in a patriarchal social system.

In tribal trust lands, the institution of chieftainship is likely to cause many tensions between democratically elected councils and chiefs. Rhodesian government officials were for many years aware of the inconsistency between local government through councils and chiefly administration. Holleman had attested the chiefs' suspicion of councils in the *Mangwende Report*. He wrote:

> It is not common for Chiefs to welcome Native Councils; they tend to distrust this instrument of local government as a potential threat to their own authority. These fears may be exaggerated but are not without foundation. For, no matter how carefully the respective fields of interest and responsibility are demarcated, there is no denying the fact that, in the total sphere of tribal government, traditional authority must now share power with a partially elected body of persons who had no formal authority before. As recently as 1959 the Chief Native Commissioner admitted in his Annual Report that Chiefs were in a 'difficult and ambiguous' position.[2]

And in 1964 the district commissioner in charge of the Shiri and Ngara chiefdoms commented to the fieldworker: 'Community development will undermine the power of the chief, and chiefs will gradually disappear. You cannot simultaneously have autocratic chiefs and democratic councils.'

In the Victoria province, which covers most of Karangaland, local civil servants introduced certain alterations into the community development structure at lower levels. They followed the Prime Minister's directive and retained councils at chiefdom level,[3] but altered the method

[1] Especially pp. 36, 51–52.
[2] *Mangwende Report*, para. 177.
[3] Prime Minister, 1965, para. 17.

of choosing councillors. According to government policy all chiefs are *ex-officio* vice-presidents of councils. That is, they hold offices similar but subordinate to district commissioners. All other councillors however are elected. To overcome the chiefs' fears that their authority would be queried by democratically elected commoners, district commissioners encouraged chiefs to nominate suitable council members. In addition they placed the community development councils under the chiefs' traditional councils, called *dare*. Since a *dare* consists of old, traditionally orientated men, it is conservative and its members tend to block innovations which younger and more educated councillors on the community development body might desire.

The Victorian experiment found widespread approval in the Ministry of Internal Affairs, and in 1969 a district commissioner from another province wrote: 'I warned the headmen that no committees would receive Government assistance unless, and until, both the committees and its members had been approved by the Chief. This strengthened the position of the Chief and entrenched his position as patron of the movement.'[1] He concluded:

> It has been my experience that since the tribal elders have been inextricably involved in the implementation of community development methods they do not resent 'pressure from below' for self-help development and, in fact, welcome it. Had they not been so involved it is my submission that they would have resented the intrusion of the community adviser and would have viewed his endeavours to arouse the dormant aspirations of the tribesmen as a threat to their traditional position. In this event the community development movement would either have died or would have led to a set of new leaders being thrown up who, having initiative, would indeed have posed a serious threat to the existing tribal system.[2]

The administrators' endeavour to win the chiefs' support for community development conforms both to government policy to strengthen traditional leaders and also to Batten's advice that the support of local leaders is essential for the success of the new development plans.[3]

The case histories of the successes and failures of community development in five chiefdoms and two purchase areas test the following hypotheses:

(i) The success or failure of community development depends on a community's relationship to the agency of change. This in turn depends on the general ideological background of the community. If the popula-

[1] Simmonds (1969), p. 11.
[2] Simmonds (1969), p. 12.
[3] Batten (1965a), p. 31.

tion of a chiefdom or purchase area is relatively well educated, national-istically inclined and served by a Christian mission which itself is critical of community development, this policy is likely to be strongly opposed by the people. The relationship between the community and govern-ment officials who implement the policy is likely to be strained. In less-educated communities whose people depend on government assistance for essential services and where nationalism is less widespread, govern-ment officials may expect co-operation from the people.

(ii) The introduction of community development depends on the attitude of the leaders towards the new policy. If the leaders support community development, community development is likely to be attempted. But unless the leaders are accepted and supported by their people, their sponsorship of the new policy is unlikely to succeed.

(iii) Affluent communities show greater interest in community de-velopment than poor communities, because they have the means to embark on community projects likely to increase their prosperity. Purchase areas in particular, which are more affluent than tribal trust lands, are likely to run successful councils.

2. REJECTION OF COMMUNITY DEVELOPMENT

(a) Council proposed to a passively conforming chief
The history of community development in Shiri chiefdom illustrates the total rejection of a government policy by a nationalistically inclined people who had lost confidence in their acting chief. Chapter three[1] traced the historical relationship between the Shiri and Ngara chief-doms. The two chiefdoms are situated in the same tribal trust land. The senior chief Ngara accepted chief Shiri into his area and made him indebted to him by giving him his daughters in marriage. Through this affinal link and positional succession chief Shiri remains son-in-law of chief Ngara and subordinate to him in local politics. The rejection of community development in Shiri chiefdom is therefore strongly in-fluenced by the total refusal of chief Ngara to co-operate with any government policy.[2]

The people of the Shiri and Ngara chiefdoms were first told about community development in September 1962, when a government minister addressed them at a large gathering and said:

Government has decided to give more power to chiefs. For some years now

---

[1] *supra*, pp. 44–45.
[2] *supra*, pp. 96–100.

your chiefs met every six months with our officials at provincial level and this year we established a Council of Chiefs for the whole country. Never before did you have such good chances of putting your requests before the Rhodesian Government. Government now plans to grant your chiefs greater powers to try court cases because it desires that you solve your own small problems.

Yet this is not all. The main purpose of my visit today is to consult you about community development. Government wants you to establish councils in which you can decide with your chiefs what kind of development you desire in your community. You have to collect some money to pay for your plans but Government will help you generously. Your plans for the improvement of your community must be approved by the district commissioner. Many meetings will be held in your area to explain everything to you. The important point to remember is that you are offered community development; it is not imposed on you. If you do not want to develop your area you can let it stagnate while your neighbouring tribal trust lands will develop fast.

The district commissioner concluded the minister's address with the words: 'You have heard weighty words and you must remember them because they are words of authority; they are the truth and nothing but the truth. You are now welcome to ask questions.'

The people eagerly availed themselves of this opportunity to present their problems to the minister. But nobody asked a single question about community development. Chief Ngara opened the discussion: 'This tribal trust land is too small for us. My people have greatly increased in number and we need more land and more cattle.' A subchief complained: 'My people are migrating to a resettlement area because I cannot give them enough land to plough. I am becoming a subchief without people.' A village headman added: 'We have been promised more land by the district commissioner but we have received nothing.' Then a commoner spoke: 'Some of our children have no land at all; they are suffering and starving.' Another subchief declared: 'I am surprised that some government officials recently told us that we could buy land in unreserved areas. When the white man came to this country he sold the land which God created. How can you sell what God has made?' These requests for land continued for a long time, but nobody asked about community development. To bring the meeting to a close the local district commissioner declared that the minister was not interested in land problems, that he had come to talk about community development, and if they had no questions about the new government policy the minister would leave. There were no questions about community development and the minister left by helicopter.

an exceptional means of transportation which greatly impressed the local people.[1]

The people of the Shiri and Ngara chiefdoms were so preoccupied with their major problem of land shortage that they could think of nothing else. They were unaware that a new and important government policy had been announced to them.

In early 1964 a community adviser was sent into the area. He visited the people, attended their meetings, and finally made friends with some teachers. He encouraged them to form a football club and promised them a football from departmental funds. The teachers agreed. They considered the community adviser a harmless man; nobody quite knew what he was sent for.

A few months later the district commissioner asked his assistant district officer to stimulate the people's interest in community development. He himself was at the brink of retirement and unwilling to initiate a new policy of which he was very critical.[2] The district officer instructed the community adviser to find out what local improvements the people desired. He was soon presented with a long list of requests, ranging from roads, bridges and dams to bore-holes. The district officer's attention was caught by a suggestion that a bridge be built in the southern part of Shiri chiefdom across a major river separating the tribal trust land from a purchase area. This bridge would give the people a quicker access to the nearest town.

The district officer asked the purchase-area farmers whether they too would be interested in the bridge, which would connect them with the tribal trust land. The farmers were enthusiastic about the project because they desired access to the mission hospital in Shiri chiefdom, and promised to construct a road through their area from the bridge to the main road.

With this assurance the district officer returned to the tribal trust land and asked the community adviser to find out what the people in general thought of a bridge. The community adviser had casual talks with the villagers at beer drinks and at work and got the impression that they had nothing against it. He found special interest among members of a newly founded co-operative society, who calculated that the new road and bridge would reduce the transport costs of maize by two shillings and sixpence per bag.

---

[1] A similar use of a helicopter by a government minister was made when a chief, Tangwena, was ordered to leave his ancestral land. Cf. Clutton-Brock (1969), p. 9.
[2] Cf. *supra*, p. 171. For similar delegations of unpleasant duties see *supra*, p. 131 and Clutton-Brock (1969), pp. 18–19.

The district officer was delighted with the findings and personally approached the missionaries, who were only too pleased with the project and promised financial assistance.

So far the people had attached no importance to the consultations. Because their chief had not been involved they considered the discussions one of the incomprehensible actions of government agents.

Finally the district officer met the local chief. He told him that his community adviser had heard that the people wanted a bridge across the river to give them easy access to the nearest town; would he agree to the people's wishes? The chief agreed, without referring the matter back to his people, and the district officer called in a surveyor and other technicians to fix the place where the bridge was to be built and to estimate the cost. The district officer asked the chief not to discuss the matter with his people before all details had been worked out. He explained that under community development the people either had to contribute money to meet half of the cost of the project or had to provide unpaid labour. The chief objected to unpaid labour because half a century ago the people had had to build roads in forced-labour gangs, and the memory of this and resentment against it was still alive. But he thought that each family could contribute one pound. He suggested that the district officer consult chief Ngara and ask whether those people of Ngara chiefdom who would use the bridge would make a contribution. He himself stayed in the background and left all negotiations to the government official.

To win local support for community development the district officer began to hold public meetings for leaders. First he addressed the African agricultural staff of the tribal trust land, then the teachers, and finally the traditional leaders. African government employees carefully listened to his technical expositions; the teachers rejected his explanations and violently opposed the new policy. By the time the district officer held a meeting for chiefs and subchiefs the teachers had already spread suspicion towards community development and the people were generally hostile to the new policy.

The district officer opened the meeting on community development for chiefs and subchiefs with a reference to dip fees.[1] This reference increased the opposition of his audience, who listened in sullen silence. When at the end of his talk he came to mention the bridge, chief Shiri asked whether he had kept his promise and discussed the project with chief Ngara. The district officer admitted that he had visited chief Ngara's village but that the chief had not been at home; consequently

[1] Cf. *supra*, pp. 98–99.

he had not yet informed him but, he added, chief Ngara had heard at the present meeting. His Karanga listeners were taken aback at this breach of etiquette and chief Shiri, in order to save face, addressed himself to the district officer's interpreter and asked him to instruct chief Ngara's 'ears', that is his son, that the people of Shiri chiefdom were interested in building a bridge across the river and asked whether chief Ngara would give his people permission to contribute money to the project.

Chief Ngara answered through his son that the plan was new to him; that he had not consulted his people; that the bridge did not concern him; and that, if government and chief Shiri wanted to build a bridge, they should do it without him; they could call the people together for a meeting but he himself was not interested in the project. With these words he took his hat, got up and left the meeting, with a rebuke to his 'son-in-law' for having reached an agreement with a government official without informing him. As soon as chief Ngara had left the meeting the people dispersed and the district officer stood in an empty hall.

The outcome of the meeting soon became common knowledge and chief Shiri was severely criticized for agreeing to build a bridge without consulting anybody. Members of the co-operative society expressed less enthusiasm than the district officer had expected because they were aware that their surpluses were too small to warrant the heavy expenditure on the bridge. Local businessmen were concerned that the bridge would ruin their stores because people would be inclined to visit the town more frequently and bypass them. A teacher asked ironically whether the chief wanted to built a monument to his name, since nobody had any use for a bridge; people had no cars, and bicycles could be carried across the river without a bridge. The people rejected the idea out of hand.

A week after that meeting the district officer called a meeting in chief Ngara's area to explain to the people the advantages they would derive in joining with the people of Shiri chiefdom in the bridge project. He invited both chiefs, and went out of his way to fetch chief Shiri by car, but bypassed the village of chief Ngara. Chief Ngara remained at home and sent none of his sons to attend the meeting. About 130 men, most of them village headmen, assembled. They had been called by the district officer without being given the reason for the meeting. When chief Shiri arrived with the district officer and found that neither chief Ngara nor his representative had arrived, he felt embarrassed, and opened the meeting with the words: '*Majinda*[1] of chief Ngara, I your

[1] *Majinda*: agnates of the chief. Often translated as 'princes'.

son-in-law greet you. I had arranged with the owner of this land to meet you here and I am very surprised that neither he nor his son has come. The district officer and I wanted to ask your help to build a bridge across the river so that our men who have joined the co-operative society can sell their crops at better prices. You know well that store-keepers kill us by paying too little for our crops and by charging too high prices for what they sell us. We want to get fair value for our crops and money and we think that the bridge will help us to obtain this. This European will tell you the details of the bridge. I, your son-in-law, have spoken.'

The district officer then explained that the bridge would cost £4,000 to £6,000 and that the people had to raise £2,000 to £3,000; government would contribute the rest.

At question-time nobody showed interest in the bridge. All pointed to the irregularity of holding a meeting in Ngara chiefdom without the chief's presence. Chief Shiri was heavily criticized for ignoring traditional custom and coming to a meeting in Ngara chiefdom with a European official. One man asked: 'Why do you call a meeting and ask our opinion when the owner of the country is not present?' Another commented: 'Has it ever been heard that our son-in-law has called us to a meeting, arranged by him and a European? Did he not get his land from us? How dare he address us in the absence of our father, chief Ngara?' The last speaker was a young nationalist who wore the symbol of African nationalism, a fur cap. The people grew excited. At this critical moment the district officer called out: 'Why do you want to wait for chief Ngara? This is your meeting. A chief is only there to agree to the wishes of his people. A chief without people is no chief. A chief must always agree to what his people want.'

But the people did not listen to him. What was at stake was not the bridge but the standing of chief Shiri, who was departing from local custom in three ways: he was presiding at a meeting of people in a chiefdom not his own without the authorization of the local chief; he had failed to inform his own people of the project; and he was allowing himself to be used by a government official to implement a policy that was generally rejected in the tribal trust land.

Chief Shiri therefore shouted excitedly: 'Do you think that I am stealing you?[1] No, I honour you as my fathers who gave me and my people our land. Realize that I did not come of my own accord; it is this European who fetched me in his car and brought me here.'

---

[1] This expression means: asking the people to change their allegiance from one leader to another. Cf. *supra*, p. 17.

One man then asked chief Shiri:

'Did you not have a private meeting with seven Europeans at the river?'

'Yes.'

'Did you ever hold a meeting with your own people about the bridge?'

'No.'

'How then can you come and hold a meeting outside your own chiefdom when your own people know nothing about the whole project? I think you have acted wrongly. You have wasted our time and the time of this government official.'

With these words the meeting closed.

A few days later members of the co-operative society held a meeting and expressed their annoyance that they had been blamed for asking for a bridge. Senior village headmen in Shiri chiefdom commented that they did not know how the idea of the bridge had originated and that if chief Shiri wanted the bridge he should pay for it himself. The district officer no longer backed the chief. He informed the research worker that after he had suggested the bridge to chief Shiri the chief began to talk about it as 'his bridge', so that the project looked just as if it sprang from the 'felt needs'[1] of the people.

Finally chief Shiri held a meeting with his village headmen. But his manoeuvres had alienated all his people. He was told that nobody in his chiefdom wanted the bridge, that he had only given his support to the idea because he was paid by the government and dared not oppose the wish of any civil servant. The headmen did not see why they should pay for a new bridge since bridges had always been built by the government in the past.

Realizing his people's strong opposition to community development and his own weakened position in the tribal trust land, chief Shiri informed the district officer that he was no longer interested in the bridge. The district officer also realized that his project would never materialize, and rather than jeopardize any form of community development he stressed in subsequent meetings to village headmen that they should forget about the bridge; the project had been shelved and its papers were already collecting dust. They should rather think of some other need which community development could satisfy.

Soon after these meetings the district officer was promoted to district commissioner and transferred to another province. By 1969 the Shiri

---

[1] Community development agents speak constantly about the 'felt needs' of the people, so as to express the voluntary character of the movement.

and Ngara chiefdoms were still without councils and no community development project had been attempted.

ANALYSIS

(i) Chapter five described the tribal trust land that contains the Shiri and Ngara chiefdoms as a marginally fertile area with a relatively well-educated population, interested in African nationalism.[1] Since African nationalism had condemned community development as a preparation for separate development along the South African pattern, the people readily listened to the teachers' suspicion of the government's new policy. In addition 85 per cent of the people were Roman Catholics, and two active mission stations exerted a strong influence in the tribal trust land. Catholic missionaries too had warned the Karanga against community development because they thought that the government was misusing it for political ends. Consequently Catholic leaders were as suspicious of the new policy as were African nationalists. Under the double influence of nationalist and Catholic leaders, the people were ideologically stimulated to reject the new policy. The first obstacle to community development in the Shiri and Ngara chiefdoms therefore arose from an opposed local ideology.

(ii) The second difficulty arose from the relationship between chief Shiri and the district officer. In a community that was generally critical of government, a chief's close association with a government official jeopardized his own acceptance by his people. Chief Shiri was a weak chief who gained security through association with strong characters. Chapter five[2] illustrated his reliance on a businessman, and his helplessness when he lost his support. The community development campaign showed his dependence on a civil servant and his identification with the latter's plans.[3]

The district officer's disregard for Karanga etiquette and local custom, especially his gross impoliteness to the senior chief, increased the structural difficulties of chief Shiri. He roused the antagonism of the Karanga, but because peasants find it difficult to accuse government officials directly, because of the great social distance between the two groups, they attacked instead the man who had allowed himself to be manipulated, chief Shiri. In stripping the chief of his prestige the people

[1] *supra*, p. 92.
[2] *supra*, pp. 93–94.
[3] He called the bridge project 'his bridge', p. 179.

stripped community development of respectability: in rejecting chief Shiri they rejected the district officer, and in rejecting the district officer they rejected the policy for which he stood, community development. Batten, stressing the close link between an agent and the policy he implements, writes:

> Every time a worker sponsors an idea which the people reject, so he decreases their confidence in himself as a person who is really able to help them. This is true even when he proposes a change that the people reject outright, for in rejecting the change, in effect they are also rejecting him: and if they think him wrong on this occasion they will be all the more ready to think him wrong on others.[1]

By continuing the past directive approach of the ministry of Internal Affairs under the new system of indirect guidance, the district officer gave the people the impression that government policy had not really changed, that the government was not concerned about their 'felt needs' but about the implementation of a new policy. The campaign greatly increased the people's suspicion of the government and led to rejection of the passively conforming chief. Had chief Shiri taken a different stand on the bridge issue, he might have kept his chiefly office.[2]

Throughout the community development campaign in Shiri chiefdom the community adviser remained in the background. People paid little attention to him, because the European civil servant held the stage.[3]

(iii) The question of the financial capability of the people to carry through a community development project was never raised. The question of whether the project would bring economic advantages was brushed aside. The very men who were expected to profit from the bridge, members of the co-operative society, repudiated the idea as unpopular, and businessmen feared for their own shops. The teacher's claim that chief Shiri seemingly desired a local monument to his name showed that people saw no purpose in the bridge. Only outsiders were interested in it: the government, the missionaries, and the purchase-area farmers. Consequently financial considerations did not cause the rejection of community development.

CONCLUSION

The main reasons for the failure to establish a council in Shiri chiefdom

[1] Batten (1965b), p. 2.

[2] Cf. *supra*, pp. 94–96.

[3] Cf. the case history *infra*, pp. 182–187, where the community adviser plays a very important role in the rejection of community development.

were, therefore, firstly, an ideology hostile to the new policy, and secondly the behaviour of the agent of change, which antagonized the local community. As a consequence of the unsuccessful campaign the position of the senior chief Ngara, who completely dissociated himself from the new policy, was strengthened, but the position of chief Shiri, who tried to co-operate, was undermined. Chief Ngara's inactivity supported his people's hostility towards government. Chief Shiri's co-operation ran counter to his people's wishes and fully convinced them that their chief did not stand for their interests but was an agent of the Ministry of Internal Affairs. Community development, which the Minister of Finance called the 'corner stone of Government policy'[1] became the stone which crushed chief Shiri.

(b) *Council proposed to an affluent purchase area*

The Guruuswa community, situated in an area of average rainfall and average soil fertility, is a relatively affluent purchase area because of the industry of its farmers. Most farmers are keenly interested in agriculture and have formed several formal and informal associations to help them increase productivity. In order of importance, these are the African Farmers' Union, which administers the community, co-operative societies, an intensive conservation area committee, and neighbourhood groups in which farmers compete with each other for agricultural excellence. Nearby mines, urban settlements and tribal trust lands provide ready markets for surplus crops. The average farmer has an income of over £200 per annum. Educationally the area is served by three primary schools from a mission in the adjoining tribal trust land.

In addition to these favourable economic and educational conditions the Guruuswa community has a peaceful political record. When nationalists gained many followers and caused local disturbances in neighbouring purchase areas and tribal trust lands, the farmers of this community showed a conspicuous lack of interest in politics. They seemed exclusively concerned with increasing the returns from their farms, and in order to do this they cultivated good relationships with the Ministries of Internal Affairs and Agriculture. Consequently their community was esteemed in civil service quarters for its co-operation. The setting, therefore, seemed propitious for the introduction of community development.

In 1965 the district commissioner informed the farmers through their African Farmers' Union that his department offered them £10,000 for local development provided they formed a local government council.

[1] *supra*, pp. 167–168.

He then explained to them the new policy. To his surprise the farmers rejected the money and refused to form a council. They argued that in the past they had been given an annual sum of money from the African Development Fund to improve their area. This money was derived from compulsory deductions from their agricultural sales. It was called the 'S Vote' and ranged between £1,000 and £2,000 per annum. The farmers expended it on road maintenance, water supplies, and community buildings. They preferred to continue using this money for local improvements rather than to form a council. When they were told that the 'S Vote' would no longer be paid and that unless they formed a council their area would receive no government subsidies for development, they showed bitter resentment of this form of indirect compulsion.

A few months later a community adviser was sent to their community. He lived in some wattle and daub huts near the extension assistant's house but was never formally introduced to the farmers. He accompanied the extension assistant on his regular duties and attended all agricultural meetings in order to learn the attitudes of the people; he made friends with them at beer drinks and visited them in their homes. Since he never identified himself people took him to be a member of the agricultural extension staff. Whenever farmers asked him: 'What is your real work?', he answered: 'I am here to help you if you have any difficulties.' The farmers were puzzled as to how the government could pay a salary to a man who did nothing but visit farmers, ask them about their troubles, and attend meetings. Some suspected that he was linked with community development.

In 1966 the district commissioner held another meeting and informed the farmers that he was still holding their £10,000. If they did not form a council immediately he had to return the money to the government. The community adviser attended the meeting but did not join in any discussion. Though some farmers seemed to show interest in the new policy the majority told the district commissioner that they were opposed to community development. A second meeting was arranged to enable those who were interested in the new policy to speak freely without being intimidated by the majority. At this meeting the district commissioner suggested that further meetings be held during which the farmers could consult his assistant, the community adviser, on the full meaning of community development. This was the first time that the community adviser's identity was publicly stated. This revelation caused surprise and annoyance among the farmers, and those who had established friendship with the community adviser came under heavy attack from their neighbours.

The community adviser organized another meeting, which aroused loud opposition. He tried to explain community development, and read relevant extracts from the Prime Minister's directive, but he was repeatedly interrupted with the words: 'Why should we try to understand something we are not interested in?' Whenever a farmer who sympathized with the new policy tried to speak, a chorus interrupted him with ironical remarks. Finally an old farmer stood up and said: 'Look at this young man: he is our son;[1] we educated him and now he is selling us to government. Our sons forget their duty to rescue us from dangers. They are interested in nothing but money and their own well-being.' After seven hours the disorderly meeting came to an end. As the people dispersed a diviner and leading farmer exclaimed: 'I stand by our fore-fathers, fellow-men; you all know me. Anyone who agrees to form a council will experience misfortune. If he should consult other diviners, let him know that my magic will be stronger.' Many ordinary farmers approved of his statement and added: 'We shall use our axes to get rid of community-development supporters.'

Opposition to community development was kept alive by discussions at beer parties, agricultural meetings and social festivities. Those who desired a council stayed away from all social functions for fear of their neighbours.

Meanwhile the community agent approached the chairman of the African Farmers' Union, the only coloured man[2] in the area, respected by Africans and Europeans alike. He suggested to him that as an influential man and progressive farmer he was likely to obtain a high position in the council, especially since he had been both divisional and branch chairman of the African Farmers' Union since the inauguration of the purchase area. After many discussions the chairman became convinced that community development would bring advantages to the purchase area and that a refusal to establish a council would seriously hinder economic progress. This consideration, not that of his own promotion, finally prompted him to support the council idea. He therefore approached those farmers who were favourably disposed toward community development. He reasoned with them that the local roads had already deteriorated to such an extent that the transportation of their produce was becoming difficult. He considered that the majority of farmers were neutral towards the new policy and that strong opposition was engineered by only a few vocal farmers. He advised them that

---

[1] That is, a member of a younger generation, irrespective of kinship ties.

[2] In Rhodesia the word 'coloured' refers to a person of racially mixed parentage, usually the child of a European father and an African mother.

if they themselves were convinced of the advantages a council would bring, it was their duty to win supporters among their neighbours. The men followed his advice and collected the signatures of twenty-seven farmers who favoured the introduction of a council. They represented 18 per cent of the whole community.

Thereupon the chairman called a general African Farmers' Union meeting. But his conversion to community development had aroused such antagonism that the meeting was boycotted by all except the twenty-seven farmers. At the meeting it was decided to invite the district commissioner and ask him whether a council could be started for twenty-seven farmers. The district commissioner attended the next meeting, but as he began to explain community development one of the dissenting farmers shouted: 'District commissioner, you are acting contrary to the constitution of the African Farmers' Union. You hold a meeting which does not have our approval. We are absolutely opposed to forming a council, and we shall never accept it.' The man was immediately led out by the district commissioner's messenger. When the district commissioner asked the farmers why twenty-seven of them wanted a council, he was told that they were concerned about the roads, which were becoming impassable. He replied that this was not sufficient reason for forming a council; that the support of 18 per cent of the community was too small to justify it; and that they should try to win more supporters. He promised to help them by arranging a tour for thirty local men to visit a well-functioning purchase area council.

Soon after these events the annual meeting for the election of office-holders on the African Farmers' Union committee had to take place. After ten years' service as chairman the coloured man failed for the first time to be re-elected. The new chairman was a man who opposed community development and therefore enjoyed a large measure of support among the farmers. About this time the ex-chairman realized that he was suffering from tuberculosis, and he retired from an active part in the affairs of the community.

For the visit to a successful council area the district commissioner instructed the community adviser to choose those men who strongly opposed community development. The community adviser found this task difficult. For two months he visited farmers, promising them a wonderful trip with 'free food, free beer, free accommodation and free transport'. At one stage he had collected a list of fifteen men who promised to accompany him; the rest refused. Yet even these fifteen were not all volunteers. Often the community adviser approached a farmer with the words: 'Your name is on the list; you have to go on the trip.' The number fluctuated because those who first agreed to go were told by their friends that their visit would indicate to their neighbours that they had changed their attitude towards the council and had become traitors; and that the trip was considered a means of brainwashing council opposition. Some reasoned however that men of character could suffer no harm; rather they would be exploiting the government, which was paying all the costs of the trip.

At last the community adviser had listed thirty farmers who seemed willing to accompany him on the trip. He informed the district commissioner and the bus was sent. To the great distress of the community adviser, however, only twenty-one farmers stood ready when the bus arrived. The community agent ran desperately into the nearest farmhouse, snatched the farm-owner's blankets and his best clothes, and ordered the wife to fetch her husband immediately. The man was bundled into the bus, which left with twenty-two farmers.

On their visit to the successful purchase area council the farmers were royally feasted and lodged. They were shown all the improvements that the council had brought to its purchase area. They noticed too, however, that their host council was situated in an area with much better soil and a higher rainfall. In spite of this observation the visit convinced a certain number of farmers that the idea of a council might bring advantages to their area.

When the farmers returned home they were greeted with shouts: 'Hello, sell-outs, have you already sold us to government?' The new chairman had stayed at home. He had not been consulted by the district commissioner about the trip and had disapproved of it.

The community development campaign officially came to a close with the final report of the delegation. A public meeting was arranged and the European extension officer, who had no official connection with community development, attended it out of interest. He had a wager with the community adviser that even if members of Internal Affairs failed to convince the people of the advantages of a council, he would succeed. About a third of all the farmers came for the meeting, more than had ever attended a community development discussion.

The delegation enumerated all the successful projects they had seen, such as better schools, better roads, more abundant water supplies and a generally high living standard among the people. One speaker stressed that he had never in his life eaten such good food as on that occasion. After these eulogies the delegates came to speak about the financial side of a council, about council rates and levies. The audience listened attentively and finally decided that a council was far too expensive, and that community development was a trick by which government tried to exploit them.

When the extension officer saw that opposition was getting the upper hand he stood up and delivered a long speech, stressing all the advantages a council would bring. He threatened that if the people refused to co-operate all government services, including those of agriculture, would be withdrawn. The people listened in silence and the extension officer thought that he had succeeded where the district commissioner and community adviser had failed.

An enthusiastic supporter of community development then asked the chairman to call for an immediate vote, since a larger number of farmers was attending the meeting than had ever done so before. The vote was taken: twenty-three farmers were in favour of community development and twenty-eight voted against. Since twenty-seven farmers had long ago signed a paper in favour of community development everybody was surprised, and the chairman once more asked those who were in favour of a council to raise their hands. Again only twenty-three hands went up. The extension officer was appalled at what he called local folly, which spends money on beer but not on development. He left the meeting in disgust. He had lost his bet; he too had failed where the district commissioner and community adviser had failed before him.

After the extension officer's departure the chairman concluded that the people had rejected the proposal to form a council and that in the future the purchase area would be administered as in the past. Local hostility to community development had won; nevertheless one farmer concluded apathetically: 'I think that our resolution carries no weight. Whatever Europeans want is always done and therefore, since Europeans want community development, it will be imposed on us.'

In spite of this prediction no council had been established by 1969. In 1968 the community adviser was transferred at his own request. His departure ended the first community development campaign in the Guruuswa community.

ANALYSIS

(i) The total rejection of community development in the Guruuswa community, which had an exceptionally friendly relationship with civil servants because of its eagerness for economic progress and lack of interest in African nationalism, startled local government officials. No ideological barriers seemed to exist to block the propaganda for community development. Nationalism had been rejected by the people themselves, and Christian missionaries had little influence in the purchase area because distance prevented them from visiting it frequently. Nor did conflicts arise through a juxtaposition of values associated with a traditional patriarchal social system and those associated with modern democracy, since the Guruuswa community had from its inception administered itself through a popularly elected committee. The influence of district commissioners and extension officers had always been strong in the purchase area because no chiefs intervened between government officials and the people. In spite of this, opposition was almost violent, and community development supporters were intimidated by their neighbours.

Two main causes led to the failure of the new policy. Firstly, the attitudes expressed by civil servants and the methods they employed roused resentment. Secondly, the civil servants' threat of withdrawing government finance and agricultural assistance unless the farmers conformed to government's request embittered the people. Both causes reveal a deep underlying suspicion among the farmers towards government, a suspicion of which civil servants had been completely unaware.

(ii) A feature to antagonize the farmers was the secrecy which surrounded the community adviser's entry into their area. New civil servants were usually introduced publicly at general meetings, but the community adviser sneaked in. In addition to his surreptitious arrival he antagonized the farmers by his overbearing behaviour. The trip he organized was interpreted by the people as a brain-washing tour. He was rejected by the people as a young educated man who had forgotten his obligations towards his elders, who enriched himself at their expense, and betrayed their interests. The young man's behaviour also drew attention to an opposition between generations: the elders, not as well educated as their sons, felt threatened by a young man who had come to their area as a complete stranger and in a sense replaced them as leaders of the community. The community adviser's position in the purchase area was quite different from the teacher's position in the tribal trust land, because the teachers were related to the local people and their elders relied on them for advice. The teacher stood together with them against government officials, but the community agent stood with the government officials against the people. In Batten's terms, the people rejected the community adviser by rejecting community development. By asking for a transfer to another area he accepted the farmers' rejection of himself.

The leading diviner's threat of supernatural punishment on all who co-operated with the new policy and departed from the ways of their ancestors at first surprised the research worker, since all purchase area farmers had long ago departed from these ways, especially the diviner himself, who was more progressive in modernizing his agricultural techniques than many of his neighbours. The appeal to the customs of their forefathers was not an appeal to revert to traditional ways of life, but a call to oppose a particular modern innovation that threatened to disrupt their accustomed modern way of life.

Just as the people of Shoko chiefdom had recourse in their succession dispute to moral arguments when structural reasons were not accepted, so the farmers of Guruuswa community appealed to intangible supernatural punishment when they had no practical means of punishing those who deviated from popular expectations.

Since there was no chief to mediate between the government and the people the chairman performed the task, and like a chief conforming to government expectations he was rejected by the people and replaced by a man who shared the majority's opposition to the new policy. The democratic administration of the area effectively prevented the introduction of an unpopular policy. The ex-chairman's simultaneous realization that he was suffering from tuberculosis increased the standing of the diviner who had threatened supporters of the new policy with misfortune. Again less tangible sanctions were invoked when ordinary force failed.

(iii) But the economic pressure seems to have been the major cause for the failure of community development. The pressure used by the district commissioner was indirect, though for that reason no less irritating to the farmers. The withdrawal of accustomed development funds threatened the prosperity of their area, and the extension officer's threat that agricultural advice would no longer be given hardened their resentment. They did not know that the agriculturalist's statement was unsupported by any government pronouncement.

Because of the threat of economic sanctions, the farmers rejected community development for economic reasons. They argued that they were financially unable to pay council rates, though objectively their agricultural income was about four times as high as that of the average tribal trust land peasant,[1] and much higher than that of farmers in a neighbouring purchase area which had a council. With an average income of over £200 farmers in the Guruuswa community form the richest community in their neighbourhood.

The hypothesis that economically affluent communities show greater

[1] Cf. *supra*, p. 36.

o

interest in community development than poor communities is not verified by this case study. The campaign for the establishment of a council in Guruuswa community showed that no real trust existed between the people and government officials in spite of a general atmosphere of co-operation and economic viability. In fact, it can be said that their very prosperity made the farmers suspicious of community development, since its announcement coincided with a withdrawal of government aid, just as it had done in the Shiri and Ngara chiefdoms.[1] Like the two tribal trust land communities, Guruuswa purchase area reacted by a total rejection of the new policy.

CONCLUSION

The local details leading to the rejection of community development in the Shiri and Guruuswa communities differed because the communities were differently structured. Yet there are significant underlying similarities. In both cases the people were basically opposed to the new policy, though for different reasons,[2] and this opposition was increased through the actions of government officials, whether European or African.

To be able to resist the pressures exerted by these officials the people in both communities sacrificed their leaders. By siding with civil servants the leaders had become alienated from the expectations of their followers. The two case histories of proposed councils show that by supporting a locally rejected policy, traditional as well as modern leaders risk their position. The final legal authority in the tribal trust lands and purchase areas lies indeed with district commissioners, but the aspirations of the people cannot be ignored. This is the crux of the intercalary position of all African leadership in modern Rhodesia.

3. COUNCILS THAT FAILED[3]

In this section two councils are studied which were established but

---

[1] *supra*, pp. 98–99, 176.

[2] The tribal trust land communities rejected community development because of their idealogy, and the purchase area community because of the threat of economic sanctions.

[3] Another well-documented council which failed·is that of Mangwende, a Rhodesian chiefdom outside Karangaland. In Mangwende the failure of the council was due to a clash between the people and their chief on the one hand, and successive district commissioners on the other. The failure was caused by the Africans' unwillingness to spend their money as the district commissioners thought most advantageous, rather than according to their own priorities. See Holleman (1968), especially pp. 247–251.

either never functioned, or after a number of years closed down. The reason is that 'what is legal is not always real; the actual facts may be bound up in personalities, social organizations, economic conditions and political movements'.[1] Legally established councils, therefore, may not always be functioning councils, as even the Secretary for Internal Affairs observed.[2]

The two councils discussed in this section failed for different reasons. The first council was unable to operate effectively from its beginning because it was imposed on the people against their wishes by a chief who did not understand the implications of community development, and the second was closed down after more than ten years because the purpose for which it had been founded had been achieved.

(a) *Council of an actively conforming pro-government chief*

Chief Shoko's struggle for power has been analysed in the social drama presented in chapters six to eight,[3] and attention has been drawn to the chief's utter dependence on European support. This dependence explains chief Shoko's attitude towards community development.

In early 1967 chief Shoko was approached by the district commissioner during one of the latter's regular visits to Shoko chiefdom, and was asked to form a council. The district commissioner stated that most of chief Shoko's neighbours had formed local government bodies and that his chiefdom was the only one that had not yet complied with the new government policy. Chief Shoko showed great interest in the policy, complimented the district commissioner on his concern for his people and assured him that his people would welcome community development. The district commissioner expressed great appreciation of the chief's confidence that he knew and controlled his people. He offered to take local delegates to a well-functioning council in the province so that the people could convince themselves of the advantages of local government. The chief agreed to send a delegation to a council chosen by the district commissioner and appointed Japheth (J7), the leader of the Shoko Museamwa community, as one of the delegates. The tour took place without any local opposition.

When the delegation returned the chief called Japheth (J7) for a private interview. He asked him to relate all he had seen in the visited chiefdom to a certain number of village headmen and to urge them to establish a

[1] Alderfer (1964), p. 93.

[2] *supra*, p. 24. According to the Secretary for Internal Affairs' Report there were six non-functioning councils in 1964.

[3] Cf. *supra*, pp. 106–165.

local council. Japheth (J7) however refused at first to address a select group; he claimed that a council concerned all the people of the chiefdom and that a public and open meeting ought to be called. But the chief argued: 'It is useless to call all the people together. I have chosen the men who will meet with us again when we put our findings before the district commissioner. To address many people causes much opposition. The few will represent the many.'

Japheth (J7) obeyed the chief's order and gave his report to a select group of village headmen. During question time people raised the following issues:

(1) It was difficult to agree on any project when many people were involved, so could each village form its own council? The chief answered that this was against government policy.

(2) Would a council enable the government to raise rates and levies on all property, including such minor items as carts, fowls and cooking pots? The question went unanswered.

(3) Would the people be allowed to give up the council if they found that it imposed too heavy a burden on them? The chief answered that it would be unwise to give up a council because a council gave them local independence; a rejection of the council would equal a rejection of self-rule. He added that if all Africans in Rhodesia were to refuse councils Europeans would write to Great Britain to inform them that Africans refused to rule themselves and that they were politically immature. A close agnate of the chief stressed that if they refused a council, neighbouring chiefs who had established council would swallow up their land and give it to their own people so that people of Shoko chiefdom would be landless.[1]

Japheth (J7) raised another issue: 'Our people, especially those of the Shoko Museamwa community, are afraid that if we form a council the chief will control everything we do. However, I have seen that in the council area we visited the chief could do nothing against the wishes of his people.' A village headman explained: 'What we are really afraid of is that if we village headmen agree to form a council our people will beat us up, because they are opposed to community development.' The chief reassured him that any commoner who beat him would be arrested; moreover because a council would bring economic advantages to the

---

[1] No such statement has ever been made by government officials. The argument shows how members of the chiefly family were quick to invent reasons to back a government proposal. Also chief Shoko's reference to international politics seems incongruous against the background of the locally focused succession dispute, which occupied the people of the chiefdom for over twenty years.

area through making government grants available to the people, the people would be pleased with their leaders once they received the first benefits from the new policy. Another village headman commented: 'The delegation was sent to a very fertile area. In our chiefdom we experience frequent droughts and are quite unable to raise the money necessary for council projects. Chief, you are endangering the well-being of your people by introducing a council.'

The chief was angered by this criticism and ordered his messenger to remove the speaker immediately from the assembly; he shouted: 'We should not fear pressure from our people. We are their representatives and they have no option but to agree to our decisions. We do not need to ask the district commissioner to explain to us the real meaning of a council. All we have to do is to tell the district commissioner that we accept it. I therefore ask for a vote.' When only eight out of twenty-nine village headmen[1] voted in favour of a council, the chief asked the remaining twenty-one headmen individually whether they really objected to a council. Through this personal questioning eight more indicated some agreement, though thirteeen still objected strongly.

The chief declared that since the majority had accepted a council those who opposed it were forbidden to attend future meetings on community development. Three of the eight headmen who agreed under pressure later admitted that they had only agreed because they were striving for a subchieftainship; they feared that if they opposed the chief their promotion would be in jeopardy.

The ordinary people of the Shoko Murewa community were opposed to forming a council. When their headmen informed them of the decision they declared that they would rather be imprisoned than live in a council area. Members of the Shoko Museamwa community, whose leader had given the report and whose area is much more fertile, were less strongly opposed to a council.

A week later the chief took the village headmen who favoured a council to see the district commissioner. The district commissioner briefly explained to them how a council should work:

'Your chief has to choose certain village headmen to form a council, and these will meet regularly each time I come to visit your area. I shall at times attend your council meetings. The councillors ought to be men who always agree with what the chief suggests. They may not raise opposition to the chief because a council is there to support the chief.

[1] Twenty-nine headmen represent less than half of the village headmen in the chiefdom.

The council must work hand in hand with the chief's *dare*.[1] No matter may be raised in the council which has not first received the *dare*'s approval. The reason is that the chief has to remain your head and the guardian of your customs. You may not forget your customs.'

He then explained that parliament had adopted community development as government policy and had decided to withdraw all aid from any area which did not form a council. He stressed that missionaries too had been warned not to provide additional educational facilities, because the people had to develop their own areas. He concluded that community development was a serious undertaking, that people should expect many problems in its early stages, but that if they persevered they could achieve many goals.

The district commissioner then asked the people whether they really wanted a council. Nobody raised an objection, and the chief stated that there was no local opposition to community development. The district commissioner congratulated the chief on achieving such unanimity among his people.[2]

The chiefdom was subsequently divided into six wards; each ward included approximately ten villages. The people of each ward were asked to elect two councillors. The chief advised local leaders[3] to nominate only those who would always agree with them. Consequently all but two councillors were either brothers or sons of senior village headmen or agnates of the chief. The two unrelated councillors were local businessmen. The villagers objected to the nominations and demanded a democratic election. They claimed that only if every man voted for the councillors would intelligent men be appointed. They objected to a local government staffed by the supporters of the chief. Their request was ruled out of order by the district commissioner and chief as being contrary to Karanga custom.

The council chairman, a minister of religion, was a close relative and supporter of Japheth (J7). Fifty years of age, he was slightly older than the other councillors, who were only in their thirties and forties. He had also received a longer education than the rest, who had attended school for only four to seven years: he had studied for ten years. As a minister

[1] The *dare* is the traditional council of a chief, consisting of his close agnates. Cf. *supra*, p. 172.

[2] It is worth noting that throughout the meeting the district commissioner and chief sat in the shade on the verandah of the district commissioner's office but all the people sat in the sun. The district commissioner spoke the African language in a very broken manner and the people felt very tired.

[3] Senior village headmen; cf. *supra*, p. 47.

of religion he followed a profession which carried prestige. Most of the other council members were peasants, apart from the local businessmen.

After their appointment the councillors were summoned to a three days' training course near the district commissioner's office. There they received two contradictory sets of instructions. The district commissioner reminded them of the Karanga custom that any villager who had a request ought to bring it to his village headman, the headman to the subchief, and the subchief to the chief. This custom was to be preserved under community development. Consequently no item might be debated by the council which had not first received the approval of the chief's *dare*. Simultaneously the district commissioner issued the councillors with booklets setting out their rights and duties. Among these was listed the councillor's duty to visit the members of his ward in order to learn from them what development projects they wanted, and then to raise their wishes at the next council meeting.

The chairman took his duties seriously and visited his ward members to find out their needs. He learned that they suffered greatly from water shortage. The chief heard of his questions and at the next council meeting issued him with a stern warning when he put forward the requests of his ward members for water supplies. The chief reminded him of the district commissioner's instructions that all topics discussed at the council ought to have the *dare*'s approval, and he rebuked him for defying chiefly authority by making independent enquiries of local needs. Chief Shoko explained: 'A council is like a son whom his father sends to plough a field. If the plough breaks down the son has to report the fact to his father and his father will see to the repair. You likewise may do nothing without my consent.' From that day onward councillors dared not talk to the people of their wards about new projects, nor did they raise any matters at council meetings. They waited to ratify what the chief put before them.

Meanwhile the chief's *dare* drew up council rates, worked out a budget and presented a list of projects to the council for debate and ratification. The projects included a clinic, a new road, a beer garden and two boreholes. The councillors had various opinions. Some argued that a nearby mission hospital sufficiently covered their needs and that bore-holes only profit small groups of villages. The most vehement discussion arose over the beer garden. People from the Shoko Museamwa community argued that it should be erected in their area because the Shoko Murewa community was far away from any main road and no money from the outside would be attracted; their own area, on the other hand, was traversed by a main road, which carried many buses to various towns and tribal trust lands, so that a beer hall near a bus stop would bring in the largest amount of cash from outsiders. Councillors of the Shoko Murewa community however argued that most men in the Shoko Museamwa community were practising Seventh Day Adventists and were forbidden to drink beer, whereas members of the Shoko Murewa community were less fervent Christians and regularly attended beer drinks. The beer hall ought then to be built in their area to serve local needs. When no agreement could be reached the chief stood up and said: 'I am the vice-president of the council and I now give the final decision: there must be a clinic and a road and a beer garden, and the beer garden must be situated in the Shoko Murewa community where I live. The bore-holes which the Shoko Museamwa community requests are not necessary.' The chief asked the secretary to put these decisions in writing and then went with the secretary to the district commissioner to inform him of the council's decisions.

While waiting outside the district commissioner's office chief Shoko met other chiefs who had come to town for the same purpose. When he saw that the other chiefs had prepared much longer lists of proposed projects he asked his secretary to add the two bore-holes for the Shoko Museamwa community to their own list of requirements. He then submitted the list to the district commissioner and was told that the government would be willing to make an advance of £400 to help the people on their first project.

From this moment onward the council activities came to a standstill. The chief forgot to recall his *dare*, and without the approval of the *dare* the councillors could not meet. One month the district officer visited the chiefdom unexpectedly on council day. He found that the chief was not at home. The councillors told him that in the chief's absence they were forbidden to hold a meeting. They added that the district commissioner's arrangement, which made the council dependent on the chief's *dare*, had 'killed' it. The district officer was greatly annoyed and sent a messenger to fetch the chief. When chief Shoko heard of the district officer's displeasure he came running home and arrived perspiring and breathless, trying to apologize. The district officer took him aside and rebuked him for the inactivity of his council. The chief called a hurried meeting of his councillors, but the district officer drove off in anger before the meeting started. The chief told his councillors that their council had received a bad reputation because it had achieved nothing. He therefore suggested that a general meeting be called to instil new life into the council. The secretary approved the calling of a meeting of all the people, but the chief insisted that a 'general meeting' consisted of those headmen whom he selected. Finally a compromise was reached and all village headmen of the chiefdom were invited.

The 'general meeting' took place in 1968, a year after the council had started. The chief opened the meeting with general announcements about rural administration, which the district commissioner had made at the previous provincial assembly of chiefs. He exhorted his people to follow good agricultural techniques, to stop drunkenness and to observe the days of rest in honour of the ancestors. He concluded: 'I am your representative, and I dislike it if you get unwittingly into trouble. I know all that the district commissioner wants because I visit him frequently. Some of you say that I am a bad chief because I have allowed you to plough land in grazing areas; but remember that your village headmen always come to me for land. You have only yourselves to blame.

And now I come to today's business. Our council is totally under my *dare*. It is only there to do what the *dare* decides. I am your god, and you village headmen are the gods of your people. This is how authority works.'

He then announced when the council rates had to be paid, and dismissed the meeting. The village headmen wondered why they had been called. They had not been given the chance to ask a single question.

The chiefdom as a whole submitted to community development. In spite of the initial strong reaction the villagers paid their council rates. Another year passed and no action was taken by the council to implement any of its proposed schemes. The secretary became frustrated in his forced inactivity.[1]

ANALYSIS

(i) The difficulties in establishing a council in Shoko chiefdom varied greatly from those in Shiri chiefdom. No opposition arose from nationalist or religious leaders, yet the people resented community development as strongly as others had done who could fall back on an opposed ideology. Preceding chapters have shown that leaders of Shoko chiefdom were orientated towards the past. The district commissioner's emphasis that councils should continue their past traditions confirmed the chief's authority.

The district commissioner's influence was strong and accepted by the people because they were used to appealing to him for help in times of drought and during their succession dispute. Most people in the chiefdom regarded district commissioners as powerful father-figures, and the constant backing which commissioners received from their head office in

[1] After Joab (J12) was replaced by his younger brother Joachim (J13), the council became active and by 1971 had completed several projects.

the capital gave the people the impression that district commissioners were indeed very powerful men. Consequently the people tried to co-operate with them. Their predisposition to comply with Government orders ought to have made the introduction of community development a smooth process.

(ii) Unlike the civil servants in the previous case history, the local district commissioner acted tactfully. He did not force the idea of community development on the people, but made them aware of the difficulties involved and left the final decision to them. In fact, no great campaign for community development was started as was done in the Shiri and Guruuswa communities. The district commissioner used his ordinary meetings with the people to acquaint them with the new policy after he had settled matters of routine administration. There was no need for pressure, since the chief was so totally dependent on government support that he could not but regard even a suggestion as binding.

And yet the district commissioner's action was decisive in the failure of the council. The reason was that he crystallized the conflict inherent in the establishment of any council between modern democratic procedures and those based on the traditional patriarchal system. No case history highlights this opposition more clearly than that of Shoko chiefdom. The crucial incident in the establishment of this council was the meeting in which the district commissioner gave his instruction to the council members: their council was to be subject to the chief's *dare*, and was unable to act without the full consent of all officials in the traditional hierarchy of authority, yet its members were to proceed as democratically elected office-bearers, sounding out the opinions of their ward members.

The ages of the council members show that they were younger than the men attending the chief's *dare*; their education too was slightly above average and three of them followed modern occupations.[1] Consequently they represented a more progressive section of the chiefdom than the *dare* members, and to subordinate them to their elders was bound to arrest progress.

This conflict was emphasized at every stage of the council's history. The people clamoured for a democratic election, but the district commissioner and chief insisted on the nomination of loyal supporters. This shows that the people of Shoko chiefdom were less orientated towards the past than their government-supported leaders. Even Japheth (J7), the leader of the opposition to the ruling family, who more than any other man had insisted on customary procedure during the succession

[1] *supra*, p. 194.

dispute, favoured a democratic council.[1] It would provide him with a chance to increase his influence. The people as a whole therefore were ready for bureaucratic administration,[2] but those with vested interests in the patriarchal system resisted it. The conflicting norms by which the councillors were asked to act paralysed them. The council might have achieved some success had not every endeavour to follow bureaucratic procedures been blocked by a recall to patriarchal norms. After all, the people did submit to the council, and paid their rates.

Apart from these conflicting norms that councillors had to reckon with, the chief's own attitude caused the council to falter. Preceding chapters have shown that chief Shoko gained the office through the help of European friends, not through the support of his own people. His dependence on outside support was so strong that he compulsively conformed to all government demands in order to retain government support. Consequently at the district commissioner's first announcement of community development he gave an *ad hoc* approval in the name of his people, and complimented the district commissioner on his efforts to foster the well-being of the Karanga.

At the same time chief Shoko insisted on patriarchal norms, and enforced them in a bureaucratic manner. He taught his village headmen how to override the wishes of their people and how to force them to obey their authority. His insistence on delegated authority by which even his village headmen became 'gods', independent of the consent of their followers, was contrary to the patriarchal system. In a moderate form unquestioned subordination characterizes bureaucratic relations, but not those of the traditional Karanga system.[3] As a bureaucrat the district commissioner instructed traditional rulers that the obedience of their subjects was the foundation of their power. This inversion of traditional values suited the chief but it roused the resentment of his followers.

The consequence of this travesty of Karanga customs was that while the district commissioner was ostensibly trying to increase the chief's authority he was in fact undermining it. The people awaited the chief's commands in apathy and obeyed them with repressed hostility. While the chief enjoyed the approval of the district commissioner, he lost the confidence of his people.

[1] *supra*, p. 192. Note the different values stressed by both Japheth (J7) and the chief in this issue and during the succession dispute. This shift proves that members of both factions are gamblers. Their choices of values and techniques are determined by the likely success they will achieve in the power game.

[2] See footnote p. 197.

[3] Contrast the district officer's argument in Ngara chiefdom that a chief must always agree with his people's wishes.

The chief's compulsive conformity to government orders became ᴉ obvious not only in the methods by which he imposed the council on his people but also by the way in which he directed council meetings. He determined which projects were to be attempted and excluded, or included items as he thought fit.[1] In the past Karanga chiefs had consulted their people. A vice-president of a democratic council had even less right to impose his will on his fellow councillors.

Had chief Shoko been a capable and enterprising man he might still have succeeded. His inactivity once the council had been established showed that he was in fact less interested in community development than his people. He was concerned that the district commissioner's orders be fulfilled to the letter, though their meaning was not clear to him. His implicit compliance with orders showed that he had internalized some bureaucratic norms, but the full implication of bureaucratic administration evaded him. This incomprehension was partially due to the district commissioner's own reluctance to sponsor democracy in the chiefdom.

(iii) Economic factors seem to have had little impact on the failure of the council. The Shoko Museamwa community, more prosperous than the Shoko Murewa community, showed greater interest in community development, but this may have been due to their confidence in their leader Japheth (J7). The people objected to the new policy and saw it as a government ruse to extract money from them; yet all paid their rates when ordered to do so. Local ability to finance community projects seems therefore to have been of secondary importance.

CONCLUSION

The two main reasons for the failure of community development in Shoko chiefdom are, firstly, the direct confrontation of patriarchal and democratic institutions brought about by the district commissioner; secondly, the chief's inability to initiate and direct local development effectively. This case history presents a paradox: chief Shoko accepts community development against the wishes of his people because as a government chief completely dependent on the administration he cannot do otherwise. Yet it is his people who show greater interest in the council once it is established. The case history of Shoko council illustrates the unwillingness of a patriarchal ruler, influenced by the authority relations of a bureaucratic civil service, to co-operate with his followers in a democratic institution for the development of his area.

[1] *supra*, pp. 195–196.

(b) *Council in an agriculturally stagnant purchase area*

The Mutadza community lives under the same ecological conditions as the Guruuswa community, yet the farm output of its residents is much lower. The reason is that 55 per cent of all farm-owners are over 50 years of age, and more than 28 per cent are 70 years and older. Old age therefore prevents farm-owners from putting heavy work into their farms, and they are not interested in modern farming techniques. The average farmer of the Mutadza purchase area reaps a harvest of less than half the value of his counterpart in Guruuswa. The response by most farmers in Mutadza purchase area revealed that they had bought their farms as an old-age insurance in order to retire from a life of labour migration.

Mutadza community differs from Guruuswa community not only economically but also politically and socially. During the time of nationalism its farmers fervently supported the Zimbabwe African People's Union, whose leader gave his last speech on one of their farms before he was restricted. The people frequently disagreed with government officials, and tensions between the community and civil servants were frequent. The police patrol the area more frequently than neighbouring areas. Associational life is at a minimum. Though Mutadza purchase area is only a third of the size of Guruuswa purchase area, it is socially divided into two groups, which are separated by a mountain ridge; no co-operation takes place across this ridge. Apart from a struggling co-operative society no formal associations exist except the compulsory African Farmers' Union and the council. The African Farmers' Union concerns itself exclusively with agricultural matters and the council with community projects, mainly road and school maintenance.

The local council was formed in 1956, some six years after the people occupied their farms, and was formally established under the Native Councils Act of 1957. The people formed the council for the sole purpose of providing education for their children because mission stations were far away and no school existed in the area. By 1968 the council school provided full primary education. Once the educational need was satisfied people lost interest in their council. It was used by ambitious men who desired local prestige; election campaigns were lively, but once a new chairman had been elected life settled down to its normal routine. Council rates were irregularly collected and council members engaged in frequent disputes with the local district commissioner. Farmers stated that they elected councillors for their ability to argue successfully with government officials.

During 1968 the council went through a crisis when the local secretary absconded with £140. He was arrested, tried and found guilty. But he had spent the money and had nothing with which to repay the farmers. His place was taken by a local man with only eight years' primary education and no knowledge of book-keeping. After some months the council books were in disorder and the auditors sent a warning to the council that unless they had their secretary trained their council would be closed. The secretary agreed to attend a course and the chairman arranged with the district commissioner to accept a government-trained secretary to take over the post until their own man had obtained his qualifications. The chairman failed to inform the councillors of his decision, and when they heard about the arrangement they raised an outcry, saying that their chairman implicitly obeyed government instructions without defending the freedom of his people to act as they wished. They insisted on retaining their untrained secretary.

Another dispute arose when the people collected dip fees from a local cattle-dip built and run by the government, whose fees were consequently to be handed over to the district commissioner. The people refused to part with the levies and threatened to dip all their cattle at the one dip which they had built themselves. The district commissioner threatened legal action if cattle were transferred from one dip to another, because the long cattle tracks would cause serious soil erosion. He warned them that he interpreted their threat as a provocation to force him to close down their council, and that its closure would be to their disadvantage.

By the time of the 1968 council elections the people seriously considered the abolition of their own council. Internal dissension, dissatisfaction with the chairman, inefficient administration, and above all an awareness that their council, long before community development was introduced into Rhodesia, was now regarded as an integral part of the new government policy, brought them to this.

The fatal election meeting was presided over by the district commissioner, who was accompanied by a community adviser and the new secretary. The district commissioner opened the meeting with the announcement that he had come to introduce to the people their new secretary. But before he could speak further several farmers raised their hands and called out: 'Why do you try to deceive us? How can you introduce a new secretary when we have seen him on the chairman's farm for several weeks? He has often accompanied the community adviser. Why is there now a community adviser in our area? Our council was established long before government thought of community development. Who of us has given you permission to replace our present secretary by a new one? We have not been consulted about these innovations and we object.' The chairman felt embarrassed, but was helped by the district commissioner, who declared: 'Either you accept the new secretary for one year or I shall dismiss your old secretary permanently.' This settled the first point on the agenda.

The district commissioner then talked privately with the chairman, and after receiving some instructions the chairman announced that the district commissioner had come to preside over the election for the new councillors, but that he insisted on the council rule that only those men were to vote who had paid the council rate.[1] At these words the farmers protested and demanded that every man be given a vote. One farmer stood up and declared that very few men in the community had paid their council rate and that those who had paid were not even present. The district commissioner tried to meet the people half way and suggested that all those could vote who promised to pay their arrears. But the farmers shouted in chorus: 'No one shall vote unless all are allowed to vote.' At this the district commissioner became annoyed and said: 'Either you want a council or you do not want it. If you no longer want your council, say so openly. There are several councils which I ought to visit; in giving you the preference I have neglected others for no good reason. Obey the rules.' The people murmured: 'We are being forced; we shall never obey rules which we resent. Why did you come if you knew you were more welcome elsewhere? Go, we do not want to be suppressed.' As the district commissioner left the hall with the community adviser and the new secretary, the people shouted after him in chorus: 'Go, go, go.'

ANALYSIS

(i) The Mutadza purchase area can be viewed as a truncated tribal system without a chief and without kinship obligations binding the farmers into a real community. Its people lacked the support that traditional values provide. No modern values had as yet been adopted by the ageing population, whose only interest in the purchase area was that it provided for their old age.

The Mutadza council failed after ten years, during which it had operated reasonably well. It had the advantage of having started long before community development became government policy and so was

[1] Native Councils Act, 1957; NAD-Form Service Information Sheet, No. 7 (1961), p. 5.

not directly affected by the negative associations which the word acquired all over Karangaland. The local ideology of opposition to government, inherited from nationalist days, consciously provoked the council to criticize government officials and policies. The government's contention that 'national politics play no part in local elections, and there are no local parties'[1] does not hold for the Mutadza community. Nationalist sentiments strongly influenced the election in Mutadza purchase area and dominated the council's activities.

The final failure of the council was due to its association with a government policy which the people rejected. The strongly nationalist-inclined population of this community had used its council to express dissatisfaction with government. Once they realized that their council conformed to government policy they repudiated it violently.

(ii) The district commissioner was seen as the embodiment of a government that denied the people freedom, and therefore he became the target of attack. He showed his power by forcing people to use the government-built cattle dip. But he lost when he stipulated that the council be run on efficient bureaucratic lines. The people thought they no longer needed the council, because the purpose for which it had been founded had been achieved.[2] Local crises, such as thefts of funds, change of secretary and the introduction of a community adviser provided the external occasion to close a council which had become redundant. Unlike the people in Shiri chiefdom, who rejected a government official indirectly by rejecting their chief, farmers of Mutadza purchase area openly encouraged the district commissioner to leave their area. They wanted to abandon their council, but forced the district commissioner to close it for them. It was a struggle for power. Outwardly the civil servant had supreme authority. In reality he acted according to the dictates of the people.

As with the leaders in all preceding case histories of councils, so the leader of the Mutadza was criticized for co-operating with the district commissioner. The closure of the council prevented an election to test whether he had lost his popularity to such a degree as to be replaced by another. His role no longer existed.

(iii) Economic considerations played no part in the failure of the Mutadza council. Though its farmers were poor in relation to farmers in the Guruuswa purchase area, they had run their own council adequately for ten years. The initial success of the council was due to the

---

[1] NAD-Form Service Information Sheet, No. 7 (1961), p. 5.

[2] They did not realise that once their council was abolished, their school would be closed. Their school was closed in 1969.

common aim of the farmers to establish a school for their children. As years passed the farmers were still able to unite in opposition to the district commissioner, but unable to unite for a community project. Their group lacked cohesion, and poverty increased their sympathy towards African nationalism and dissatisfaction with the European government.

CONCLUSION

The Shoko and Mutadza councils failed, but they failed for different reasons. Shoko council had been imposed by the chief against the people's will, and once imposed their co-operation was forbidden. The chief himself 'killed' the council through his inefficiency. Mutadza council had been started by the initiative of the people because they wanted to achieve a common purpose. It was 'killed' by its association with government policy. As in the case of councils that failed to be established, councils that were established foundered partly because of the attitudes of civil servants. In each case local leaders were defeated with the defeat of the council itself.

P

CHAPTER 10

Successful Community Development

1. INCIPIENT COUNCILS

Functioning councils can be subdivided into two categories: those that have just been established and show signs that indicate future success, and long-established councils that have proved themselves successful. Incipient councils may have been established with or without the consent of the people. If they have attempted or even achieved certain community projects this activity has been taken as a sign of probable success in the future. Whether a chief is pro- or anti-government, he has an equal chance of controlling a successful council. However, no successful council has been recorded of a weak government chief who lacked his people's support. Pro-government chief Mhofu succeeded in imposing a council on his people against their will because he was strong enough to override their objections; the anti-government chief Nzou convinced his people that a council would bring them advantages. Both councils were established under the Rural Councils Act in 1967.

(a) *Incipient council of a pro-government chief*

Chief Mhofu's case history has been discussed in chapter five.[1] His chieftainship has never been bothered by succession disputes because the present ruler still stands very close to the founder of the chiefdom. Consequently he is strongly backed by the traditional system.

In 1966 the district commissioner held several meetings in Mhofu chiefdom to which all the people were invited. He explained to them the new policy of community development, but the people showed no interest. Because the strongest opposition came from ordinary villagers the district commissioner suggested to the chief that further meetings be held for village headmen only and that commoners be excluded. When the people heard that their headmen went alone to attend meetings on community development they urged them not to agree to the new policy; some even added that if the headmen were to agree the council would be a council of village headmen, but not a council of the people. At first the headmen supported their people's request and refused to form a council.

[1] *supra*, pp. 77–80.

The chief became irritated at their opposition and threatened to depose all village headmen who objected to community development and appoint others who would obey his directive. Many headmen took fright and sat silently through further discussions. The chief took their silence[1] as consent. He asked the district commissioner to send some of the local village headmen to visit a well-functioning council to convince them of the advantages of community development. The tour was arranged and the ministry of Internal Affairs paid the expenses. As in the case of delegates in the previous chapter, they were impressed with the achievement of the council they visited but they too noted that it was situated in a much more fertile area. They gave a favourable report on their return, and the chief thought that they would agree to form a council. The villagers however were still opposed to a council, and when the headmen were again called for a meeting with the district commissioner and chief, the people instructed them to vote against a council.

The district commissioner presumed that the people had agreed to form a council, and proceeded to give final instructions. The headmen sat in silence. Finally one of them got up, clapped his hands respectfully to the chief and addressed him by his kinship term: 'My sister's son, it is absolutely necessary that you should understand your own people. Our silence means opposition. All of us reject community development.' He sat down and the district commissioner, ascertaining that the man had expressed the general feeling of the meeting, left, saying that he was not interested in the development of Mhofu chiefdom; economic and social progress were to be matters of local concern.

The district commissioner's departure disturbed the chief. He deposed his mother's brother as village headman and threatened to remove in like manner all headmen who opposed community development. Several headmen, afraid of losing their positions, suggested that the district commissioner be recalled and a council constituted. The chief took money from his own purse and sent a delegation to the district commissioner to invite him for a final meeting. At this meeting the council was established. Everybody agreed; no criticism was raised.

The area was divided into six wards, each consisting of some ten to fifteen villages. The councillors from each ward were appointed by the local village headmen. No villagers raised opposition to the appointments, which were made on the basis of the councillors' past co-operation with their chief and village headmen, their abstention from nationalist politics, and their general esteem in the community. Education was

[1] *supra*, p. 83.

considered unimportant except in the case of the chairman. A government-trained secretary was sent by the ministry of Internal Affairs and the people paid £10 towards his monthly salary of £30. The government paid the rest.

The council was gazetted in 1967 and was made a grant-in-aid by government to start the first project, a clinic, which all the people urgently desired. But immediately problems arose. The people had been promised that once they had established their council they could collect the local dog tax and take over cattle-dipping, which would entitle them to collect the dip fees. When they asked to take over this service they were told that since the year was already advanced these rights would be handed over to them only in 1968, and that the government would collect the taxes and fees for the current year. If they wanted to make money they could double the dog tax and collect the excess charge. The councillors agreed. By doubling the dog tax and imposing a levy on all land and cattle holders, including widows, the council was able to raise £350 in the first year. But they were unable to construct a clinic because they had first to build a house for their secretary, which cost them £366. The clinic ranked uppermost in their list of priorities for 1969, followed by a beer hall. To cut down costs the people reclaimed a deserted store and hall, once built by the department of Conservation and Extension for agricultural shows, and decided to convert the first into a clinic and the second into a beer hall.

By 1968 the council had its second secretary, because the government auditors of the council's accounts found that the first secretary had embezzled £70. He was convicted and imprisoned.

The people submitted silently to the imposition of the council and paid their rates regularly, though with resentment. Whenever they brought their contributions to the secretary they said: 'Here is your money', and when the secretary tried to convince them that it was not his personal money but that he brought it to the council's bank account in town, they did not believe him. One man commented: 'Our money is for the secretary and government. In recent times they call government "saving bank", but it is still government.' Because in the local town the bank is opposite the office of the ministry of Internal Affairs people believe that all their contributions go to the government. The general belief is that the council belongs to the district commissioner, its president; the chief, its vice-president; and the secretary, who gets part of his monthly salary from it.

Through the silent submission of the people public services in Mhofu chiefdom slowly improved.

ANALYSIS

(i) Mhofu chiefdom, with its long history of co-operation with government, seemed ideologically suitable for the introduction of community development. No nationalism has ever alienated the people from their chief or the administration. People and government have worked in harmony, and the people are proud of this record. And yet, like all other communities, the people bitterly resented community development.

(ii) The district commissioner served again as the 'spearhead' of the new policy. He did not use direct pressure, yet he nevertheless compelled the chief to form a council. The chief's embarrassment at his people's opposition implies that he felt bound to carry out the district commissioner's suggestion. The district commissioner's advice that commoners should be eliminated from discussions of community development in order to reduce opposition demonstrated to the chief the government's determination to have councils constituted. He complied with the undemocratic method of winning support for a democratic institution. All along he ignored his people's wishes and followed government instructions. He was a pro-government chief by conviction. Yet government let him down. The refusal to allow his people to collect the local dog tax and dip fees, and the suggestion of doubling the former to raise some funds, roused local resentment. The villagers obeyed, but concluded: 'The council is the council of the district commissioner, of the chief, and of the secretary.' Community development was not their affair. It had been asked for by the government, whose local representative was the district commissioner; it had been accepted and forced on them by the chief, who stood close to the district commissioner; and it provided a living for the secretary through their own contributions. This statement neatly summed up the view of the people. They submitted to community development in silence because they had no alternative. But it remained an alien government policy with which they did not identify themselves.

As in communities in which councils failed, the council of Mhofu chiefdom destroyed local peace because it led to the deposition of the chief's mother's brother as senior village headman. The Karanga regard their mother's brothers with friendly familiarity, and the relationship customarily involves giving advice to leaders. The old man had acted in conformity with local custom and his deposition from village headmanship ran counter to local kinship norms. His deposition offended the people because their chief was known for his insistence on the traditional way of life.

When the people decided against the chief's plan and won the village headmen to their side, they placed the latter in an intercalary position. This freed the chief to side with the administration. Though the headmen sympathized with their people, they could only lose by opposing their chief. Karanga village headmen are generally without education or wealth, and their only claim to public recognition lies in the fact that they are village headmen. Hence they are reluctant to risk their office. In submitting to the chief they increased the chief's prestige, and the chief, in fulfilling his responsibility as a government employee, won the approval of his superiors. Consequently the chief gained from establishing a council both at home and in government circles. This case history confirms the hypothesis that if a leader who is accepted by his people accepts the government policy of community development, community development is likely to be implemented successfully.

(iii) Economic considerations played a minor role in the establishment of Mhofu council. In spite of the initial financial difficulties and setbacks, the people struggled through because they were accustomed to obeying orders.

CONCLUSION

The case history of Mhofu council shows that in a peaceful and relatively uneducated community, which has never shown great interest in modern politics, any new policy can be introduced with a minimum of opposition, given that the chief is won over first and that he has power to force his people into submission. It may be asked, however, whether a council which is forced upon a community through direct or indirect pressures of an administrator qualifies as a local government institution designed to fulfil the 'felt needs' of the people.

So far all case histories of community development have shown strong local opposition. Even the council in the Mutadza community declined rapidly when it was brought into association with community development. Because the feeling against community development is so widespread among rural Karanga, the remaining two case histories of councils are of special importance. They operate with at least a moderate consensus of the people. They reveal certain factors which turn local opposition into support.

(b) *Incipient council of an anti-government chief*
The characteristics of chief Nzou have been described in chapter five.[1]

---
[1] *supra*, pp. 100–103.

Chief Nzou is an educated man whose interests transcend those of his chiefdom. Nevertheless he shares the concern of most traditional office-holders for his own safety. Consequently he suffers from a conflict of interests which imposes a great strain on him. His attitude towards community development reflects his personal dilemma.

Chief Nzou's forced resignation as president of the Chiefs' Council, because he had supported majority rule, reduced his opposition to government policies. He said: 'I shall try to be quiet in order to preserve my position. I have made my views sufficiently clear. I told government officials that people distrust chiefs and that this is the reason why they prefer majority rule to chiefly administration.'

After his resignation several district commissioners approached chief Nzou, suggesting that he should form a council, but both the chief and his people were hostile to community development. In 1966 a new district commissioner arrived and called a general meeting in Nzou chiefdom, which was attended by the chief, subchiefs, village headmen and commoners, including several women. The chief opened the meeting with the words: 'The district commissioner wants to speak to you about community development. He knows the subject better than I; therefore I have no comment to make. The district commissioner.'

The chief sat down, and the district commissioner gave a long ex-planation of community development. At the end he asked for questions. A subchief stood up and exclaimed at the top of his voice: 'Chief and district commissioner, we, the people of Nzou chiefdom, do not want a council. We are all against it. Some keep quiet for fear of authority but they all think as I do.' At this the people broke into loud cheers and the women ululated. The district commissioner assured them that he would not force a council on them. The chief remained utterly silent. At last the meeting dispersed.

After this initial failure the district commissioner held private dis-cussions with the chief. He also sent leading men to him, especially those engaged in business, to convince him of the benefits that community development would bring to his chiefdom. The most influential per-suader was a neighbouring chief who stood to chief Nzou in the traditional relationship of 'father' by positional succession and who shared chief Nzou's political aspirations. This chief admitted that he had brought himself to form a council because the district commissioner had interfered with his plans to open a clinic, which his people had already started to build. Chief Nzou too had planned to build a clinic with his people and to improve primary schools, and was disturbed to learn that he would not be allowed to proceed with these projects unless he formed a council. To test the neighbouring chief's statement he made official applications to start his community projects, but all were turned down. Chief Nzou bitterly resented the indirect pressure exerted by government. At the same time, however, he was attracted by the large grants of money given to councils. He carefully weighed the pros and cons of community development and finally changed his mind. He called a second meeting with the district commissioner and the people.

When the people had assembled they shouted in chorus: 'We do not want a council.' But this time chief Nzou took part in the discussion. He pointed out that all their development projects had been turned down because they did not have a council; but their neighbours, who had a council, had not only been allowed to proceed with their projects, they had even obtained large government grants. The people persisted, however, in their refusal. The chief saw that no agreement could be reached at that meeting. He asked the district commissioner to leave and to let him discuss the matter privately with his people.

During the following days chief Nzou held informal talks with his close agnates, subchiefs and important village headmen. He asked the subchief who had formally opposed the council in the first meeting to withdraw his statement, pointing out that as a member of the chiefly family he ought to work hard to develop the land of his ancestors. Chief Nzou succeeded in convincing all his leading relatives of the advantages which community development could bring to their land, and asked them to go to their areas and in turn to persuade village headmen and commoners of its usefulness.

Some time passed, and the chief's agnates succeeded in their task. As their reports reached the chief he called for another meeting with the district commissioner, himself, his subchiefs and the village headmen. On this occasion the decision to establish a council was finalized. This decision was announced to the people in a public gathering. The chief declared that the council had already been formed and that no opposition or criticism was acceptable. The people grumbled that the council had been founded in spite of their opposition, but no one dared to oppose the chief openly.

Elections for councillors took place. The chiefdom was divided into its nine school communities, and each school community, consisting of some ten to fifteen villages, elected one councillor. Councillors were chosen by public discussion, and not nominated by the chief or his headmen. At one stage of the election the position of councillor was regarded as regular employment, and preference was given to men with little income. Those with adequate land and several head of cattle were told to give the opportunity to earn some money to their poorer neighbours.

Even the candidature of women was considered. One nominee was a prosperous business woman; she lost the election because the men were reluctant to give a new public office to a woman. No woman had held a public office in their chiefdom in the past, and a combination of two innovations seemed risky to them. Moreover the woman was unrelated to the local people. Since women possess no registration certificates some men expressed fear that she might abscond with the money and nobody would be able to trace her. The business woman was willing to accept the position, and annoyed to be called a 'stranger', since she had lived in the chiefdom for many years; she also felt insulted at the suggestion that she might run away with council money. Yet the very fact that the election of a woman had been considered is outstanding for Karangaland and shows that the people of Nzou chiefdom are more progressive than many of their neighbours.

The composition of Nzou council differed significantly from the composition of Shoko council. A free election was held, and of the nine councillors elected only three were related to the chief. The chief's son was elected chairman; with twelve years' schooling he was the most educated man on the council.

Another councillor was a brother of the chief and a third the chief's sister's son. All the others were unrelated. Outstanding among the 'strangers' were a teacher and a young man in his late twenties. These two, together with the chief's son, were the only councillors who dared to engage in arguments with the district commissioner. The older men were silent, only speaking when they were asked for their opinion. All councillors were married and had several children; that is, they had adult status in their community. The free election in Nzou chiefdom may account for the under-representation of the chief's relatives on the council. Also the people's endeavour to give positions to poorer people excluded the wealthy members of the chief's family, most of whom had larger fields and herds of cattle.

The first friction occurred in the council when the district commissioner as president refused to listen to suggestions by councillors that had not first received the approval of the chief's *dare*. On two occasions the chief himself raised requests. Once he proposed to discuss an educational topic, which the district commissioner turned down because the *dare* had not approved it. Another time the chief pleaded for bilharzia control in his chiefdom, and again the district commissioner refused because the *dare* had not yet considered the scheme. The chief was annoyed at these delaying tactics. On one occasion it was three months before essential stationery could be purchased because the *dare*, consisting of illiterate old men, did not see why things ought to be put into writing. When the council proposed that a typewriter be bought and the *dare* refused, the secretary had to travel regularly to the district commissioner's office to type the minutes; his bus fares came to £4 a month. In exasperation the chief ordered that the typewriter be bought immediately and that the decision of the *dare* be ignored. This caused a breakthrough in council procedures. In the future, whenever the district commissioner asked whether the *dare* had given its consent, the chief answered 'yes', even though the *dare* members knew nothing about the project. The chief and his councillors argued that those serving on the *dare* were only interested in the past, and not in progress. They knew, moreover, that *dare* members were subservient to the district commissioner because they felt inferior to him and did not have the courage to dispute with him.

A *modus vivendi* was therefore found in Nzou chiefdom. Whenever the chief and his councillors agreed on a project, the chief empowered the council to act without consulting the *dare*. The district commissioner was ignorant of this local variation of council procedure in his district, and in this way projects were planned and executed.

Within a year of its establishment Nzou council collected £850 in rates from all land-holders. People did not understand that the money was council rates, thinking that it was a land tax since only land-holders had to pay. Consequently they brought their money as soon as the pay day was announced for fear of losing their right to cultivate. Like the incipient Mhofu council, people in Nzou chiefdom were forbidden to take over cattle-dipping and to collect the dog tax before the next financial year. They calculated that dip fees in their chiefdom would bring in a revenue of £817 and dog tax £275 per annum. People attributed the delay in the grant of this income to government dishonesty, and expressed doubts that they would ever be allowed to collect these levies. Their budget was therefore smaller than they had anticipated, and the distrust between people and government continued.

Within a year of its establishment the council erected a six-roomed prefabricated clinic, which was opened in 1969. The people wanted to build a still larger clinic, but were prevented by a transfer of responsibilities for African health services from the ministry of Health to the ministry of Internal Affairs.

The council planned a second project, but had not completed it by 1969. They wanted to build a beer-garden, from which they expected an annual profit of £145. Many villagers however raised objections on financial and moral grounds. They argued that a certain type of millet suitable for beer sold at 18 shillings a bag in local stores, but when brewed into beer fetched £2 to £3. People feared that once the beer-garden was established most people would buy their beer there and thus deprive local brewers of a steady income. Councillors already planned to pass a by-law forbidding home brews in order to favour the council project. People also thought that a beer-garden at a bus stop would bring in many strangers, who might corrupt local youths and girls. The councillors accepted this objection but promised that the entrance to the garden would be guarded by reliable villagers, who would prevent young men from town disturbing local peace.

As soon as the council was established, chief Nzou launched a vigorous campaign to take over local schools from the African Reformed mission, with the aim of developing lower primary schools into upper primary schools and eventually establishing a secondary school in his chiefdom. This plan too was delayed by the administration, but in 1968 the people were promised that the schools would be handed over to them in 1969.

Within less than two years of its establishment Nzou council had completed one major community project and initiated a second. The driving force behind the council was the chief. The more chief Nzou achieved, the more the ordinary people supported him. By 1969 all but the very old commented approvingly on the activities of their council and were proud of their new clinic.

ANALYSIS

(i) Nzou council is the first of the councils to register success and the approval of its people. There are certain factors that distinguish this council from those previously considered.

Nzou council was established in a strongly nationalistic area, by a chief who was widely known for his anti-government sentiments. He enjoyed the support of most of his younger subjects, and successfully ignored the old who disagreed with him. His strong personality silenced the latter and impressed the former. Consequently the chief's opinion was widely accepted.

(ii) The district commissioner played the same role in Nzou chiefdom as in the other council areas. Through indirect pressure he tried to win the chief's consent. But he could not manipulate chief Nzou. The chief's original silence—a most important weapon which all Karanga know how to interpret—showed his people that he stood on their side. This gave him an initial advantage. Chief and people were opposed to community development and resented the government's refusal to allow them to build their own clinic. But the resentment was shared, and this prevented alienation between chief and people. Unlike chiefs Shoko and Mhofu, chief Nzou tried to convince local leaders, and did not silence them, though he too eliminated popular opposition from time to time. In contrast to the other chiefs, chief Nzou allowed a democratic election of councillors, which guaranteed them wide support. The free election allowed vocal younger men to gain positions on the council.

Free elections and the first successful project of the council won the chief the almost unanimous support of ordinary villagers. The misunderstanding that identified council rates with land taxation guaranteed a fast rate-collection, which in turn facilitated the speedy provision of social facilities. Had administrative difficulties such as the prohibition against collecting dog taxes and dip fees not intervened, progress would have been even faster. But this obstacle bound chief and people still closer together in their opposition to government.

Popular support for the democratically elected council finally enabled chief Nzou to overcome the structural obstacles that the district commissioner had erected by subjecting the council to the traditional *dare*. This undemocratic device, designed to protect the position of the chief under a system which in principle worked against traditional authority, obstructed its purpose. The chief was one of the most progressive men in the chiefdom. As head of the *dare* and vice-president of the council, chief Nzou felt free to make decisions in the name of both. In fact his identification with the council was closer than with his *dare*. Because he was a chief against the wishes of the old people,[1] his position in the *dare* was weaker than his position in the council, on which younger men had a strong voice. It can be said that the council gave a chief who favoured majority rule his first opportunity to work within a more democratic framework and to modernize his chiefdom. The democratic framework, however, did not necessarily guarantee that he acted in a democratic way because his suggestions were generally accepted, though it seems that his suggestions met with approval. His real opponent was the district commissioner. His lies to this civil servant succeeded in satisfying both the people and the administrator. Development became possible.

(iii) Financial considerations played some part. The people had already planned to engage on community projects and knew that they could

[1] He superseded his father's brothers. Cf. *supra*, p. 100.

finance them. Consequently the offer of government grants greatly influenced the chief in starting a council.

CONCLUSION

Three important criteria distinguish Nzou council from those already discussed, and contribute to its success. Firstly, the people of Nzou chiefdom were already conscious of the need for local development and had already planned to build a clinic before community development started. Secondly, the community had confidence in its leadership. This confidence was generated by a long history of resistance on the part of that leadership to government attempts at intervention in community affairs. Thirdly, the chief successfully eliminated the structural obstacle which made the democratic council dependent on the traditional *dare*. This made community development more like what its theorists meant it to be: a concern of the community to improve its material conditions. A progressive anti-government chief led democracy to victory in his chiefdom.

Chief Nzou was the first chief to accept a council without endangering his position. He was never suspected of subservience to government. His circumvention of the district commissioner's order proved his independence of European expectations. He increased his prestige by erecting the first African-built clinic in the tribal trust land.

2. A SUCCESSFUL COUNCIL

The Shumba community was included in this fieldwork after all the other studies had been completed because none of the communities originally chosen had a well-established, well-functioning council. The province in which most of the communities are situated has only two chiefdoms with highly successful councils. The one which was often used by district commissioners to persuade men from other tribal trust lands to establish a council of their own was situated in an exceptionally fertile and high rainfall area, and its inhabitants belong to a different tribal group from the Karanga. Consequently this council was judged unsuitable for comparison. The other council was selected because it was situated in an area sharing the same rainfall and soil conditions with the Shiri, Ngara, Shoko, Guruuswa and Mutadza communities, and similar ones to those of the Nzou and Mhofu communities. People of Shumba chiefdom are Karanga and belong to the same tribal groups as members of the other communities. The Shumba community shares similar educational facilities with most other sample communities, and all denominations operating in other tribal trust lands and purchase areas have followers in the Shumba community. The labour-migration rate of 50 per cent is also typical for Karangaland. Consequently no variables are introduced that distinguish the Shumba people from the other groups.

Shumba council was started as early as 1947, a time when district commissioners were advised to experiment with councils and promised promotion if they succeeded.[1] For many years the council provided local district commissioners with an extra source of money and labour to develop their area; the people themselves were hardly aware how their council operated. The district commissioners, as chairmen, made the development plans and the people agreed. The council, therefore, gave administrators an extra dimension in which to exercise their authority.[2] The council was the council of district commissioners.

This changed in 1958 when a new district commissioner took over the tribal trust land. He was dissatisfied with the way the local council was run, and handed over the chairmanship to an elected Karanga. From 1960 onwards he withdrew even more and encouraged the people to take the council into their own hands and to decide for themselves what they wanted their council to do.

As soon as the district commissioner ceased to direct local development, council activities came to a standstill. For four years no more rates were collected. When the district commissioner did not issue reprimands the people began to realize that the council was really theirs, and not the council of the district commissioner. For the first time they became interested in it and gradually again began to collect rates. At the beginning of 1968 the council had £10,494 in hand, and it seems that the money turnover during the year amounted to about £80,000. One reason for this large sum available to the council was that the council area covers two chiefdoms, which are divided into eighteen subchiefdoms. Consequently the number of people paying rates to the council is very high. In the past the council area was still larger because it included another tribal trust land and a purchase area.

The first council buildings, costing about £150, were erected near the district commissioner's office, but in 1967 the people rebuilt their council in the centre of the tribal trust land on a more lavish scale. Their new council buildings had six rooms, which cost £903. Next to it they erected

[1] Information from a senior district commissioner. Cf. *supra*, p. 14.
[2] Cf. Lee (1967), p. 144, for similar processes in other colonies.

a council-owned bottle store, costing £350, and a beer-garden, costing £400. During 1968 they installed an electric plant worth £42 at the council building. By then the council site had become the social centre of the area. The council also built a clinic, whose annual running costs were over £400. During 1968 it built two more, one of which was almost complete by the time the fieldwork was done. It had already cost £600. In addition to these buildings, the council bought furniture costing about £400 and a lorry worth over £1,000, and it installed a telephone. Two trucks were purchased for regular council work in the tribal trust land, and accommodation for council staff costing up to £500 was completed. In 1968 the council repaired old bore-holes built by the government and graded local roads.

To perform its many tasks, in 1968 the council employed a staff of 120 people. Of these eighty attended to local cattle dips, twenty-seven were labourers on council projects; the rest were drivers, nurses, attendants at the bottle store and beer-garden, or they performed other duties on council property. Their monthly wages amounted to £800, that is £9,600 per annum.

To obtain the necessary money the council taxed every vehicle in its area, including regular buses which passed through the tribal trust land. Since 1964 the council had been allowed to collect dip fees, which brought in about £9,165[1] a year, and dog tax. The beer-garden serves as a centre for refreshment and food, and those who regularly sell meat there pay one shilling a day to the council. During 1967 £2,000-worth of beer was sold, and the total turnover of the beer-garden was in excess of £3,000. The bottle store had an annual turnover of almost £2,000. Additional money was collected from council rates and hospital fees. Both men and women paid a council rate of five shillings a year. Local women pay one shilling for attending the clinic and local men two shillings. All outsiders pay two shillings and sixpence. Because the government contributed £1 for every £1 locally collected, government contribution was high.

Shumba council's large budget enabled it to show interest in various local enterprises. It gave £150 to a chief to build his court house, and made a donation to a mission hospital to buy X-ray equipment. Two mission schools received money contributions for local extensions.

Council meetings are lively. They deal with the day-to-day administration of the area. One typical council meeting dealt with the following items: the women's clubs asked for £100 to finance their social activities; a subchief asked for £300 to build a court house; three businessmen

[1] This figure indicates that the area of Shumba council is about ten to eleven times as large as the area of Nzou council. Cf. *supra*, p. 214.

applied for licences to open a mill and grocery shops in a newly opened township, employees complained that in the past years they had not received their normal leave and asked for money compensation. All topics were discussed at great length and every opinion was heard. Finally the councillors reached a compromise or unanimous decision.

The lively activities of Shumba council suggest that it has the full support of the people. Yet the council, like many others, had to weather many difficulties. Three council employees absconded with sums of money worth £20, £50 and over £1,000. All were convicted and imprisoned, but no money was returned to the council. People also complained about council employees, especially those in the bottle store and beer-garden, that they did not give the full measure of the goods purchased, and opened late in the day. A warning from the council secretary brought the salesmen to order. Accidents on council transport due to careless driving also caused serious losses. One lorry-driver had repeated warnings by the council that he would have to pay for any further damage to a council vehicle; he committed suicide after another accident because he was unable to pay for the damage.

People of the Shumba community often complain about their council and its heavy financial demands. Yet all agree that it has brought them benefits, additional dip tanks, clinics, a new township, educational and agricultural improvements, and above all local employment. Jealousies exist between the various subchiefdoms of the council area because each demands priority for development works and those served last complain of being neglected. Criticism has however been subdued. Ordinary villagers have been interested mainly in the amount of money that their council controlled, and have calculated how many more services they could demand. Never during the time of research did people seriously express a desire to close their council. On the contrary, people and councillors alike looked forward to extending their development plans.

The efficiency of council members grew steadily, and by 1968 three-quarters of all councillors had undergone a government-sponsored training course to equip them for their posts. The local district commissioner was feared but respected by the people, and generally complied with their suggestions for improving the area. He stayed in the background and did not dominate their activities. The district officer, however, who occasionally deputized for the district commissioner, provoked resentment among the people. They regarded him as unreasonable and domineering. On one occasion chief Shumba threatened that if the district officer continued to dominate proceedings he would close the council. To prove their determination the two chiefs and several subchiefs wrote a combined letter to the district commissioner complaining about the actions of his representative.

Because the council had been in existence for over twenty years people did not associate it with community development. Teachers, civil servants, businessmen and ordinary villagers alike objected to community development. When it was pointed out to them that their council was very effective community development they concluded that the council had originally been imposed on them by a district commissioner and their chief, but that it had become their very own. If it looked like community development, this was purely accidental.

It is likely that the success of the council has come in part from the character of the councillors. Of the seventeen councillors seven are 'strangers', the rest are related to either chiefs or village headmen. This is a relatively high percentage of strangers and implies that Shumba council is run fairly democratically.

The chairman is a subchief who is respected by his people for his personal qualities. He has a high reputation as a fair judge in court cases because he never accepts bribes. Although he has built a prison near his residence in which he detains criminals before handing them over to the police, he is trusted and loved. He is outspoken, fairly well educated, having had full primary education, and is admired for his clear reasoning. Recently he introduced a new African independent church into the tribal trust land; so in addition to being a subchief and council chairman he has also become a religious leader. The weekly meetings of his church regularly bring about 300 people to his village.

The secretary, who is only 33 years old, has served longest on the council. He is trusted by all, ever ready to help them and loved for his good humour. Chairman and secretary work hand in hand.

The treasurer is new and has just completed his accountancy training. He takes the place of one of those who absconded with money, and is keen to establish a reputation for honesty.

All council members keep in close touch with the people, ask them what assistance they require from the council, and inform them of council decisions. In this they differ greatly from the councillors in Shoko chiefdom.[1] The people in turn confide in them and lodge with their ward representatives complaints against certain council employees. The councillors' power to dismiss council employees gives them some measure of control over the employees and guarantees that they perform their tasks to the satisfaction of the people.

[1] Cf. *supra*, p. 195.

ANALYSIS

(i) Shumba council is an exceptionally well-functioning council. Internal Affairs officials in the province rank it second in Karangaland. National statistics indicate that few councils in Rhodesia can compare with its efficiency. The Secretary for Internal Affairs' Report for the year 1967 records that the seventy-six councils in Rhodesia had £96,641 cash in hand in January 1968,[1] which gives an average of £1,272 per council. Since Shumba council alone had £10,494, or more than eight times the average amount, many councils must possess far less than £1,000. Established for over twenty years, and functioning well for at least five. Shumba council has become part of the local community structure and has been as fully accepted by the people as have local schools. People were so accustomed to it when the new ideology of community development was announced that they, like most other Karanga, expressed their dislike of the new concept and realized only on reflection that their council actually represented this policy. Even nationalist-inclined residents in the community supported it.

(ii) The reason for the success of Shumba council lies largely with the district commissioner. In the late 1950s he skilfully withdrew from council chairmanship and convinced the people that the council was their own personal concern. This removed the apathy and antagonism with which people had originally regarded the council. It ceased to be 'a council of the district commissioner and the chief'. The discretion of later district commissioners consolidated the success. The confidence with which people handled an unpleasant district officer proves that they were not overpowered by the actions of an individual civil servant. Their council had existed long before this man came into their area and was in no way associated with him. The absence of direct or indirect pressure by civil servants marked a significant difference between Shumba council and those councils that failed.

A second criterion that distinguishes Shumba council from the others is that no district commissioner has ever attempted to subordinate it to a chief's *dare*. This would in fact have been difficult, because two chiefdoms were served by the one council. This freedom from the control of old traditional councillors removed Shumba council from the intercalary position in which Shoko council and others found themselves. Nzou council, which has likewise rid itself of the control of the *dare*, is the only other council that promises to develop strongly in the future.

The subordinate role played by traditional leaders in Shumba council

[1] S.I.A., 1967, p. 23.

indicates that people and leaders alike accepted the democratic institution. The fact that a subchief was chairman was not a result of
traditional status: he was chosen for his personal qualities. Chief
Shumba, vice-president of the council, remained inactive. He lacked the
support of many tribesmen, who wanted another candidate to fill his
office. He is generally drunk, and people claim that his court decisions
are determined by favouritism. Thus the chief contrasts sharply with his
subchief, who is known for his strong and upright character. Apart
from those functions exclusively entrusted to chiefs, such as hearing
court cases and allocating land, the council has replaced the chief as the
focus of local interests. It is through the council that people find employment and that improvements on an ever larger scale are made. The chief
stands in the background. Through their councillors people have a
stronger control over their community life than they had in the past, and
the office of councillor carries great prestige and power. Councillors
make decisions determining the well-being of the community and so
contribute to the formulation of new values. The unanimity or compromise with which they decide local improvements guarantees that
development is not paralysed. As Bailey observes, disagreements in
small face-to-face communities would arrest local action.[1]

Because a new structural relationship evolved between chief, council
and people, the council functioned smoothly. In contrast to the Shoko
communities, no traditional institution blocked democratic procedures.
The chief's weakness gave democracy a chance. Popular discontent
existed, but seemed to form the natural background music to the successful council orchestra. It provided a stimulus to do better.

(iii) Economic factors proved no problem. The people of the Shumba
community have identical incomes with those of the Shiri and Ngara
communities, yet they were able to pay council rates. Although not
wealthier than other tribal trust lands, and in fact much poorer than
purchase area farmers, the people of Shumba community collected
large sums of money which considerably improved their social facilities.
One reason for this success is the large population of the council area.
Even small contributions by many people enabled council to dispose of
substantial sums.

CONCLUSION

Shumba council functioned with even greater approval by the people
than Nzou council. Both communities genuinely experienced 'felt
needs', which they believed their councils could meet. Both councils

[1] Cf. Bailey (1965), p. 5.

were directed by strong personalities, Nzou council by chief Nzou as
its vice-president and Shumba council by a subchief as its chairman.
Both leaders had multi-structural supports in the educational, religious,
traditional political or modern political spheres. This enabled them to
draw on a large number of followers to back them in their various
activities, including council leadership, and lent greater weight to their
opinions and suggestions. Opposition from the patriarchal system was
in both cases eliminated: chief Nzou was himself the traditional ruler and
the driving force in the council, and chief Shumba was so weak and
little respected by his people that he could not arrest council proceedings.
Nor did he want to interfere because he was not interested. In both
successful council areas therefore there existed no conflict between
traditional and modern leadership. An important dimension in which
the Nzou and Shumba councils differed is that whereas Nzou council,
just like Mutadza council, won support from the people by forming a
strong opposition to government, such opposition was no conscious
element in the Shumba community. Shumba council was mature and
successful enough to focus local loyalties on itself without external
provocation.

3. REVIEW OF HYPOTHESES

The seven council histories presented in chapters nine and ten reveal a
very complex interplay of factors leading to the success or failure of
community development. These demand a reformulation of the original
hypotheses.[1]

(i) An important criterion for the success or failure of community
development is the relationship of a community to the agency of change.
Community development has been so universally rejected by Rhodesian
Africans that the opposition of church leaders and nationalists in some
communities cannot be regarded as a sufficient cause for the failure to
establish councils. It might account for the failure of community
development in the Shiri and Ngara chiefdoms and in the Mutadza
purchase area, but it does not explain its failure in the Shoko and
Guruuswa communities, nor the success of Nzou council. The case
history of Nzou council shows rather that local attitudes towards
government can be manipulated by leaders so as to either boycott or
co-operate with a new policy.[2]

[1] *supra*, pp. 172–173.
[2] For example, co-operation in a community hostile to government can be seen as
a means of exploiting government for local advantages. Cf. the Nzou and Guruuswa
council case histories, *supra*, pp. 210–215, 182–187.

More important than abstract ideologies are the concrete relationships between people and government agents. In the areas where councils failed or were rejected, civil servants had acted provocatively and were openly or indirectly attacked by the people. In successful council areas government officials were either pushed into the background or withdrew of their own accord to allow the people to organize their own communities. Spicer observes that all societies constantly undergo change and that no society is inherently resistant to change. He suspects that if a group consciously resists an effort to alter its culture, the relationship between the agent of change and the people must be unsatisfactory.[1] The case histories of unsuccessful councils show that the indirect pressure exerted by civil servants hardened the opposition of the Karanga to the introduction of councils and community development. The first hypothesis may therefore be stated as follows: *Popular ideologies affect the success or failure of a new government policy. But more important are the concrete relationships between people and government agents.*

(ii) The success or failure of councils depends to a large extent on the attitude of local leaders towards community development, but more still on their relationship with their own people. Whether leaders adopted or rejected community development was not solely determined by their general attitude towards government. Even anti-government chiefs like chief Nzou adopted a council, and the Guruuswa purchase area, known for its people's general co-operation with government officials, rejected it. If a leader's attitude coincided with that of his people, as did that of chief Ngara, no conflict arose. If a popular chief, like chief Nzou, and to a lesser degree chief Mhofu, could carry his people with him, community development had a chance of success. Yet when leaders who lacked popular support adopted a policy rejected by their people, as did chief Shiri, the leader was rejected together with the policy he had adopted. Conformity to government demands undermined the position not only of chief Shiri, but also of chief Shoko and the chairmen of the two purchase areas. Uninfluential leaders therefore broke down under the challenge of community development, but popular chiefs increased their influence. The attitude of unimportant local leaders towards a new policy is irrelevant, as the case history of Shumba council shows.

The second hypothesis therefore reads: *The success or failure of a new government policy depends on the attitudes of local leaders only if the leaders are the true spokesmen of their people and enjoy popular support. If*

---

[1] Cf. Spicer (1952), p. 18.

the interests of leaders and their followers diverge greatly, their sponsorship of a new policy remains ineffective.

Yet this hypothesis has to be extended. The structural compatibility or incompatibility of social institutions is important. Structural compatibility alone does not determine the success of a council. The absence of a patriarchal political structure in purchase areas was not in itself sufficient to open the way for community development. In fact the farmers of the Guruuswa and Mutadza purchase areas were more outspoken in their opposition to the new policy and the civil servants who introduced it than people who lived under patriarchal social systems. Unrestrained by local norms, they freely asserted their right to choose their own form of local administration.

Structural incompatibility, on the other hand, does affect council efficiency. When democratic councils were subordinated to patriarchal institutions they generally failed. The history of Shoko council shows that if a modern democratic institution is subjected to a patriarchal institution, the former is unable to develop initiative or to achieve goals.

The case history of Nzou council confirms the crippling effect of the subordination of a democratic to a patriarchal institution. Only after chief Nzou had freed the council from the traditional *dare* did development become possible. The disadvantages of mixing democratic and patriarchal norms showed themselves also in the selection of councillors. Councillors who were nominated because of their ascribed status in the traditional system proved less acceptable and successful than elected councillors who held their position because of achieved status. These findings contradict the opinions of some civil servants who ascribe the success of community development in Rhodesia to the fusion of patriarchal and democratic institutions.

The second part of this hypothesis therefore states: *The fusion of patriarchal and democratic institutions leads to the failure of a new policy. Only if democratic elements are free to operate according to their own principles can the modernization of African rural areas be achieved.*

(iii) In spite of the general claim by most Karanga that they are financially unable to run a council, economic factors seem least important for the success or failure of a council. Affluent communities like Guruuswa purchase area showed no more interest in community development than poorer tribal trust lands, and even communities at subsistence level attempted to form councils when forced to do so by chiefs or civil servants.

The third hypothesis is therefore: *Economic prosperity prior to the introduction of a new policy like community development is not a significant factor.*

Two chapters on community development have been included in this study of Rhodesian chiefs in order to illustrate some of the new functions that modern chiefs have to perform and the new roles in which they have to meet their people. For several decades chiefs had to reconcile the conflicting demands made on them by people and government. Under the new policy of community development they are placed at the intersection point of three structurally contrasted systems of social organization: they are patriarchs in their traditional society; they are junior civil servants in the bureaucratic hierarchy of the Ministry of Internal Affairs; and they are vice-presidents of (ideally) democratically elected councils. Such a fusion of contradictory roles in one social position necessarily leads to the atrophy of Karanga chieftainship as a patriarchal institution. At the same time it hinders the transformation of patriarchs into efficient bureaucrats or democratically elected leaders. The reason is that chiefs obtained their office because of their genealogical position rather than because of special talents fitting them for their role as administrators. As long as the 'test of ancestors' rather than the 'educational certificate'[1] determines leadership positions, neither an efficient bureaucracy nor democracy can evolve.

---

[1] Cf. *supra*, p. 3 and Gerth and Mills (1961), p. 241.

Conclusion

This book has analysed how the patriarchal position of Karanga chiefs has increasingly acquired bureaucratic overtones and incorporated elements that are incompatible with its nature. Max Weber has pointed out the structural incompatibilities between patriarchal political systems, which are characterized by personal relationships among office-holders and people, and bureaucracies, characterized by impersonal relationships. He has stressed that whereas patriarchs are simultaneously political leaders, organizers of economic activities and officials in religious cults, bureaucrats have influence in only one particular sphere of social life. A bureaucrat is evaluated for his efficiency, and efficiency forces him to specialize. Patriarchs, on the other hand, are leaders because of their kinship ties with a large number of their followers, and the sacred character of their office. Patriarchs are no specialists, but they regulate many aspects of their followers' lives.

The different role-content of patriarch and bureaucrat is to a large extent determined by the scale of the society in which they function.

The concept of scale is not new. It was first developed by Godfrey and Monica Wilson in 1945. For various reasons it fell into disfavour, but it still appears useful in this context, for reasons which will become clear in what follows.

Only in small-scale societies can one man assume leadership in several distinct activities, such as politics, economics and religion. As the scale of a society increases, especially in a mass society, authority must be delegated, personal contact between rulers and ruled becomes impossible, and specialization is essential for the smooth running of the society. The distinction between a patriarchal and a bureaucratic society may therefore be seen as a distinction in scale, and a transition from patriarchy to bureaucracy is likely to occur as the scale of a society increases.

If a society grows steadily over time, the transition may be smooth. But if the scale is suddenly extended through outside intervention, the social organization of a traditional society may need major re-adjustments. The political unit can no longer regard itself as a family writ large, it loses its sacred character, and the basis of authority is likely to shift outside its own small universe. According to Weber, personal tribute is replaced by salaries and taxes, paid by and to an impersonal agency, and the educational certificate rather than a test of ancestors determines political and administrative office. The introduction and the early chapters of this book have shown how through the incorporation of formerly autonomous chiefdoms into the new country of Rhodesia the scale of these chiefdoms was rapidly extended. A country-wide network of communication made possible a centralized administration of all areas, and the introduction of the cash economy and education into African communities increasingly exposed them to the influence of western society.

In particular three aspects of the increase in the scale of the Karanga's universe affected the position of chiefs: firstly, economic and social differentiation among a formerly egalitarian people; secondly the extension of the political and administrative system; and thirdly, the penetration of the traditional political system by European institutions. Each of these extensions in scale added to the factors affecting the basis of chiefly authority and made more complex the chiefs' relationships with their people.

1. INCREASE IN SCALE DUE TO ECONOMIC AND SOCIAL DIFFERENTIATION

In the past, Karanga society consisted of small autonomous political units, and social life took place within a strictly circumscribed geographical area: the stockaded village and its surrounding arable land and hunting grounds. Local communities numbered some thousand people,[1] who were related to each other by kinship bonds. All engaged in peasant agriculture, and economic specialization was at a low level. Even smiths and other traditional craftsmen were peasant cultivators. A common religious cult based on ancestor worship united the people. The oldest man was at one and the same time political leader, head of the extended family, in charge of economic activities, and director of religious worship. The leader therefore filled many roles, but all were integrated with each other. The social life of the people revolved within their community. Political ties, often transformed into affinal relationships,[2] linked small communities to each other without endangering each other's autonomy.

[1] *supra*, p. 56.
[2] *supra*, p. 45.

With the arrival of European settlers the many small patriarchal societies were drawn into a much larger political unit, the new colony of Rhodesia. Economically, Karangaland became greatly differentiated. Peasant agriculture remained important, but 39 per cent of the people's income was derived from other economic activities.[1] People were drawn into the modern cash economy. They sought employment in the highly capitalized sector of Rhodesia's dual economy, which is controlled by Europeans, but they remained rooted in their own rural communities.

Agents of change, such as Christian missionaries, enabled the Karanga to enter the European labour market by offering them academic education and training in new crafts. In this way the people began to differentiate themselves from each other economically and some were able to obtain higher rewards from European employment than others. Above all, missionaries presented Africans with a new religion and philosophy of life. Localized ancestor-worship was replaced by a world religion.

This increase in the scale of economic activities, new values and religious beliefs was facilitated by the construction of roads and the introduction of new means of transportation and communication. Small-scale patriarchal communities became small cells of new country-wide political and economic systems.

This increase in the scale of the social environment affected all sections of Karanga communities, but some adapted themselves faster, some more slowly to the changing conditions. Men with a stake in the past, such as chiefs, were more reluctant in the face of innovations[2] than people with little traditional standing. Consequently commoners were often more educated than chiefs and obtained higher rewards on Rhodesia's labour market. Change therefore took place unevenly, tensions arose between traditionalists and progressives, and a decline in consensus set in concerning cultural goals and the norms by which these were to be achieved.

In all the communities studied in this book, the material and ideological preconditions for bureaucratization have been established, but in none have they been sufficiently developed to allow an elaborate bureaucratic system to take the place of the traditional patriarchal system. The pre-bureaucratic epoch of Karangaland has given way to a semi-bureaucracy, but traditional forces are still strong enough to remain a significant impediment in the way of thorough-going bureaucratization.

[1] *supra*, pp. 38–39.
[2] *supra*, pp. 58–59.

The increase in the scale of the people's social life and the introduction of bureaucracy has opened a new era for the Karanga. Because of its efficiency bureaucracy is likely to gather momentum and to create new institutions and privileges, which in turn will perpetuate it and extend the scale of social expectations still further. The educated and wealthy Karanga, who have no stake in the patriarchal system, see in bureaucracy their best chance of social advance. With powerful agencies of change supporting their aspirations, such as Christian missions and even certain aspects of government administration, these men are committed to bureaucratization and will abandon patriarchal institutions.

2. INCREASE IN THE SCALE OF POLITICAL AND ADMINISTRATIVE SYSTEMS

It is argued that an increase in scale need not have disturbing effects in a society if it proceeds smoothly and uniformly.[1] The growth of Karanga chiefdoms in the first half of the twentieth century[2] did not in itself adversely affect the position of patriarchal rulers, since the growth was organic. It increased the chief's prestige and underlined the traditional value of a large following.

More far-reaching changes occurred when the traditional political system was incorporated into the administrative bureaucracy of a government department. Suddenly the scale of political units increased from about a hundred square miles[3] to some 150,820 square miles.[4] The chiefs were at first loosely, later more intimately affiliated and integrated into government administration, but the effective local rulers became European civil servants with chiefs as their assistants.[5] Increase in scale of the political unit therefore decreased the status of former patriarchs.

A further challenge to traditional authority occurred when its base was removed to an alien political system. Though the people retained a strong voice in the selection of chiefs, final authority to appoint and depose traditional rulers was assumed by the Rhodesian Government.[6] Through their frequent appeals to civil servants to solve local con-

[1] Cf. G. and M. Wilson (1968), pp. 133–134, and *supra*, p. 228.

[2] *supra*, pp. 46–48, 56–58.

[3] According to district commissioners' records, the average size of Karanga chiefdoms is some 100 square miles. The estimate is derived from detailed figures covering seven chiefdoms.

[4] *Rhodesia in Brief* (1969), p. 1.

[5] *supra*, pp. 10–11.

[6] *supra*, pp. 62–63.

troversies, the people recognized the new authority and accepted it as legitimate. Through this shift Karanga chiefs became an extension of the bureaucratic administration controlled by Europeans, but the traditional system still persisted because civil servants decided to recognize claims based on traditional succession rules.

This alteration made chiefs simultaneously patriarchs and bureaucrats. They were tied by different but equally strong and important bonds both to their people and to government. Chapters four and five[1] analysed the dilemmas of chiefs who tried to harmonize dual and often opposed loyalties. Their traditional relationship to their people and their descent from the founder of their chieftainship imposed on them the obligation to represent and fight for their people's interests. Their inclusion in the bureaucracy of the Ministry of Internal Affairs turned them into semi-bureaucrats and imposed on them the duty to implement government policies.

This combination of structurally conflicting roles in the persons of old, often illiterate, elders,[2] bred a confused self-understanding in the chiefs. Their self-images[3] and case histories[4] show that many are unsure whether to act as heads of patriarchal systems or as bureaucrats responsible to senior administrators. Whether they accommodated government demands or whether they forcefully adopted an anti-government attitude, many broke down under the strain and many lost their positions. Weber's observation that a most acute tension centres round the position of the former patriarch when he has to become a bureaucrat[5] is fully borne out by the Karanga case material.

The question arises whether the role conflict of chiefs is due entirely to what Weber calls the antagonism between patriarchalism and bureaucracy, or whether it is not greatly exacerbated in Rhodesia by a difference in scale between Karanga chiefdoms and government bureaucracy. Weber observed tensions between the Prussian monarch of his time and Prussia's bureaucracy and commented that the political head might be reduced to a dilettante by his civil servants who possessed expert knowledge. Yet Tsarist Russia too was administered by a highly developed bureaucracy and the monarchs could rely on the advice and efficiency of the civil servants. The latter did not undermine the monarch's position.

An important difference in the relationship of monarchies and chiefdoms towards bureaucracy is that monarchies were territorially

[1] *supra*, pp. 55–105.
[2] *supra*, p. 59.
[3] *supra*, pp. 64–74.
[4] *supra*, pp. 77–105.
[5] *supra*, p. 4.

coextensive with their bureaucracies, whereas Rhodesia's bureaucratic administration extends far beyond local chiefdoms. In fact it forms the unifying bond between the many chiefdoms of the country, as well as between African chiefdoms and European political units. As a result Rhodesia's bureaucratic administration has swallowed up local chiefdoms.

The scale of political societies, therefore, as well as succession rules, which keep political office in certain families, account for the antagonism between patriarchal and bureaucratic social institutions. Karanga chiefdoms are threatened by bureaucratic administration because they are very small. Small rulers cannot run their own bureaucracies and draw advantages from them as the larger traditional rulers of Prussia or Russia could.

3. INCREASE IN SCALE DUE TO A PENETRATION OF THE PATRIARCHAL SYSTEM BY EUROPEAN SOCIAL INSTITUTIONS

The scale of Karanga political experiences was extended still further when apart from having recourse to government officials people appealed to various sections of the European community, such as farmers, lawyers, and parliamentarians, to assist them in their power struggle. The help of these men was enlisted at first to wrest a political office from government,[1] but later to exclude competitors whose claim was based on traditional succession rules.[2]

Their appeals to European outsiders, who had no right (either in the patriarchal or in the bureaucratic system) to appoint Karanga chiefs, bear witness to the strains and stresses that the traditional system experienced. Chapter six[3] noted that confinement in a small territory, which hindered the process of fission and migration, accentuated internal segmentation. That in spite of these pressures the traditional system still maintained itself is a proof of its vitality.

The ready intervention of Europeans in a local succession dispute shows that in spite of legislation separating the races territorially and socially,[4] African and European neighbours co-operated, and European institutions offered their services to African clients. There exist many links across the colour line, though the relationship is never one of

[1] *supra*, pp. 123–131.
[2] *supra*, pp. 131–140.
[3] *supra*, p. 110.
[4] *supra*, pp. 11–12.

equality. Rather, Africans look up to Europeans for help and Europeans condescend to their African clients with 'benevolent paternalism'.[1] The multiracial character of Rhodesian society has certain advantages for both Africans and Europeans and enlarges the scale of social interaction for both groups.

Uneven social change in the educational and economic spheres caused opposition between the traditional and progressive elements in Karanga society. So, too, the greater readiness of one section of a chiefdom to appeal for help to wider segments of European society intensified opposition between competitors for a traditional office. It turned a competition for leadership into open conflict, which appears to have no solution.

The introduction of alien institutions into a patriarchal system is likely to have still greater repercussions when the agency introducing it is government itself, rather than individual Europeans acting at the request of interested Karanga. Weber remarks that both patriarchal and bureaucratic political systems are hostile to democracy, because all systems of domination aim at power, whereas democracy demands a larger participation in government by the people.[2] The government policy of community development expected African chiefs to accept and co-operate with the democratic institution of councils.

Various sociologists observe that the same conditions that favour bureaucracy also favour democracy. Lipset, for example, writes that 'growing industrialization, urbanization, wealth, and education favoured the establishment of a democratic system',[3] and Neal likewise observes that 'in order for democratic forms to work out in practice there must be a modicum of general education, and, if not economic well-being, then at least the absence of widespread poverty'.[4] The spread of the cash economy and education paved the way therefore for democratic processes at the local level. The strongest opposition to a democratic council could be expected from those who had least participated in the modern economy, and who had the greatest stake in the patriarchal system: the chiefs. Government reports[5] stressed the chiefs' resistance to the new policy, and councils were only accepted on a wider scale when their democratic character had been transformed into one of service to traditional institutions.[6]

[1] C.N.C., 1956, p. 2, and *supra*, p. 16.
[2] Gerth and Mills (1961), p. 231.
[3] Lipset (1964), p. 46; Cf. *supra*, p. 49, and Gerth and Mills (1961), p. 227.
[4] Neal (1964), p. 187.
[5] *supra*, pp. 18–19, 24; S.I.A., 1959, p. 158, S.I.A., 1964, p. 28.
[6] *supra*, p. 172.

A democratic council was a new concept to the Karanga. In their traditional society men could influence the political life of their chiefdom by discussing their problems with their leaders, and the leaders, if they wanted to remain in power, had to take note of their followers' desires. If they alienated their people, the latter could leave the chiefdom and settle with another chief who took greater note of the people's wishes. Migration was, therefore, one of several effective sanctions through which the people controlled their leaders. Today migration is no longer possible and people have lost their control over their chiefs.

Chiefs were never absolute rulers but were advised in their decisions by a council of elders.[1] These elders, however, held their position not because of their wisdom and popular support but because of their genealogical connection with the chief. All councillors stood in a special relationship to the ruler and none held exactly the same rank. The council, like the rest of Karanga society, was hierarchically structured. No one was equal to anyone else.

When this strongly hierarchical and traditional body, whose members were drawn from a narrow range of chiefly kinsmen, was confronted with a democratically elected body on which every commoner could serve, the equilibrium of the patriarchal system was again disturbed. Yet again traditionalists and progressives were pitched against each other: where the traditionalists won, the democratic institutions foundered, as the case history of Shoko council shows.[2] Where, however, traditional rulers were weak and the progressive element strong, as in Shumba chiefdom, the democratic institution gradually replaced the patriarchal authority in many aspects of community life.[3] The more efficient, influential and powerful a democratic institution becomes, the greater is its threat to a patriarchal ruler. Insecure leaders cannot tolerate such an institution,[4] though strong rulers can increase their power through it, as the case history of chief Nzou and Nzou council shows.[5] The comment of the district commissioner quoted in chapter nine ('You cannot simultaneously have autocratic chiefs and democratic councils'[6]) epitomizes an awareness of the structural incompability between patriarchalism and democracy. In spite of the failure of many councils—and many more community development projects have failed

[1] That is, the *dare*. Cf. *supra*, p. 194.
[2] *supra*, pp. 191–197.
[3] *supra*, pp. 217–221.
[4] Cf. Lipset (1964), p. 115.
[5] *supra*, pp. 210–217.
[6] *supra*, p. 171.

than have succeeded—the case histories of several councils reveal that many Karanga are more willing to accept true democracy and bureaucracy than their chiefs.[1] This may be due to their greater involvement in Rhodesia's wider social and economic systems than their rulers experience. The case history of Nzou council indicates that if the people were allowed to find their own *modus vivendi* in a confused world, the conflicts within modern Karanga society would be more readily resolved. The government's protection of chiefs, however, arrests the political evolution of Karanga society and hardens the radical opposition between those who look back to the past and those who look forward to the future.

[1] Cf. e.g. the history of Shoko council, *supra*, pp. 191–197, especially pp. 195–197.

APPENDIX A

All the communities referred to in this study are given fictitious names. The names of chiefdoms are traditional clan names, but never the names of clans to which the communities predominantly belong. Karanga clans are mostly named after animals. One chiefdom in this study, which is divided into two opposed sections, is referred to by Karanga praise-names, none of which refer to the local communities concerned. Praise-names are very difficult to translate into English.

The purchase areas described in this study are named after a well known Karanga locality and the nickname of a group.

The following is a list of the fictitious names of the communities with, wherever possible, their English translations.

NAME OF THE COMMUNITY	ENGLISH TRANSLATION
Chiefdoms and Subchiefdoms	
Hove	Fish
Shiri	Bird
Ngara	Crocodile
Shoko	Monkey
Shoko Murewa	Murewa Monkey
Shoko Museamwa	Museamwa Monkey
Nzou	Elephant
Mhofu	Eland
Shumba	Lion
Purchase Areas	
Guruuswa	Tall Grass
Mutadza	You have done wrong

R

APPENDIX B

All the names given to the actors in the social drama described and analysed in chapters six to eight are fictitious in order to conceal the actors' identities. European actors are given the popular British surnames Thomson, Williams and Smith. African actors are given names taken from the Bible, both because Biblical names are common among the Karanga, and also because a pattern is followed in the name-giving which requires many names to start with certain letters. Such names were not available in sufficient numbers in the indiginous language.

To facilitate the memorizing of the genealogical positions of the actors, the generations are numbered from A to K, and all men belonging to a certain generation are given a name starting with the letter of their generation. Thus all men of the seventh generation, G, bear a name starting with G. This rule does not apply to the two women recorded on the genealogy.

In addition, within each generation a man's seniority is indicated by numerals. Thus (G2) signifies a man of the seventh generation, G, who is the second oldest member recorded on the genealogy in that generation.

The fictitious names within each generation are arranged in alphabetical order. When, therefore, two men are discussed, for example Gamaliel and Gilead, the names themselves indicate the genealogical seniority of Gamaliel. To facilitate the use of the genealogy, each name is followed by a letter and numeral in brackets, indicating an actor's exact position on the genealogy.

The following is a list of the names used in the social drama:

List of Actors in the Social Drama

Abraham (A1)	Fagiel (F1)
	Faltiel (F2)
Benjamin (B1)	Feleg (F3)
	Fenez (F4)
Caleb (C1)	Finon (F5)
David (D1)	Dinah (F6)
Eber (E1)	Gad (G1)
Enoch (E2)	Gamaliel (G2)
Ephraim (E3)	Gatam (G3)
Esau (E4)	Gazer (G4)

Gerar (G5)
Gershom (G6)
Gethan (G7)
Gether (G8)
Gilead (G9)
Gamar (G10)
Gideoni (G11)
Gomer (G12)

Hadad (H1)
Hadoram (H2)
Ham (H3)
Hamuel (H4)
Hanoch (H5)
Haran (H6)
Hareph (H7)
Havilah (H8)
Helon (H9)
Hirah (H10)
Homam (H11)
Hul (H12)
Huppim (H13)
Hur (H14)
Husham (H15)
Hushim (H16)

Jabeth (J1)
Jachin (J2)
Jacob (J3)
Jahleel (J4)
Jalam (J5)
Jamin (J6)
Japheth (J7)
Javan (J8)
Jehu (J9)
Jeremiah (J10)
Jethro (J11)
Joab (J12)
Joachim (J13)
Jonathan (J14)
Joseph (J15)
Joshua (J16)

Kedar (K1)
Kedemah (K2)
Kemuel (K3)
Kenan (K4)
Kenaz (K5)
Keturah (K6)
Kiriath (K7)
Kohath (K8)
Korah (K9)

APPENDIX C

African Primary Education and Councils

During the period from 1955 to 1970 government policy towards African primary education underwent several changes. In the 1950s until 1962 the Rhodesian government was concerned about African education and intent on maintaining its high standards. During these years almost all rural schools were run by Christian missionaries who charged low school fees for the upkeep and extension of these schools while the government paid the teachers' salaries. In urban areas government controlled most schools, and at these no school fees were charged. Many Africans desired the abolition of school fees in rural areas and in some areas which had a council, like the area of chief Mangwende, people pressed for permission to open their own schools. Such permission, however, was only reluctantly given; in most cases it was refused because both government and missionaries feared that in African controlled schools standards would fall.[1]

With a change of government in 1962 and the new government's decision to make community development the corner stone of its policy, as also of the new government's ambivalent attitude towards educated Africans, the government's policy towards African primary schools and councils changed. In all schools school fees were now charged. From 1962 onward until the mid 1960s, government encouraged Africans to form local councils and promised that if they did so they could take over responsibility for local schools. By this time, however, Africans were no longer interested in this offer. They knew that they would not only have to pay school fees but that, if the missionaries relinquished the schools, they would have to raise more money than they had done in the past. Moreover, they were highly critical of the new policy of community development. It is this period which is described in this book.

Towards the late 1960s and in 1970, the time this appendix is written, a further development occurred. Government then forced Africans to take over their own schools: missionaries were forbidden to make any extension to their primary schools and to open any new schools. When this pressure did not lead to a speedy adoption of community development, government announced that from the end of 1970 onward

[1] This led to serious conflicts in one of the well established African councils in the late 1950s and early 1960s and its final closure. Cf. Holleman, 1969, especially pp. 292–320.

it would only pay 95 per cent of the African teachers' salaries, and that this government 'contribution' towards African primary education would in stages be further reduced, first to 90 per cent. If the Christian missions were unable to make up the deficit of the teachers' salaries, they had to hand over the schools. The majority of Christian missionaries declared that they were financially unable to pay increasing shares of their teachers' salaries, and prepared to hand over African primary education to those ready to take on responsibility for it. Few councils took over any significant number of schools; the parents still objected to council schools and government declared itself ready to sponsor schools for a limited period until councils could be formed. In government sponsored schools parents have to collect money to pay the five per cent of the teachers' salaries and children whose parents refuse, or are unable, to pay, may not attend schools except in cases of special concession. If no councils are formed within a period of five years, the schools will be closed.[1] The fear expressed by missionaries and African parents and teachers that educational standards in African primary schools will fall under this policy, was declared unfounded by government officials.

[1] African Education Amendment Act No. 38, 1970.

BIBLIOGRAPHY

ABRAHAM, D. P. (1966) 'The Roles of "Chaminuka" and the Mhondoro Cults in Shona Political History', in STOKES, E. and BROWN, R. (eds.), *The Zambezian Past*. Manchester, Manchester University Press, 28–46.

ALDEFER, H. F. (1964) *Local Government in Developing Countries*. McGraw-Hill Book Co.

AQUINA, Sister Mary, O.P. (1966) 'Christianity in a Rhodesian Tribal Trust Land', *African Social Research*, 1, 1–40.

AQUINA, Sister Mary, O.P. (1967) 'The People of the Spirit: An Independent Church in Rhodesia', *Africa*, XXXVII, 203–219.

AQUINA, Sister Mary, O.P. (1968) 'Simbabwe gestern und morgen', *Die Katholischen Missionen*, 5, 146–155.

AQUINA, Sister Mary, O.P. (1969) 'Zionists in Rhodesia', *Africa*, XXXIX, 113–137.

BAILEY, F. G. (1965) 'Decision by Consensus in Councils and committees', in BANTON, M. (ed.), A.S.A. Monographs *Political Systems and the Distribution of Power*. London, Tavistock Publications, 1–20.

BARBER, J. (1967) *Rhodesia: The Road to Rebellion*. Oxford University Press.

BARNES, J. A. (1955) 'Seven Types of Segmentation', *Rhodes-Livingstone Journal*, 17, 1–22.

BATTEN, T. R. (1965a) *Communities and Their Development*. Oxford University Press.

BATTEN, T. R. (1965b) *The Human Factor in Community Work*. Oxford University Press.

BECK, C. and MALLOY, J. M. (1964) *Political Elites*. Geneva, Sixth World Congress.

BLANC, R. *Handbook of Demographic Research in Under-Developed Countries*. C.C.T.A., 36.

BLAU, P. M. (1964) *Exchange and Power in Social Life*. New York, John Wiley & Sons Inc.

CLIFFORD, W. (1966) 'Community Development as a Movement and a Policy', in APTHORPE, R. (ed.), *Social Research and Community Development*. Lusaka, Rhodes-Livingstone Institute, 1–18.

CLUTTON-BROCK, G. (1969) *Rekayi Tangwena*. Gwelo, Mambo Press.

CUNNISON, I. (1956) 'Perpetual Kinship: A Political Institution of the Luapula Peoples', *Rhodes-Livingstone Journal*, 20.

EVANS-PRITCHARD, E. E. (1940) *The Nuer*. Oxford University Press.

FALLERS, L. (1955) 'The Predicament of the Modern African Chief: An Instance from Uganda', *American Anthropologist*, 57, 290–305.

FALLERS, L. (1963) 'Equality, Modernity, and Democracy in the New States', in GEERTZ, C. (ed.), *Old Societies and New States*. The Free Press of Glencoe, 160–218.

FRANKENBERG, R. (1957) *Village on the Border*. London, Cohen & West.

GANN, L. H. (1965) *A History of Southern Rhodesia*. London, Chatto & Windus.

GARBETT, G. K. (1966) 'The Rhodesian Chief's Dilemma: Government Officer or Tribal Leader?' *Race*, 8, 113–218.

GERTH, H. H. and MILLS, C. WRIGHT, eds. and trans. (1961) *From Max Weber: Essays in Sociology*. London, Routledge and Kegan Paul.

GETZELS, J. W. and GUBA, E. G. (1954) 'Role, Role Conflict, and Effectiveness: An Empirical Study', *American Sociological Review*, 19, 164–175.

GRAY, H. (1968) 'Machiavelli: The Art of Politics and the Paradox of Power', in KRIEGER, L. and STERN, F. (eds.), *The Responsibility of Power*. London, Macmillan, 34–53.

GREEN, J. M. (1967) 'What is Community Development?' in *Community Development 1963*. Salisbury, University College of Rhodesia, Faculty of Education, Occasional Paper 3, 1–11.

HOBBES, T. (undated edition) *Leviathan*. Oxford, Basil Blackwell.

HOLLEMAN, J. F. (1968) *Chief, Council and Commissioner*. London, Oxford University Press.

HOWMAN, R. H. G. (1969) 'Economic Growth and Community Development in African Areas', *NADA* (Salisbury) X, 3–8.

INKOMOYAHLABA (1965) 'An Historical Tour', *NADA*, IX, 61–69.

KAEGI, W. (1968) 'Freedom and Power in History', in KRIEGER, L. and STERN, F. (eds.), *The Responsibility of Power*. London, Macmillan, 220–229.

KRIEGER, L. and STERN, F., eds. (1968) *The Responsibility of Power*. London, Macmillan.

KUPER, L. (1965) *An African Bourgeoisie*. Yale University Press.

LEE, J. M. (1967) *Colonial Development and Good Government*. Oxford, Clarendon Press.

LEWIS, I. M. (1968) *History and Social Anthropology*, A.S.A. Monographs. London, Tavistock Publications.

LEYS, C. (1960) *European Politics in Southern Rhodesia*. Oxford, Clarendon Press.

LIPSET, S. M. (1964) *Political Man*. London, Mercury Books.

LLOYD, P. C. (1967) *Africa in Social Change*. Penguin African Library, AP 22.

LLOYD, P. C. (1968) 'Conflict Theory and Yoruba Kingdoms', in LEWIS, I. M. (ed.), *History and Social Anthropology*, A.S.A. Monographs. London, Tavistock Publications, 25–62.

LOUCH, A. R. (1966) *Explanation and Human Action*. Oxford, Blackwell.

LUTHULI, A. (1966) *Let My People Go*. London, Fontana Books.

MAFEJE, A. (1963) 'A Chief Visits Town', *Journal of Local Administration Overseas*, 2, 2, 88–99.

MITCHELL, J. C. (1964) Foreword to VAN VELSEN, J. *The Politics of Kinship*. Manchester, Manchester University Press.

MORTON-WILLIAMS, P. (1968) 'Fulani Penetration into Nupe and Yoruba in the Nineteenth Century', in LEWIS, I. M. (ed.), *History and Social Anthropology*, A.S.A. Monographs. London, Tavistock Publications, 1–24.

MOUZELIS, N. P. (1967) *Organisation and Bureaucracy*. London, Routledge & Kegan Paul.

MURPHREE, M. W. (1969) *Christianity and the Shona*. London, Athlone Press.

MURPHREE, M. W. (1970) 'A Village School and Community Development in a Rhodesian Tribal Trust Land', *Zambezi*, 2, pp. 13–23.

NEAL, F. W. (1964) 'Democracy', in GOULD, J. and KOLB, W. L. (eds.), *A Dictionary of the Social Sciences*. London, Tavistock Publications, 187–188.

PARSONS, T. (1951) *The Social System*. London, Routledge & Kegan Paul.

PASSMORE, G. C. (1966) *Local Government in Southern Rhodesia*. Salisbury, University College of Rhodesia.

POSTON, R. W. (1962) *Democracy Speaks many Tongues*. Harper & Row.

RANGER, T. (1966) 'Traditional Authorities and the Rise of Modern Politics in Southern Rhodesia, 1898–1930', in STOKES, E. and BROWN, R. (eds.), *The Zambezian Past*. Manchester, Manchester University Press.

RANGER, T. (1968) *Aspects of Central African History*. London, Heinemann.

RAYNER, W. (1962) *The Tribe and its Successor*. London, Faber & Faber.

RENNIE, J. K. (1966) 'Settlers and Missionaries in South Melsetter 1893–1925'. Salisbury University College of Rhodesia, Department of History (unpublished).

ROBINSON, K. R. (1966) 'The Archaeology of the Roswi', in STOKES, E. and BROWN, R. (eds.), *The Zambezian Past*. Manchester, Manchester University Press, 3–28.

ROMAN CATHOLIC CHURCH (1963) *The Catholic Directory of Southern Africa*. Cape Town, The Salesian Press.

ROTBERG, R. I. (1966) *The Rise of Nationalism in Central Africa*. Harvard University Press.

SIMMONDS, R. G. S. (1969) 'Self-help in the Mangwende Chieftainship', *NADA*, X, 9–13.

SITHOLE, N. (1959) *African Nationalism*. Oxford University Press.

SJOBERG, G. (1964) 'Community', in GOULD, J. and KOLB, W. L. (eds.), *A Dictionary of the Social Sciences*. London, Tavistock Publications, 114–115.

SOUTHERN RHODESIA CHRISTIAN CONFERENCE (1962) *Statistical Record as at 31st December, 1962.*

SOUTHERN RHODESIA CHRISTIAN CONFERENCE (1964) *Survey Report on Adult Literacy and Christian Literature in Southern Rhodesia.*

SPICER, E. H. (1952) *Human Problems in Technological Change*. New York, Russell Sage Foundation.

STOKES, E. and BROWN, R., eds. (1966) *The Zambezian Past. Studies in Central African History*. Manchester, Manchester University Press.

SUMMERS, R. (1961) 'The Southern Rhodesian Iron Age' (first approximations to the history of the last 2000 years). *Journal of African History*, 2, 1–13.

THOMSON, H. C. (1898) *Rhodesia and its Government*. London, Smith, Elder & Co.

TILLICH, P. (1967) *On the Boundary*. London, Collins.

TINDALL, P. E. N. (1968) *History of Central Africa*. Longmans.

TURNER, V. W. (1957) *Schism and Continuity in an African Society*. Manchester, Manchester University Press.

WHEELER, D. L. (1967) 'Gungunyane the Negotiator: A Study in African Diplomacy'. Salisbury, University College of Rhodesia, Department of History (unpublished).

WILSON, G. and M. (1968) *The Analysis of Social Change*. Cambridge University Press.

VANSINA, J. (1965) *Oral Tradition*. London, Routledge & Kegan Paul.

WRATHALL, J. J. (1969) 'The Tribal Trust Lands: Their Need for Development', *NADA*, X, 92–99.

YUDELMAN, M. (1964) *Africans on the Land.* Harvard University Press.

ACTS OF PARLIAMENT

All published by the Government Printer, Salisbury, Rhodesia.

SOUTHERN RHODESIA *Native Tax Ordinance,* No. 21 (1904).

SOUTHERN RHODESIA *Native Affairs Act,* cap. 72. Consolidated 1st June, 1928.

SOUTHERN RHODESIA *The African Affairs Act,* cap. 92.

SOUTHERN RHODESIA *The Land Apportionment Act,* cap. 257 (amended 1941).

SOUTHERN RHODESIA *The Industrial Conciliation Act,* cap. 246.

SOUTHERN RHODESIA *The African Land Husbandry Act,* cap. 103 (1951).

SOUTHERN RHODESIA *African Councils Act,* cap. 95 (1957).

SOUTHERN RHODESIA *The Local Government Act,* cap. 124.

RHODESIA *The African Affairs Amendment Act,* No. 44 (1966).

RHODESIA *Rural Councils Act,* No. 61 (1966).

RHODESIA *Tribal Trust Land Act,* No. 9 (1967).

RHODESIA *African Law and Tribal Courts Act,* No. 24 (1969).

RHODESIA *African Education Amendment Act* No. 38 (1970)

OTHER GOVERNMENT PUBLICATIONS

All published by the Government Printer, Salisbury, Rhodesia.

SOUTHERN RHODESIA (1913–1962) *Reports of the Secretary for Native Affairs and Chief Native Commissioner for the Years 1913–1962.* Presented to the Legislative Assembly 1914–1963.

FEDERATION OF THE RHODESIAS AND NYASALAND *Annual Report on Education for the Year 1962.*

SOUTHERN RHODESIA *Second Report of the Select Committee on Resettlement of Natives.* Presented to the Legislative Assembly on Tuesday, 16th August, 1960.

SOUTHERN RHODESIA *Report of the Mangwende Reserve Commission of Inquiry, 1961.*

SOUTHERN RHODESIA *Report of the Commission Appointed to Inquire into and Report on Administrative and Judicial Functions in the Native Affairs and Districts Courts Departments,* 1961. (Robinson Report).

SOUTHERN RHODESIA *Second Report of the Commission of Inquiry into the Organisation and Development of Southern Rhodesia Public Services,* 1961. (Patterson Commission).

SOUTHERN RHODESIA *Chiefs and Chiefs' Courts; African Local Government,* ed. Leaver, NAD Form Service Information Sheet, No. 7, 1961.

SOUTHERN RHODESIA *1961 Census of the European, Asian and Coloured Population.* Central Statistical Office, Salisbury.

SOUTHERN RHODESIA *Final Report of the April/May 1962 Census of Africans in Southern Rhodesia.* Central Statistical Office, Salisbury, 1964.

SOUTHERN RHODESIA *Report of the Southern Rhodesia Education Commission 1962.* Presented to the Legislative Assembly, 1963.

SOUTHERN RHODESIA *African Education, Southern Rhodesia.* Annual Report by the Secretary for the year 1962.

RHODESIA *Reports of the Secretary for Internal Affairs for the Years 1963 to 1967.* Published 1964–1968.

RHODESIA *The Demand for Independence in Rhodesia. The Domboshawa 'Indaba'.* 1964.

RHODESIA *Local Government and Community Development: The Role of Ministries and Coordination. Statement of Policy and Directive by the Prime Minister,* 1965.

RHODESIA *Economic Survey of Rhodesia for 1965,* 1967.

RHODESIA *Parliamentary Debates* (Hansard) 1967.

RHODESIA *African Education. Annual Report by the Secretary for the Year 1967.*

RHODESIA *Annual Report on Education for the Year 1967.*

RHODESIA *Rhodesia in Brief.* Ministry of Information, Immigration and Tourism, 1969.

RHODESIA *Report of the Constitutional Commission, 1968* (Whaley Report).

RHODESIA *Quarterly Statistical Summary,* No. 4, February, 1968.

RHODESIA *Proposals for a New Constitution for Rhodesia,* 1969.

NEWSPAPERS

Moto. Gwelo, Mambo Press.

The Rhodesia Herald. Salisbury, The Rhodesian Printing & Publishing Co.

The Sunday Mail. Salisbury, The Rhodesian Printing & Publishing Co.

Index